12 A

SHOPPING AND RETAILING TOURISM

SHOPPING AND RETAILING TOURISM

Mahesh Chandra Singh

CENTRUM PRESS
NEW DELHI-110002 (INDIA)

CENTRUM PRESS
H.O.: 4360/4, Ansari Road, Daryaganj,
New Delhi-110002 (India)
Tel: 23278000, 23261597, 23255577, 23286875
B.O.: No. 1015, Ist Main Road, BSK IIIrd Stage,
IIIrd Phase, IIIrd Block, Bangalore-560085 (INDIA)
Tel: 080-41723429
Email: centrumpress@gmail.com
Visit us at: www.centrumpress.com

Shopping and Retailing Tourism

First Edition, 2010

ISBN 978-93-80540-04-7

PRINTED IN INDIA

Printed at Mehra Offset Press, Delhi

Contents

Preface

Shopping has traditionally been considered a subsidiary activity to travel– people shop when travelling, to buy souvenirs and presents, but it has not been the primary purpose. However, in recent years, with the relative decreasing cost of travel, this concept has changed. Retail tourism has become a popular leisure pursuit and statistics indicate that this is likely to be a continuing trend. This article looks at the rise in retail tourism and provides advice to destinations on how to exploit this growing market.

Tourism in Dubai is an important part of the Dubai government's strategy to maintain the flow of foreign cash into the emirate. Dubai's lure for tourists is based mainly on shopping, but also on its possession of other ancient and modern attractions.

Dubai is the most populous emirate of the seven emirates of United Arab Emirates. It is distinct from other members of the UAE in that revenues from petroleum and natural gas account for only 6% of its gross domestic product. A majority of the emirate's revenues are from the Jebel Ali Free Zone (JAFZ) and now, increasingly, from tourism.

Dubai has been called the "shopping capital of the Middle East." The city draws large numbers of shopping tourists from countries within the region and from as far as Eastern Europe, Africa and the Indian Subcontinent. Dubai is known for its souk districts. Souk is the Arabic word for market or place where any kind of goods are brought or exchanged. Traditionally, dhows from the Far East, China, Sri Lanka, and India would discharge their cargos and the goods would be bargained over in the souks adjacent to the docks. Dubai's most atmospheric shopping is to be found in the souks, located on either side of the creek, where bargaining is part of the buzz.

Modern shopping malls and boutiques are also found in the city. Dubai Duty Free at Dubai International Airport offers merchandise catering to the multinational passengers using Dubai International Airport.

While boutiques, some electronics shops, department stores and supermarkets may operate on a fixed-price basis, most other outlets consider friendly negotiation as a way of life.

Dubai's numerous shopping centres cater for every consumer's need. Cars, clothing, jewellery, electronics, furnishing, sporting equipment and any other goods will all be likely to be under the same roof.

This groundbreaking companion offers readers an opportunity to reassess key themes in contemporary tourism studies in the light of recent theoretical developments in tourism studies and the social sciences, as well as dramatic changes in the operating environment for tourism. The book also sets an agenda for future tourism research.

—Mahesh Chandra Singh

1

Cross Border Tourism and Shopping

Introduction

To what extent have governmental policy and economic factors, such as trade treaties, sales taxes, recession, inflation, and exchange rates, influenced cross-border tourism and shopping patterns of Canadians in the United States over the 10-year period 1985-1994? This paper analyzes macro-level economic and political variables, and explores the implications for cross-border shopping and tourism.

Cross-Border Tourism Defined and Measured

Essentially, two travel populations are represented within the definition of "tourist."

They are the *traditional tourist* who visits the United States to recreate, to "winter over" in the south, or to engage in heritage visitations. Then there is the more recent phenomenon of Canadians visiting the United States primarily to shop. We can refer to these *shoppers* alternatively as *day trippers* or as *same-day visitors.*

To this end, the tourism industry is defined here to address these two tourist streams through the use of five selected U.S. Standard Industrial Classification (SIC) codes and associated expenditures. They are defined as follows:

1. The traditional cultural/recreational tourist—SIC 5947: Gift, Novelty, and Souvenir Shops; SIC 70: Hotels, Rooming Houses, Camps, and Other Lodging; and SIC 79: Amusement and Recreation Services.
2. The shopper—SIC 53: General Merchandise Stores, including department stores, variety stores, outlets, and malls.

An expenditure made by both groups—at least one time—before returning to Canada during a visit to the United States is SIC 554: Gasoline Service Stations. Collectively, these five SIC codes are used to measure sales taxes (of various types), employment, and payroll. The traditional SIC code 58, Eating and Drinking Places, is excluded because nonresident and resident activity are too confounded to segment.

The unit of analysis for this study is the U.S. county. Two types of counties are identified: *pass-through* and *destination.* A pass-through county is contiguous to the Canadian port of entry, whereas a destination county is further removed from the border and may have the attraction of either a recreational or shopping experience. Both traditional tourist and shopper are channelled through border ports of entry.

In some cases, there is no pass-through county because the destination is within the county contiguous to the border. In this study eleven counties are defined as destination counties, and eight as pass-throughs. Eight border states are analyzed, consisting of Maine, Vermont, New York, Michigan, Minnesota, Montana, North Dakota, and Washington, and nineteen counties contained therein. Canadians returning to Canada are counted at fourteen ports of entry located in six border provinces: New Brunswick, Quebec, Ontario, Manitoba, Alberta, and British Columbia.

National and Economic Policy: A Ten-year Retrospective

In the ten-year period represented by this study, many policy factors contributed to changing the cross-border environment in which tourism occurs. However, which political and economic factors appear to be most influential?

To answer this question, the following developments have been examined: the Free Trade Agreement (FTA) between Canada and the United States, which became operative January 1, 1989; the North American Free Trade Agreement (NAFTA) between Canada, Mexico, and the United States, which took effect January 1, 1993; and issues involving recession, inflation, and currency exchange rates.

An additional factor arose on January 1, 1991, when a Canadian manufacturers' sales tax was replaced with a national value-added tax of 7%, referred to as the Goods and Services Tax or more popularly as the "GST." It was designed to move Canada's broad-based National Sales Tax from the point of origin of a good to the point of destination of a good, that is from producer to consumer, and to tax services as well. It was also intended to make Canadian manufactured goods more competitive through zero-taxing exports. Finally, it sought to tax imports at the same rate as domestic products. The GST is collected at the border upon re-entry to Canada. As the term GST implies, the tax is also placed on services.

Similar to the GST, as a value-added tax, is the Provincial Sales Tax or "PST"— which each province, except Alberta, had in place before passage of the national GST. Unlike the collection procedure of the GST, an honour system of payment was initially employed, with the consumer volunteering payment of the tax, for example, upon arrival at home sometime after crossing the international border.

But with the flood of shoppers to the south in the early 90s and with apparent traveller under-reporting, provincial and federal revenue authorities began conferring in 1992 with the intent of empowering federal Canadian custom officials to collect (along with the GST) the PST, which varies by province. Although nine of Canada's ten provinces have a provincial sales tax, only three have that tax collected by the federal government: Manitoba, New Brunswick, and Quebec.

Negotiations are currently under way with the province of Nova Scotia for federal collection of the PST. If agreement is reached, among other implications, cruise ships which operate between the Maine ports of Portland and Bar Harbour on the one side, and Yarmouth, Nova Scotia on the other, are likely to see some slight decrease in Nova Scotian tourist expenditures in Maine.

Undoubtedly, collection of these duties, along with anticipation of searches and seizures at the border, has a dampening affect on Canadian expenditures in the United States—particularly on a regional basis.

Canadian Ports of Entry, and U.S. Counties of Destination

Canadian Visitors to the United States. Visitor counts to the United States increased from 1985 to a peak in 1991, and have declined through 1994. Canadian visitors in 1994 numbered 54.3 million, having declined 25 million or by about a third from the 1991 level of 79.3 million.

They were crossing the border at levels earlier attained in the 1988/1989 time period. Both the peak of Canadian visitors to the United States (79.3 million) and the highest value of the Canadian dollar (U.S. $0.8726) occurred in 1991. And in 1991, as the FTA was first implemented, both Canada and the United States came out of recession. Since that year, both nations have avoided recession, and the FTA continues its tariff reduction schedule.

Despite the border enforcement of GST and PST, Canadian visitors to the United States at 54.3 million in 1994 number 45.1% more than they did in the beginning of the study period at 37.4 million. Although travel to the United States has peaked (at least for the time being), the count of north-to-south visitors remains historically high.

Figure 1, which compares Canadian visitor counts to the United States with the exchange rate of the Canadian dollar, indicate a direct relationship between the exchange rate of the Canadian dollar and visitors to the United States.

That is, the higher the exchange rate of the Canadian dollar, the greater the number of Canadian visitors. Earlier economic literature supports this finding. During the period 1985-1994 both values peaked in 1991, with 79.351 million cross-border visitations and an exchange rate (U.S. dollar per Canadian dollar) of $0.8726.

Figure 1

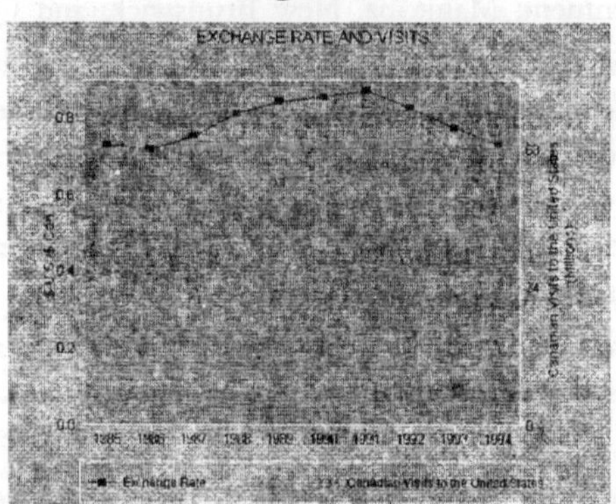

Shoppers: Same-Day Visitors. Looking at national data produced by Statistics Canada (Figure 2) in the ten years represented in this study (which uses the classifications of "Same-day," "Overnighters," and "Total"), Canadian visitors to the United States peaked in 1991. Although increasing, "traditional" recreational/cultural tourists have demonstrated a more moderate growth rate than have same-day shoppers.

We suggest that trips of more than one day are planned in advance, and therefore are less sensitive to short-term change in economic factors such as exchange-rate fluctuations. In terms of visitations, same-day trips, as a surrogate measure of shopping, are still more important today than they were in 1985. While some drop has occurred from the 1991 peak because of exchange rates, GST, and federal collection of PST, the economic impact of shopping continues to be a major factor in the activity patterns of Canadians in the United States. This is true even with the development of other factors, including the price of gasoline approaching a condition of cross-border parity and of tobacco prices dropping with the new Liberal government of Canada.

Figure 2

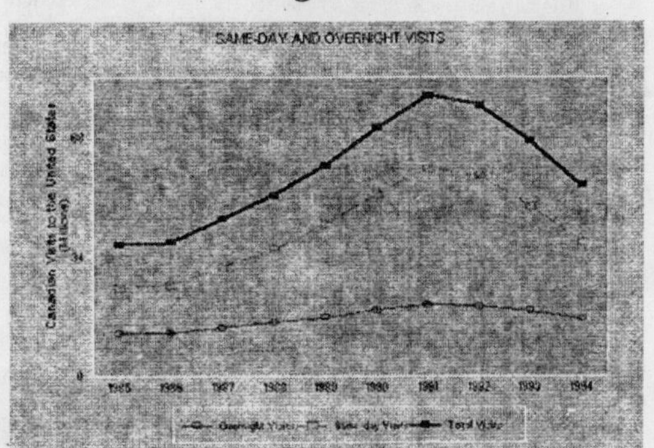

Selected Regional Changes in Canadian Visitor Patterns. The central/ eastern province of Ontario and the far western province of British Columbia are the least impacted by the exogenous economic and political factors discussed above. Other regions have done less well, as indicated by the ports of entry sampled. In the east, for example, the port of entry at Rock Island, Quebec, experienced a cumulative ten-year slide to where cross-border counts were down by 31% from 1985. St. Stephen, New Brunswick (the primary port of entry between the Maritimes and New England), continues to experience a downward trend from 2.1 million visitors in 1991 to 1.5 million in 1994. In each of these two provinces, the PST is collected at the border. Another factor is the relatively high PST rates of the Maritime Provinces. If further PST-collection agreements are entered into with the federal government, for example, by Nova Scotia, tourism activity to the south will at least be marginally impacted.

Economic Impact of Canadian Visitors in the Unites States

Canadian travel southward has employment implications on the U.S. side of the border. This study has investigated those effects on employment, associated with the previously mentioned five SIC codes. In the analysis, I use 1,535 observations, or data points, of employment in nineteen U.S. counties over nine years. These data are profiled in Figures 3 and 4.

Figure 3

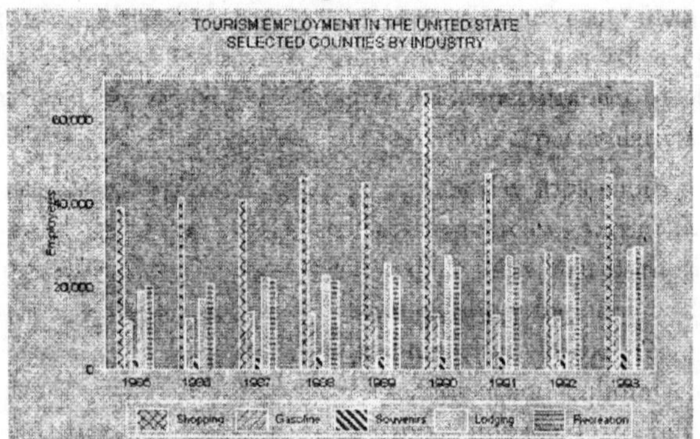

Figure 4

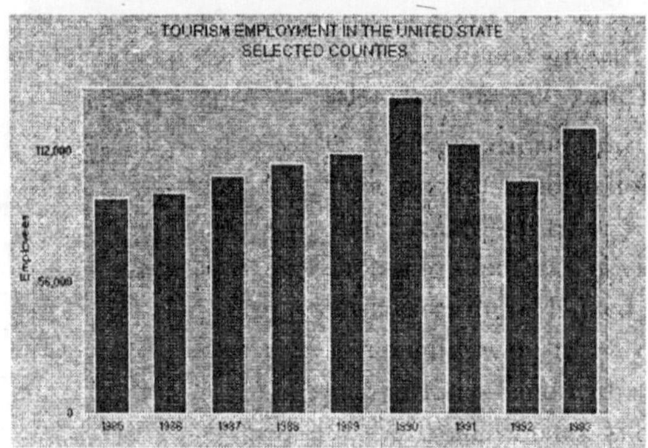

Macro-factors and Tourism: Some Observations

Ten years of data demonstrate that the most important factor affecting cross-border trips to the United States is the value of the Canadian dollar, which as of late 1995 appears to have stabilized. Other factors also affect cross-border trips and associated expenditures.

For example, the FTA may have increased Canadian awareness of U.S. goods and services. Tax policy in the form of the GST in 1991 modified an invisible manufacturers' tax into a visible sales tax, thus encouraging Canadians to go south to shop. Federal collection of the PST has also affected the amount of cross-border visits—and may more so, if additional federal/provincial agreements are written. Particularly impacted by federal collection of PSTs is the northern New England region, which shares a border with two of the three provinces that have PSTs federally collected, and with the possibility of a third province—Nova Scotia—being added. In essence, tax and monetary policies are countering the intentions of free trade agreements. Regional income, too, has a role. Those populations in regions that have the greatest concentration of income are the most likely to travel to the United States, particularly from Ontario and coastal British Columbia.

Same-day trips south for the primary purpose of shopping are not likely to increase, and in fact may continue to show a slight decrease. The data show that both same-day shopping and overnight traditional tourism shopping activity will continue to decline, but that the rate of decline is likely to be greater for shopping than for the more traditional recreational and cultural activities. Those places likely to continue to be most impacted are represented by shopping malls, and towns or cities with a large concentration of factory outlets. Those places which provide services other than shopping are likely to continue to experience some continued growth in gasoline sales, small retail (souvenir/gift) sales, lodging sales, and recreational and cultural sales.

If Canadian and provincial government debt were not reduced, the value of the Canadian dollar would decrease. This would probably result in decreased visitations to the United States for recreation and for shopping—and with obvious implications for borderland tourism-related businesses in the United States. Perhaps too, if the question of Quebec sovereignty were to be resolved, then too the Canadian dollar would gain ground—and with similar implications for cross-border visitations to the United States. While the government of Canada has no doubt realized a reduction in purchases by Canadians in the United States through rigorous enforcement of the GST, PSTs, and liquor and tobacco duties through border collections, these taxes do not have as much of an impact on a decrease in visitations to the United States except on a regional basis, as does the exchange rate. This is particularly true with both the New England states (especially the northern ones) and the Maritime provinces, which continue to trail in the recovery from recession of their respective nations.

Replacing the Manufacturers' Sales Tax with the GST was based on a two-part rationale: to increase Canada's broad-based tax collections, thus negating a need to increase income taxes, and to draw down the federal debt without having to resort to international borrowing. In 1991, when this tax replacement occurred, the Canadian dollar was trading at a high of U.S. $0.8726. This provided the impetus to go south to avoid the GST. Subsequently, the government of Canada moved to enhanced revenue collection methods at the border. It had no choice. American dollars being spent by Canadian shoppers were, in large part, dollars borrowed with interest in international financial markets. It was a downward spiral. Thus, over time, a condition approximating parity between two border states is a *sine qua non* of a sustainable border economy.

Moving more towards a condition of exchange rate parity would constitute a much more complex political and economic process than would be either a reduction in the GST or PST rates, or an altogether elimination of border collections. From the perspective of policy, a need exists for a cross-border dynamic which is roughly in balance. Continued cross-border trade is a condition of an ascending economy. For it to continue, economies on both sides of the border need to remain competitive. And such competition needs to be conducted within a context of cross-border political collaboration on matters of trade and tourism.

Tourism Activities and Shopping Preferences

Tourism is widely recognized as one of the world's largest industries. Shopping, a preferred tourism activity, is acknowledged as a primary means of generating tourism revenue and contributing to economic development. Shopping centre and mall managers are escalating efforts to attract tourists and increase the number of dollars they spend by specifically marketing malls as tourist destinations. Besides shopping, tourists also exhibit strong preferences for other tourism activities during their travels. In this research, investigation of tourists' shopping preferences was integrated with tourism activities to which they attached importance. The purpose of this research was to identify tourism activities sought during travel and to compare tourists in regard to their preferences for shopping venues, mall characteristics and product criteria. Three groups of tourism activities were revealed in the analysis: Outdoor-oriented activities; cultural, historical and arts-oriented activities; and sports-oriented activities. For each group of tourism activities, travellers with high and low "importance" scores were found to differ significantly in their shopping preferences. Outdoors tourists wanted to shop in tourist, craft and speciality stores, attached importance to the aesthetic features and uniqueness of malls, placed value on mall entertainment, and searched for mementos and gifts. Culture, History and Arts tourists looked to craft and speciality venues for shopping, were tuned to mall aesthetics and differentiation and focused on quality and artistic features of products they bought. Sports tourists attached importance to shopping at malls, attended to mall safety, navigation and sales associates' knowledge and sought entertainment and educational experiences while shopping at malls.

While they travel, tourists spend approximately three to four times more than the average shopper at shopping centres and malls according to the Travel Industry Association of America. As a result, shopping centre and mall managers are escalating their efforts to attract tourists and increase the number of dollars they spend by specifically marketing shopping centres and malls as tourist destinations. Because research on tourism retailing has only recently begun and attention is continuing to escalate, there appeared to be a justified need for investigation on the shopping preferences that tourists exhibit during their travels.

Given that there are many types of retail shopping venues competing for the same tourist consumer dollars, it is important to understand the preferences of different tourist groups and how these preferences can be used by retailers and shopping centres who target tourists for strategy development. A number of scholars have categorized travellers based on their preferred travel activities. One question that remained unanswered is whether different "types" or market segments of tourists approach shopping in different ways during their travels. For example, do travellers in different tourism activity segments vary in where they want to shop, the features that attract them to shopping malls and the criteria they consider when making purchase decisions? This investigation sought to provide practical and usable answers to these questions for retailers and shopping centre managers who target tourists.

Literature Review

The travel industry once considered retail shopping centres and malls to be competitors, not partners, for consumer dollars, according to William Norman, president and CEO of Travel Industry Association of America (TIA). Today, not only do shopping and travel go hand-in-hand, but shopping is also a cause to travel as reported by a recent survey, "The Shopping Traveller," by TIA. Retailers, shopping mall executives and tourism officials are taking notice of this phenomenon. The TIA report points out that 60% of U.S. travellers identify shopping as their favourite travel activity and that for half of tourists shopping is either the primary or secondary purpose of their travels. Further it was found that shopping expenditures on travel excursions were greater than $500 for 22%, averaged $333 and overall generated approximately $37.3 million for retail purchases during tourist travels in 1999. Tourists claim that travel is not complete without shopping. They also preferred and patronized more unique stores and malls that represent the destination they visit. Finally, 62% preferred more traditional malls, 50% sought downtown urban shopping districts and/or strip centres and 38% preferred outlet centres. Interestingly, tourists purchased more everyday lifestyle items, such as clothing, rather than souvenirs, from shopping centres and malls.

Because tourists are spending notably higher amounts of money than average shoppers at shopping centres and malls during their travels, shopping centre and mall managers are escalating their efforts to increase tourists and the number of dollars spent by strategically marketing shopping centres and malls as destinations for tourists. Included in those efforts to attract more tourists to shopping centres and malls is the new strategy of adding "tourism directors" to mall management executive staffs. Other strategies include targeting leisure travellers through special events, using strategic advertising and building relationships with convention and visitors' bureaus, hotels, state, tourism offices, airlines and tourism associations.

The physical design of the shopping centre or mall is also strategic. For example, at a major regional mall in the southeastern United States, a state's five diverse geographic regions are reflected in the physical attributes of the shopping centre: coastal, urban, plains, Piedmont and mountains. This strategic approach gives the visitor a "taste" of the entire state in which they are visiting and its heritage. Often referred to as providing an authentic "sense of place," this is considered a vital strategy for marketing a shopping centre as a destination site to tourists. Another strategy used by shopping centre and mall managers is to attract tourists by marketing shopping as a major tourist activity alongside golf, dining and arts and culture in major tourism areas. With the increased emphasis on shopping as a travel-associated activity, shopping centres, malls and retailers who consider tourists to be a major consumer group are increasing their efforts to develop a more thorough understanding of the tourist market. Market segmentation, the process of subdividing a large group of consumers into smaller groups based on distinctive characteristics, is useful to identify and profile distinct types of tourists.

An understanding of the various types of tourist consumers will provide shopping centres and mall managers with valuable information necessary to differentiate among competitors. In an effort to better identify and analyze tourist target market segments, researchers have developed typologies that profile tourist groups.

Four distinct tourist types were identified by Littrell et al. (1994) ethnic, arts and people) history and park; 3) urban entertainment; and 4) active outdoor. These profiles serve as a foundation for new investigations of the linkages between patronage and purchasing behaviour and the travel activities of different types of tourists. Littrell et al. (1994) suggest that expanded research on these tourist types would provide guidance to shopping centres and retailers in developing strategies for attracting tourists.

Obtaining a better understanding of the various groups of tourist consumers is important for any shopping centre in developing strategies for attracting tourists to their shopping centres. The purpose of this research is in response to an applied need among shopping centres and retailers to obtain a more thorough understanding of the shopping behaviour of tourists by identifying linkages among tourists with different preferences for travel with where and how they want to shop.

Purpose and Objectives

The purpose of this investigation was to identify various tourist consumer groups with similar preferences for travel and to compare and contrast them in regard to their shopping preferences during their travels. This research is timely in that tourism is one of the world's largest industries, which now acknowledges shopping as a primary means of generating tourism revenue. As shopping centres escalate their efforts to compete for tourist dollars, market segmentation through the development of distinct tourist segments will help shopping centres achieve a stronger competitive advantage.

Specific objectives for this study were to:

1) Identify and describe groupings of tourism activities.

2) Compare and contrast tourists with high and low importance scores for each type of tourism activity on a series of shopping variables, including shopping venues, mall characteristics and criteria for product purchases when they travel.

Method

Both qualitative and quantitative research techniques were used to gather the data necessary to accomplish the objectives. The researchers developed two instruments for data collection using the research literature related to tourism typologies and purchasing behaviour as the foundation and point of departure. The first instrument was an interview discussion guide which was used to gain information from a small sample of shopping centre managers, convention and visitors' bureaus and tourism agencies in order to establish validity for the mail survey. Information gathered using this instrument was then incorporated in the development of a survey questionnaire that was mailed to a sample of U.S. consumers. The questionnaire was designed to gain knowledge on travellers' preferred travel and shopping activities.

Sample for the Interviews

For the first step of data collection, 20 managers of shopping centres, directors of tourism agencies and convention and visitors' bureaus were invited to participate in personal interviews. These tourism professionals were from two regions of the United States, the Southeast (12 from South Carolina, Georgia and Tennessee) and the Midwest (eight from Iowa, Minnesota and Nebraska). Names of respondents were selected through perusing the telephone yellow page directories and from the Internet. Criteria for participation required that the professionals either be in a management position at a large, regional shopping centre/mall that was considered to be a tourist destination, or be a director or manager of a tourism agency. Ultimately a total of 13 respondents participated in the interviews, eight from the Southeast and five representing seven malls from the Midwest.

Sample for the Survey: A mailing list was purchased from a list brokerage firm, Survey Sampling, Inc. in Fairfield, Connecticut. A stratified random sample of 1,500 individuals was drawn from throughout the United States. Of the two strata, one-third was men and two-thirds women, all over the age of 17. Selecting a higher percentage of women was guided by results in previous research where 67% of tourism shoppers were women. Of the 1,500 questionnaires mailed, 86 (6%)

were returned non-deliverable because of an incorrect or non-forwardable address or because the person was deceased. An additional 12 (.8%) were under the age of 18 (n=4) or returned the questionnaire with statements indicating that they did not wish to participate in the research (n=8). From the remaining 1,402 questionnaires, 290 were completed and returned for a response rate of 21%.

Instruments

Discussion Guide for Interviews: A discussion guide of eight open-ended questions was developed. Questions ranged from initial broad inquiry related to trends in tourists' shopping over the past five, years and differences in tourist and non-tourist shoppers, and narrowed down to more specific questions that helped identify tourist market segments and tourists' shopping preferences at malls.

Questionnaire for Survey: After the results of the preliminary interviews were compiled the questionnaire was developed to measure the variables of interest to the study, including a list of vacation activity options, questions to determine shopping preferences and demographic questions to understand the make-up of the participants better. Respondents rated questions for importance of travel activities, mall characteristics and product criteria on a 5-point Likert scale with 1 being *very unimportant* and 5 being *very important.*

Procedure: In the first phase of the study, interviews were conducted with tourism professionals in order to increase the validity of the survey questionnaire. The interview process provided an avenue for active dialogue, between the participants and the researchers related to perceptions and concerns of importance to tourism professionals. Each potential participant received a cover letter of introduction explaining the intent and value of the research, requesting their participation in the study and assuring their anonymity. One week after the invitations were mailed, the tourism professionals were contacted by phone to confirm their participation. The day before the appointment, an additional confirmation phone call was placed to confirm the date, time and place of the interview. The interviews took place at the respondents' places of business. Prior to the beginning of the interviews the purpose of the study and the procedures were explained and anonymity was reassured. An audio recorder with a microphone was employed to collect data accurately for each interview. The length of the interviews varied between 60 and 90 minutes.

In the second survey phase of the research, potential respondents received a cover letter explaining the purpose and importance of the research, as well as a guarantee of anonymity, along with the questionnaire. One week after the first mailing, a reminder post card was sent to all non-respondents. Two weeks after the initial mailing, a second replacement questionnaire was mailed to all who had not yet responded.

Data Analysis

First, frequency and mean analyses were run to gain an overview of the sample characteristics and their shopping behaviour while travelling. Questions addressed the length of their last trip, how far they travelled from home, how much time and money was spent shopping during their travels, with whom they shopped and the number of trips taken in the year 2001. Demographic questions were analyzed related to gender, age, ethnic background, education, household income and family composition.

Factor Analysis: For the first stage of the quantitative analysis, four Principle Component factor analyses with Varimax rotation were carried out to reduce the number of items for tourist travel activities, shopping venues, mall characteristics and product criteria. The objective of factor analysis is to reduce a larger set of items to smaller groupings of internally consistent items. An assumption of factor analysis is that observed variables are combinations of some underlying hypothetical or unobservable factors. Factor analysis was employed in an *exploratory* manner, in that the researchers did not specify beforehand how many underlying dimensions or factors existed for each of the four variables.

For each of the analyses the conceptual clarity of the items within each factor, the strength of the factor loadings, scree plots and Eigenvalues over one served in making decisions on how many and which factors to retain. Items with factor loadings of at least and with a minimum difference from loadings on other factors of at least were retained to define the factors. Each factor was given a name based upon the salient theme that carried through the items. Cronbach's *alpha* coefficient of inter-item correlation was calculated for each factor grouping to determine the internal reliability. A Cronbach's *alpha* of was determined to be the lowest acceptable parameter for internal consistency.

Other Analyses: Once the factor groupings were formed, further analysis was carried out on each of the factors from the Principal Component analyses: travel activities, shopping venues, mall characteristics and product criteria. Additive scores were developed for each factor and computed for all participants. Finally, frequencies, means and standard deviations (SDs) were figured for the total of the newly grouped items in the factor.

For the purpose of comparing travellers with difference levels of importance given to travel activities, two groups were identified for each tourism activity factor: one group that gave greater importance for each set of activities and one group that indicated lower importance for the same set of activities. Criteria for inclusion into either group was that the high and low groups be approximately one standard deviation from the mean and that each group contain at least 50 respondents. Additive scores were then developed for the factors related to 1) the type of shopping venue where tourists prefer to shop during their travels; 2) the mall or shopping centre features that travellers prefer; and 3) the reasons why tourists buy certain products.

Analysis of Variance: Finally, using one-way analysis of variance (ANOVA), each group of tourists (based on high and low importance for a group of activities) was compared for their means on importance given to shopping venues, mall features and product characteristics. A.05 level of significance was employed in the ANOVA assessments.

Results

Sample Characteristics: Respondents for the study were primarily female at 75.4%, with male respondents being 24%. The ages of respondents ranged from 18 to 90 years; however, the average age of 55 years indicated an older group of travellers. Sixty-two percent of the respondents were over the age of 50. Caucasian-European-Americans represented the majority of the sample at 79.3% (n=230), followed by African-Americans at 6.6% (n=19), Ilispanics at 3.1% (n=9), Native Americans and Native Hawaiians at 1.4% (n=4) each and Asian-Americans at 1% (n=3).

Education levels ranged from completing less than 12 years of high school education (4.3%, n=12) to completing a graduate degree (19.7%, n=57). Overall, 42% had completed college, while nearly 53% were high school graduates or had earned some education beyond high school. More specifically, over 25% (n=71) had completed high school, 27% (n=75) had earned 1-3 years of technical, vocational school or college education, nearly 16% (n=44) had completed college and finally, nearly 6% (n=17) had some graduate education.

The majority of respondents (84%) had children, with two children being the average number. Having grandchildren was almost evenly split at 51.6% who had grandchildren and 49.4% who did not have grandchildren. Of those who had grandchildren, the average number was two.

Over half of the respondents reported that their total annual household income for 2001 was less than $50,000. More specifically, 19% (n=47) reported earning less than $25,000 a year, while 32.8% (n=81) earned between $25,000 and $49,999. In contrast, 43% of the respondents had household incomes over $50,000. In this group, 18.6% (n=54) reported an annual income of $50,000-$74,999, while 13% (n=32) stated that they earned $ 75,000-$99,999. And finally, 11.4% (n=33) indicated that they earned a total household income of over $100,000 in 2001.

The respondents were active travellers. During 2001, they took an average of 2.17 in-state trips of over two days, 2.72 trips out-of-state and trips out-of-country. On their most recent trip, the travellers were gone from home for an average of 8.18 days. Sixty-six percent travelled over 300 miles and another 19% journeyed between 150 and 300 miles. When asked about their shopping behaviour on the most recent trip, 27.8% shopped over seven hours, 29.2% shopped between four and six hours, 30.7% shopped for one to three hours and 12.4 percent shopped for less than one hour. Not only did the respondents shop, but they also made purchases. Sixty-four percent spent over $100 with 28% spending in the $200 to $500 range and another 15.1% committing over $500 to their purchases. When the respondents shopped, they tended to shop with a companion, rather than alone. Two-thirds shopped with an adult female. In contrast, a smaller percentage (21.7%) shopped with children. In summary, a typical respondent in this study was a 55-year-old, white female who had completed both high school and some post-high school education. She had two children but was as likely as not to have any grandchildren. Her annual household income could range from $25,000 to $75,000. The typical respondent took several trips in 2001, two in-state and two to three out-of-state, often travelling up to 300 miles and staying away from home for a little over a week on a recent trip. When travelling, the respondent shopped for at least four hours but likely more, and spent a minimum of $100 on her purchases. She did not shop alone, choosing instead to shop with another woman companion.

Tourism Activity Factors

The first objective of the study was to identify and describe groupings of tourism activities. Based on the factor analysis, tourists' preferences for activities grouped into five internally consistent and distinctive groupings. However, using the *alpha* score criterion of only three of the factors had acceptable reliabilities and were retained for further analysis. Total variance explained by the 5-factor solution was 49.1%. Outdoors Tourism included travel activities that were outdoor-oriented, such as visiting places designated as wilderness or natural areas and state or national parks. Camping, hiking, back packing, bicycling and visiting rural countryside areas were also distinguishing activities of this grouping. Culture, History and Arts Tourism encompassed attending cultural or ethnic festivals, visiting galleries, museums, historical or cultural heritage sites and travelling to archeological ruins. Finally, Sports Tourism included items that measured active participation in travel activities such as extreme sports (snowboarding, rock climbing), winter sports (skiing, snowshoeing, snowmobiling), golf or tennis, as well as attending sports events such as football, baseball or basketball.

High and Low Preference Groups for Tourism Activities

The second objective of this investigation was to compare and contrast tourists with high and low importance scores for each type of tourism activities on a series of shopping variables, including shopping venues, mall characteristics and criteria for product purchases when they travel. Given that two of the five tourism activity factors generated from the factor analysis did not have acceptable reliability, only three activity factors were analyzed further to determine tourists' level of preference for each activity: Outdoors tourism, Culture, History and Arts tourism and Sports tourism. The scores for high and low groups, along with the criteria (range, mean, SD) used for forming the two groups for each of the three activity factors. In order to conduct the comparison among groups of travellers, it was first necessary to conduct factor analyses on items measuring the importance respondents placed on various shopping venues, mall features and product characteristics.

The factor analysis for shopping venues resulted in three factors accounting for 51% of the variance. All factors exhibited acceptable reliability above. One group of venues, Tourism Stores, included a variety of stores frequented by tourists, including hotel, resort, or airport gift shops; camping area general store visitors' centre; and shops at various tourism destinations. Sporting goods and outdoors stores were also included in the Tourism Stores grouping. Six additional shopping venues were included in a second factor, titled Craft and Speciality Stores. These venues included craft fairs, antique shops, craft shops, art gallery and speciality gift and home decor stores. The third factor, Malls, included both shopping malls and outlet malls.

For the mall characteristics factor analysis, a 3-factor solution accounted for 55.1% of the variance with all factors exhibiting acceptable reliabilities of greater than. The first factor, Easy Shopping included mall features related to safety, accessibility, parking and ease of mall navigation. Additional items included stores offering bargains, salespersons with product knowledge and a chance to get away from the traveller's everyday routine. The second factor, Aesthetics and Differentiation, encompassed the external and internal design of the mall and its atmosphere and authenticity of appearance as related to nearby tourism sites. That the mall was convenient to tourist sites and offered shopping different than that at home were also features included in this factor. The final factor, Family and Entertainment, included a range of activities and forms of entertainment, including movies, restaurants and opportunities for learning through exhibits and special events.

The final factor analysis on product characteristics resulted in a 3-factor solution that covered 55.9% of the variance; all factors had acceptable reliabilities of over. One set of criteria, Design, Differentiation and Quality, gave importance to product design, colours, innovation and quality. The criterion that a product was different from what could be purchased at home was also included in this factor. A second factor, Mementos and Gifts, included criteria of gift giving for children and adults and that products purchased during travel served as mementos of a trip or representations of events attended. Finally, the items in the third factor, Practicality and Display, addressed issues of whether a purchase would be easy to care for, clean, pack and carry. The criterion of whether a product could be used in the home was also included in the factor.

Comparison of High and Low Preference Groups

Each of the tourism analyses revealed distinctive patterns and significant differences in their shopping preferences between those who placed higher importance versus those who placed lower importance on the tourism activities. For Outdoors tourism, respondents who gave great importance to the outdoors when they travelled were also significantly more likely than those with lower scores to give attention to shopping in tourism stores and in craft and speciality stores. However, they were less likely to want to shop in malls. When high Outdoors tourists shopped in malls, they wanted the mall to be attractive inside and out, authentic to the tourism area and offer a pleasing atmosphere different than at home. Also, as compared to travellers with low preference for outdoors tourism, those with higher scores wanted the malls to offer entertainment, activities, dining and educational events for themselves and their families. As they shopped, high outdoor tourism participants looked for mementos of their trip and products that could be used as gifts.

The high and low preference groups in the Culture, History and Arts tourism group also revealed significant differences in preferences during their travels. For Culture, History and Arts tourism, travellers who awarded great importance to these activities also chose craft and speciality stores for their shopping. Like the tourists with high scores for Outdoors Tourism, these tourists were also less likely to shop at malls than those with low preference for cultural and historic activities. Not surprisingly, as a group of travellers focused on culture and the arts, they gave importance to art-related characteristics for malls and for product criteria. Tourists who placed high importance on Culture, History and Arts tourism activities were particularly tuned to the aesthetics and atmosphere of a mall, while also valuing differentiation from shopping at home.

Shopping in a mall environment that mirrored the area's cultural and historic attractions also appealed to this group. When shopping, these tourists looked for products that were high quality, well-designed and new and innovative. That the purchases could serve as mementos or gilts were also important shopping criteria. Of particular note, the high Culture, History and Arts tourists were the only tourists to give significant attention to the design and quality of products.

Finally, the high and low importance groups for Sports tourism activities revealed yet another pattern for shopping. Similar to the other analyses, those travellers who gave greater importance to sports activities when they travelled also chose to shop at both tourism stores and craft and speciality stores. However, of the three travel activity groups, they were the only group that attached greater importance to shopping at malls than those with lower scores for these activities. Likewise, they were the only group to give greater weight to shopping at a mall that was safe, easy to locate and navigate and where sales associates were well informed about their merchandise. While travellers with high Sports tourism scores valued the aesthetics of a mall, their mean score for the family and entertainment factor was the highest of all groups, indicating a significant preference for entertainment, education and family activities as part of the shopping experience. Similar to the other two analyses, travellers who placed high importance on Sports tourism also identified whether a product could serve as a memento of a trip or a gift to be important criteria when making shopping decisions.

Typically Female Features in Hungarian Shopping Tourism

"God, I adore shopping abroad", sighs Rebecca Bloomwood, the heroine of Sophie Kinsella's popular Shopaholic books, and goes on to explain the advantages of doing shopping abroad: "you can buy things you can't get at home, you can name-drop when you get back, and foreign money doesn't count, so you can spend as much as you like". Although Rebecca is far more obsessed by shopping than the average person, her reasoning strikes a familiar chord with many shopping tourists throughout the world. In this paper, an attempt is made to analyse the typically female features of Hungarian tourists' shopping behaviour in order to understand the emotional and rational characteristics of this particular tourist segment.

Sixteen years after the collapse of the socialist regimes in East Central Europe, the region is still considered as one of the prominent areas in international shopping tourism. Although accession to the European Union has affected both the opportunities and the motivations of shopping abroad, the political and economic consequences of the 10-year-long preparation process have not significantly reduced the scale of international shopping tourism. As market studies indicate, Hungary has remained a major shopping destination for incoming travellers – particularly for day trippers arriving from the neighbouring countries – while Hungarians also show a willingness to travel abroad with the specific motivation to buy goods and, to a smaller extent, services.

Before the change of regime, pleasure shopping in Hungary was limited, due to the inadequate quality, range and marketing conditions of Hungarian goods. Opportunities for shopping abroad were also rather narrow, as a result of travel restrictions and enormous differences between eastern incomes and western prices. Therefore, many Hungarians replaced actual shopping experiences with browsing catalogues of Western European department stores, and a culture of so-called "virtual shopping" flourished. Consequently, when the opportunities to travel to the West widened in the late 1980's, hundreds of thousands of Hungarians "invaded" neighbouring Austria to buy modern consumer electronics and other household appliances. During one month in 1989, Hungarian shopping tourists spent in Austria the near equivalent of the country's total annual GDP in foreign currency. The era's shopping tourism was commonly called "Gorenje tourism", after a particularly popular brand of freezer purchased in large numbers by Hungarians. Although today's customers are not confined to the supply of local retailers, since most consumer goods have become available online, people nevertheless seem to be willing to set out and travel hundreds of kilometres for a better deal or for a more enjoyable shopping experience. As several researches have indicated, those rejecting online shopping tend to emphasize the lack of ability to personally check and try the selected goods as one of the major disadvantages of virtual shopping, i.e. they prefer to touch rather than to click on the monitor.

Shopping and Tourism

Although shopping has been long acknowledged as a major tourist activity, the extent and characteristics of shopping tourism have only recently become the subject of academic research and discussion. To date, research papers in this field have focused on a variety of themes, such as the role of shopping precincts in destination planning and development, service quality and shopping satisfaction in tourism, the characteristics and structure of tourists' shopping behaviour, the social and economic consequences of shopping tourism development and the tourist shopping phenomenon, the characteristics of souvenir purchase and the role of souvenirs shopping in destination image formation, or the motivations for, and benefits of, participation in shopping tourism.

When discussing the relationship between the phenomena of shopping and tourism, a distinction should be made between shopping tourism and tourist shopping. Shopping tourism is travel with the primary motivation of purchasing goods and services (stimulated by a favourable price-quality ratio, a wider range of supply or the added value of temporarily escaping a routine living environment), whereas tourist shopping is part of most trips as a very important leisure pastime. In quantitative terms, cross-border demand dominates the global shopping tourism sector, due to the utilitarian nature of the travellers' motivation. Cross-border shopping is common along nearly all borders in Europe; it also plays a significant role in the Americas, primarily on the USA– Canada and the USA–Mexico borders. In Europe, the cross-border shopping phenomenon has received most attention in the Denmark–Germany, Ireland–Northern Ireland, Switzerland–Italy and East-Central European contexts.

Although shopping as an additional activity enjoyed at the destination visited is a more frequent tourist pursuit than taking a trip with shopping as the primary reason to travel, both aspects of tourism play a major role in destination development and both have a significant impact on travellers' and local residents' quality of life. A destination's popularity among shopping tourists is influenced by a variety of factors including the availability of merchandise, the price-quality ratio of goods, and the area's specific features such as characteristic local products, famous shopping areas, themed shopping facilities or well-publicised shopping festivals. Leisure shopping is a universal tourist activity that usually adds to the overall attractiveness of a destination. As several researchers have pointed out, shopping on holiday may even appeal to people who normally do not particularly enjoy the activity at home. However, when assessing the relationship between tourists' socio-demographic characteristics and their shopping behaviour, several studies suggest that female travellers are generally more likely to be involved in shopping tourism. Therefore, after a brief description of the major characteristics of shopping tourism in Hungary, the paper focuses on the typically female features of outbound Hungarian shopping tourism.

Shopping Tourism in Hungary

In 2004, 17,558 millions Hungarians travelled abroad. Considering that the country's population is just over 10 million people, this figure means over 1.7 border crossings for each Hungarian citizen. The majority of outbound Hungarian travellers were day visitors, i.e. did not spend a night abroad.

When assessing the motivations of Hungarian outbound travellers, a significant relationship is experienced between the purpose of a trip and the length of stay: shopping plays a dominant role in one-day visits, but only 2.4% of Hungarian tourists take longer trips abroad with shopping as their primary motivation.

The geographical distribution of shopping tourism demand indicates that distance significantly affects travel behaviour: typically, Hungary's neighbouring countries prove to be the major destinations of one-day outbound shopping tourism. In 2004, the number of Hungarian arrivals reached or exceeded app. 2 million in Austria, Romania, Slovakia and the Ukraine, and several hundreds of thousands visited Serbia–Montenegro, Slovenia and Croatia. While these data are in close correlation with the population figures of Hungarian minorities living in these countries (i.e. VFR – visiting friends and relatives – is also a significant motivation of day trips), travel to these destinations – particularly to Romania and the Ukraine – is highly stimulated by the availability and range of inexpensive goods.

Slightly surprisingly, non-neighbouring countries such as Poland, Germany, Italy, Switzerland and the United Kingdom also feature among the shopping tourism destinations of Hungarian day trippers. However, as larger distances make travel more expensive, in these cases, fashion and status also play an important role in affecting travellers' decisions, and typically purchased products tend to be of rather high value.

In 2004, Hungarians spent 578 billion HUF abroad, out of which 108 billion HUF (18.7%) was spent by shopping visitors, with an average daily spending of app. 10,000 HUF per person (less than 40 EUR).

Research Methods

In 2005, a questionnaire-based survey on the shopping habits of Hungarian tourists was conducted by the Geographical Research Institute of the Hungarian Academy of Sciences in cooperation with Kodolanyi Janos University College (KJUC). A structured questionnaire based on close-ended questions was implemented through face-to-face interviews with respondents, conducted by interviewers from the KJUC who were selected according to their academic achievements and survey expertise. Participation was limited to adults (over the age of 18) who in the past five years have made at least one trip abroad. In total, 2473 questionnaires were evaluated. Although a convenience sampling method was used, the sample may be considered representative to the Hungarian population as the data were weighted by gender, age and region of permanent residence. 26.5% of the convenience sample were between the age 18–

26, 40.3% between 27– 39, 26.5% between 40–59, and 6.8% above the age of 60. 42.6% of the respondents were male and 57.4% female. Concerning participants' permanent residence, although the majority came from Central Hungary (including Budapest) (50.9%) and the Western part of the country (30.7%), all Hungarian regions were represented. In the interpretation of the survey findings, cross-table analysis was used to separate male and female habits and behaviour. Replies were categorised as typical and atypical for women. Those activities and factors were considered typically female where the ratio of women participating in certain activities or influenced by certain factors was higher than that of men. Typically female behavioural characteristics are seen above the line, while atypical features are seen below the line.

Female Features in Hungarian Shopping Tourism

A significant relationship exists between respondents' gender and their level of participation in tourist shopping (÷2=86868.424, sig.=0.000): during their trips abroad, female respondents were more likely to be involved in tourist shopping than male travellers. However, app. 95% of both genders did at least some shopping while travelling, and no significant difference was experienced between men and women concerning the share of shopping expenses compared to their total travel budget: in both cases, shopping expenses accounted for 25% of the overall spending.

When assessing the reasons for not always participating in tourist shopping, women were most likely to be affected by the unfavourable price levels, and the language barrier experienced in a foreign environment. The lack of leisure time also limited female respondents' shopping activities, although male participants felt similarly constrained by their pre-planned and pre-booked programmes. It should also be pointed out that women were much less likely to visit a place that did not offer any shops or any products worth buying, which might be related to their more shopping-oriented destination choices, but might also be explained by their more sophisticated skills to discover a shopping opportunity.

Tourists travelling abroad often purchase souvenirs and gifts in order to make their experiences tangible and to be able to share them with friends and relatives. Female respondents were more likely to buy products for themselves and their family member travel companions, as well as for their relatives left at home, while men and women were almost equally willing to buy any goods for friends and colleagues. Generally, the closeness of personal relationships affects both genders' shopping behaviour. The difference between men and women might be partly explained by the traditional female role of caring for others and anticipating others' needs.

Although the majority of Hungarian travellers did not make use of any specific information source when choosing goods on their trips, a few differences might be experiences between male and female respondents. On the one hand, women seem to be more affected by personal advice. It is interesting, however, to notice the different levels of trust expressed towards different kinds of people: both female and male respondents were most likely to rely on relatives' and friends' recommendations. Guides and fellow travellers – who represent the same cultural background and might have been considered as "being on the same side" by the respondents – were also relatively highly trusted compared to local people's suggestions, the latter often perceived as sales-and profit-oriented.

On the other hand, women's choices were more strongly influenced by promotional messages including advertisements and product catalogues. Altogether, female travellers seem to be slightly more conscious shoppers, since they used more information sources and were more likely to plan their purchases abroad or at least ponder the range of available goods.

Although no significant differences exist between men and women according to the main factors affecting their product choice abroad, female travellers proved to be slightly more rational in their shopping behaviour, since they were more motivated to make a purchase by lower prices or by the lack of certain goods or certain brands in Hungary. Women were also a little more likely to be influenced by the general need of buying certain products, i.e. they needed a new pair of shoes or a new coat anyway, so they bought them while being abroad.

The better price-quality ratio of specific goods or brands influenced both genders' product choice, with male travellers being slightly more value-conscious in their decisions. Similarly, men and women were almost equally affected by the unwritten rule of having to buy something abroad, as over 75% of the survey participants admitted that they simply did not want to return home empty-handed. Shopping as a tourist activity may already start on the journey to the destination, and may influence the whole stay as well as the return journey home. However, most respondents preferred to do their purchases in the destination, with men and women slightly differing in the inclusion of shopping in their general programme schedule: while female respondents were more likely to regard shopping as a valuable activity on its own right, males were more inclined to have it done as part of their other programmes.

Tourist shopping, due to its highly social nature, may be strongly influenced by the milieu of the shopping venues, thus it is particularly important to understand travellers' preferences and choices of such venues. As demonstrates, ordinary shops used mainly by members of the local population proved to be the most popular type of shopping venue among female respondents, followed by traditionally tourist-oriented gift shops and street vendors. Women's preferences are partly explained by their higher level of price sensitivity on the one hand, since shops aimed mainly at the local population may be perceived as more favourable choices among budget-conscious travellers.

The popularity of gift shops on the other hand may be related to female respondents' relatively high willingness to buy products for themselves as well as for family members and other relatives, as these venues are usually seen as the most suitable places for buying destination-specific souvenirs. In addition, gift shops are also generally able to satisfy those tourists' needs who do not have any specific goods on mind, but do not want to leave the destinations without having made any kind of purchase either.

As the survey results suggest, the most significant differences between male and female tourist shopping behaviours exist with respect to the range of purchased goods. Women were far more likely to buy clothes, shoes and accessories including jewellery (which might be seen as slightly surprising, since high-priced diamond rings are rarely bought for oneself, but the response category in the survey included all kinds of fashion jewellery as well). Clothes, shoes and accessories are generally considered popular travel purchases, since they satisfy the consumer's aesthetic needs and may be worn in public, thus providing an opportunity for the wearer to discuss travel memories, to gain status among peers by "name-dropping", or simply to be reminded of the trip and the destination. The second category of products that female travellers were more likely to purchase includes sweets, toys and smaller gifts –

goods that are typically bought for friends and family members, including children.

The fact that women also showed a slightly higher interest in buying art, decorative objects and interior design products is also in line with the traditional role of women as homemakers. In addition, as the survey results show, stereotypical social roles still rather prevailing in Hungary are further reflected by male travellers' significantly higher involvement in purchasing alcohol, consumer electronics and other technical equipment as well as fuel.

In order to study male and female travellers' price-sensitivity and "bargain-hunting" characteristics, respondents were asked to indicate the distance they were willing to travel in order to buy otherwise necessary products sold at certain price discounts. As, a significant relationship exists between the original price of the product, the discount to be received and the distance that participants were willing to travel. In addition, the results of an ANOVA variance analysis suggest that gender is significant in explaining variations in distances that respondents were ready to travel to find a bargain (in case of 25% discount: F=24886.012, sig=0.000; in case of 50% discount: F=6865.135, sig=0.000).

The survey results demonstrate that although women's participation in tourist shopping seemed to be more affected by price levels, male respondents proved to be more attracted by bargains: although the difference in travel distances was a moderate 2.84 km in case of a 25,000 HUF product sold at 50% discount, on average, men were willing to travel almost 12 km more to buy either a 50,000 HUF or 100,000 HUF product at 50% discount.

However, both genders proved to be highly rational in their decisions: when comparing the costs of travel (i.e. fuel consumption) with possible savings, on average, travel expenses amounted to only 12–17% of the savings realised by buying the product away from home.

2

Tourist Shopping Experiences and Satisfaction

Naturally, shopping as one of the most important tourism activities has an important economic impact on host communities, as it requires the spending of money for leisure purposes. However, the effects of shopping may not be limited to economic gains for local, regional and national economies. The products purchased by tourists for different reasons may help a destination develop a favourable image in the mind of tourists and their friends and relatives, because people in general, and tourists in particular, tend to share their experiences through photos, videos and items they purchased while away. Thus, in addition to using tourism as an alternative economic growth strategy, developing various components of the industry (e.g. shopping) may be used as a political tool to promote an auspicious image on the international stage. This might suggest that a well-managed tourist shopping experience may function as a tool for building a more favourable image of tourist destinations. In this context, Fodness (1994) implies that understanding the motivation of tourists visiting a destination is important for marketers to develop a better image for the destinations and products they promote, and to assess their service quality. Thus, from a holistic point of view, using every element of the tourism product contributing to the overall travel experience is essential for establishing a better destination image and achieving differentiation among many commodiffed destinations around the world.

Against this background, the principal objective of this study is to examine the tourist experience of shopping and tourist perceptions of shopping attributes in the context of Cappadocia, Turkey, with reference to price, destination characteristics, merchandising, authenticity, service quality, and the shoppers' personal characteristics. Before this, however, it is opportune to shed some additional light on the phenomenon of shopping and tourists' shopping experiences.

Tourist Shopping Experiences

The 'experience' is a complex combination of factors that shape tourists' feelings and attitudes towards their visiting and spending time in a destination. Shopping as an important component of travel is a mixture of perceptions of products, services and places. In fact, the tourist-shopping experience is the sum of tourist satisfaction or dissatisfaction gained from the individual attributes of products and services purchased.

Service and merchandise provided by retailers and vendors are an important part of the destination experience. In this regard, shopping refers to a contemporary recreational activity involving looking, touching, browsing and buying, which helps fulfil people's need for enjoyment and relaxation and which helps tourists escape from their daily routines.

Research shows that various factors influence tourists to shop or not to shop and make their experience satisfying or not. According to Keown (1989), cultural, economic and lifestyle factors clearly affect tourists' propensity to buy. According to most research, the most important variable in stimulating tourist shopping is price differentials between home and the destination. For example, Hong Kong and Singapore are well-known shopping destinations, particularly for duty-free goods, owing largely to their price advantage on both imported and locally made products.

The cultural structure of the destination community and other place characteristics are also seen as a factor affecting tourists' shopping behaviours and experiences. Although shopping functions as a leisure tourist activity, it also creates a significant opportunity for visitors to become exposed to the host culture. In particular, locally made handicrafts and souvenirs designed as tourist products may reflect elements of indigenous cultures. In fact, despite changes in art works wrought by tourism, through long-term shopping patterns and behaviours of tourists, these items can become symbols of local culture. The majority of the tourism product is intangible, but shopping provides tangible ways to experience the destination vis-a-vis the purchasing of souvenirs and gifts for friends and relatives, with these items even contributing to the satisfaction of travellers' psychological needs. Part of the experience also deals with aesthetics, where tourist shoppers are able to examine, feel and think about items even if shopping is not a principal reason for their travels. Tourists typically commemorate their experiences with souvenirs.

Souvenirs become a symbol, or memento, of their travels for themselves and others. Many tourists also exhibit self gift-giving so that they can position their trophies at home or at work to remember and remind others of their visit to interesting destinations.

It has also been noted that product selection and in-store atmosphere should match target shoppers' expectations, since these can influence tourists' emotions and behaviours related to shopping. Retailers endeavour to induce positive consumer reactions by changing in-store environments that titillate the senses, such as music, scent, climate, employee appearance and colour. Likewise, attractive and high quality retail displays and designs can make the tourist shopping experience more enjoyable and motivate visitors to spend more on shopping. Alterations in retail settings and design are carried out to provide satisfying shopping experiences, to protect a favourable store image, and to alter consumers' mood, perceptions and satisfaction levels. Thus, retailers tend to prepare their stores as theatres that carry customers into different, extraordinary and exciting shopping environments.

Useful and appealing handicrafts can be an interesting attraction and effective form of guest entertainment while they become a source of income for local artisans. The authenticity (perceived or otherwise) of these crafts and other retail products in relation to the local area is one of the most important elements in purchasing pursuits, as tourist shoppers are more often than not interested in locally made items that are typical or indigenous to the destination. 'Authenticity is typically viewed as a socially constructed notion that can be heavily influenced by producers, sales clerks, social traditions and consumers' own experiences and knowledge' (Timothy, 2005) and includes buyers' perceptions of originality, historical and cultural integrity, aesthetics, crafts people, functional use and materials utilised.

Shopping is a social phenomenon and involves much more than simply the acquisition of products. As a result, salespeople play an important role in creating the shopping experience. Jones' (1999) study found that salespeople helped create an enjoyable experience by being courteous and helpful. Likewise, results of a study by Heung and Cheng (2000) indicate that staff service quality had the most important effect on tourists' levels of satisfaction with shopping in Hong Kong, followed by product value and product reliability.

Personal attributes, such as cultural and ethnic background, also influence shopping experience and behaviour. According to a study of differences in shopping satisfaction levels between Asian and Western travellers' expectations and perceptions of shopping in Hong Kong, there was a significant difference between the two groups. It was found that western travellers were more satisfied with all the individual attributes than Asian travellers. It was noted that western travellers might in fact be better treated as a result of their relatively higher level of purchasing power than Asian travellers. Choi and Chu (2000) and Kozak (2001) also reported that nationality and demographic features could impact tourists' levels of satisfaction as consumers. Others have noted similar cultural influences on types of merchandise purchased, amounts of money spent and levels of enjoyment.

There are certainly many other variables that influence the tourist shopping experience, but those mentioned above have received relatively little treatment in the tourism literature. The discussion above suggests that various venue, destination, service and merchandise, and shopper attributes influence the shopping experience of tourists. Although there are a few studies that cover some venues, many regional factors affecting tourists' perceived satisfaction with shopping have been ignored. This study, therefore, aims to examine tourists' perceptions of shopping culture, staff service quality, product value and reliability, physical features of shops, payment methods, tourists' pre-and post-shopping experience, their expectation from overall shopping experience, shoppers' individual characteristics as consumers which contribute differently to overall shopping satisfaction and experience of tourists. It also examines the effect of cultural differences between tourists as buyers and shop operators as sellers on the shopping experience of visitors. By examining these issues, with special reference to a major tourist destination in the Cappadocia region of Turkey, this study will provide policy recommendations for marketing local tourist destinations in a better way by using shopping as an additional tool.

The Cappadocia Region

Cappadocia is located in the Central Anatolia region of Turkey. Its name was probably derived from Katpatuka — land of the beautiful horses, in the Hittite language. When the Hittites lived there, Cappadocia covered a larger area, but it is now a triangular area bordered by the cities of Kayseri, Nevsehir and Nigde in the centre of the Anatolian plateau. The history of Cappadocia began some 60 million years ago, when the ancient volcanic mountains, chief among them the noble Erciyas, the Hasan and the Melendiz Mountains, spread their volcanic ashes over the area. In the course of several millennia, rain and wind eroded the tufa, creating unusual valleys, fissures, canyons and cones, shaping the interesting and unique Cappadocian tuff-coned landscape. For hundreds of years, humans have dug into the soft but firm tuff to create dwellings, monasteries, churches and underground cities.

In the region are relics of various prehistoric and historic civilisations. Neolithic people (8–7 millennia BC) settled there in Hacilar and Catalhoyuk. Hatti culture (2500–2000 BC) thrived during the Bronze Age, and in the second millennium BC, the Hittites settled in the region, as did the Assyrians (2000–1800 BC), the Phrygians (1250 BC) and the Lydians (334 BC). In AD 17, the region became a Roman province, under whose rule early Christians selected the Goreme Valley and Urgup for building churches in the year 53 AD, which were decorated with impressive religious frescoes. During the seventh century, the emergence of iconoclasm, Byzantine persecution, caused the Christians to move away and seek refuge in caves and underground towns they had dug. The region was annexed to the Ottoman State in 1446. Today, despite the growth of tourism, agriculture remains the largest economic sector as it creates jobs for 70% of the local population. Additionally, 15% of the local population are traders, 10% have independent businesses, while the remaining 5% are employed in other areas. Between the 1950s and early 1980s, local people established small-scale tourism businesses such as accommodation facilities, cafes, shops and restaurants by converting some parts of their individual dwellings. The central government designated Cappadocia an important region for tourism and gave generous fiscal incentives to support medium-and large-scale tourism investments in the area. Unfortunately, the local people have not benefited fully from the government's generous incentives for the tourism industry, since many lack the necessary capital and skills to be effective tourism entrepreneurs. As a result, relatively large capital owners outside the local community have invested successfully in the region's tourism industry. The majority of the local population has had to invest and work in tourism on a small scale. For local residents, shopping has been one of the main income sources from tourism, because tourists' retailing patterns are based primarily on the purchase of handicrafts produced in the area by local artisans.

There are many shopping opportunities in Cappadocia. Goreme and its famous valley are situated right in the centre of Cappadocia, where an open air museum and numerous churches make up a large monastic complex. There are underground cities in Kaymakli, Derinkuyu and Ozkonak. Avanos is a small Cappadocian city of artisans situated on the banks of the river Kizilirmak—the 'Red River' — Turkey's longest river. The water is coloured by red clay deposits used to make Avanos' famous pottery. Every year in the summer Avanos and its artisans celebrate with a festival where the finest ceramics are displayed. In town the streets give way to workshops, and the roadsides are inundated with vases, amphora, earthenware pots of varying sizes, mugs and plates. Other artisans in Avanos are involved in weaving carpets. There is a weaving school in the city, where apprentices learn the ancient arts of weaving and dyeing wools and silks. In addition to carpets being produced in workshops, many women weave carpets at home as well. These products often appear on the streets, flanked by old buildings and houses. In the centre of town there is an unusual monument depicting two women kneeling at a loom and a potter at work. Avanos is a well-established venue for tourist shopping. Uchisar is called 'Pigeon Valley' based on its historical pigeon lofts. In this area, tourism has boosted local handicrafts, including the production of carpets, which are distinguished by simple multicoloured geometric patterns. Urgup is home to many small shops and stores selling a wide range of products from carpets to ceramics and small souvenirs. Other souvenirs can be bought in Soganli and its valley.

Soganli's women make handicrafts typical of these areas, such as dolls in national costumes, wool gloves, and colourful and elegant puppets. Briefly, in Cappadocia, tourists generally buy local products, such as carpets, ceramics, precious stones and jewels, other souvenirs and items of clothing, especially leather.

Research Methods

This study employed a survey questionnaire that was based on a comprehensive review of the relevant literature, opinions of academicians and experiences of the authors. It was conducted through face-to-face interviews with tourists in the Cappadocia region. A draft of the questionnaire based on the literature was sent to and discussed with many shopping academics via the Internet. These global discussions contributed to the development of the questionnaire. Based on the feedback, the questionnaire was further enhanced by improving expressions, removing some items and adding new ones. Following this academic consultation, a pilot test was implemented. Finally, the questionnaire involved open-ended, multiple-choice and Likert-scale questions. The questionnaire consists of four sections. The first section included a study of the tourists' general travel experiences; favourite shopping areas in Turkey and tourists' spending patterns; budget for shopping; kinds of products they bought; purpose of shopping and travel; and payment methods. The second section explored issues related to shop features and personnel/service factors affecting tourist shopping satisfaction levels. Section three included questions related to tourists' perception of local shopping culture, product reliability, availability of shopping information, respondents' level of trust for tour guides and shop owners, and other items reflecting tourist shopping behaviour. The fourth section elicited demographic information.

The above process, including a wide-ranging multidisciplinary literature review which established a conceptual framework, and feedback from the pilot test and connections with other academics, has ensured content validity and construct validity for the data collection instrument employed for this research.

Moreover, the scale (questionnaire) was tested for reliability using Cronbach's alpha (d"4" = 0.81 for the second section and d"4" = 0.74 for the third section). As noted above, a pilot study was done with a sample of 20 tourists, resulting in a Cronbach's alpha of 0.77 and 71 respectively. 'As a rule of thumb alpha should be least 0.70 before we say the scale is reliable'. In brief, the result of reliability analysis of the items suggests that there is an acceptable level of internal consistency among the variables. Through this process, the questionnaire developed for this research was deemed reliable.

Although the literature from business studies, retailing, tourism, sociology, psychology and economics led the research design, site-specific personal experience and cultural proximity of the principal researchers have provided extraordinary input to shape the overall research structure. For example, although the current literature on shopping issues focuses on the various factors affecting customer satisfaction, it ignores cultural differences between sellers and buyers. This particular study attempts to highlight this relatively less-studied issue, along with an examination of more traditional factors affecting shopping experiences and satisfaction levels. Nonetheless, given the difficulties of collecting data about cultural differences, this study's contribution in this regard is limited.

Sampling

According to statistical figures from the Tourism Ministry of Turkey (2003), some 343 331 foreign tourists stayed in Cappadocia in 2002. This was the population for this study. Tourists taking at least a one-day tour in the region arranged by one of the local travel agencies were culled as the sample. There were no statistical figures on what percentage of foreign tourists visited Cappadocia by local tour. Therefore, from the population of 343 331 foreign tourists, the sample size was calculated as 384 by employing the formula utilised by Ryan (1995), which requires a decision about what population proportion to use. For example, 'If there is not a priori inclination, as in the case of this research, then the value of $p = 0.5$ is often used'. 'This assumes a 50/50 split on the variable for a more skewed population, which would require a larger sample than one that has a 20/80 split on the variable for a more homogenous research population'. Sampling error or allowable error is conventionally accepted between 1 and 10%; however, it is suggested that sampling error should be carefully assessed in light of the nature of the derivation of the population proportion and other aspects of the initial data. On the basis of the argument given above, this research accepted a 6% allowable error. At the 95% confidence level, Z score or standard deviation is again conventionally accepted as 1.96. This means that we can be 95% confident that the results in the population will be the same as in the sample plus or minus the sampling error.

According to the above formula, the calculated sample size of 384 was the required number for a representative of sample. So, by utilising a purposive sampling approach, 400 questionnaires were distributed to foreign tourists to strengthen the representativeness of the population. Data were collected in July and August 2003, the highest tourism season in the region. The principal investigators visited almost all of the local travel agencies and gave them survey questionnaires to be distributed to the tourists taking a local tour through their firms. A brief written explanation was given to the tour guides on how to conduct the survey questionnaire. The tour guides were asked to give the questionnaire to the tourists to complete after the tour and while on the way to their hotel or in travel agency offices while waiting for transport to leave the region. In total, 378 out of 400 questionnaires were completed and returned. This represents a response rate of 94.5%.

Findings

In light of the above conceptual issues, the field research was conducted to determine the following: the importance of shopping as a travel motivation factor; tourists perceptions of shopping culture; staff service quality; product value and reliability and physical features of shops; payment methods; effects of cultural differences on shopping satisfaction; and tourists' expectations from the overall shopping experience.

Demographic Profile

Demographic profiles of the respondents (e.g. age, gender, education, income) and previous experiences could influence their attitudes, perceptions and motivations and affect their travel decisions. For example, some observers have argued that there is an essential difference between male and female attitudes towards shopping. Women are generally more positive about shopping than men and in turn they spend more money shopping than men do. In this study, the gender distribution of respondents was 62.2% female and 37.8% male. The three dominant age groups of the respondents were 26–35 (44.4%), 36–45 (29.9%) and 15–25 (19.6%) whereas the age group 46–55 (4.8%) and senior travellers aged 56 years and older made up the smallest group, representing 1.3% of respondents. In terms of level of education, 18.5% of the respondents had primary school, 18.5% high school, 57.7% college or university, and 5.3% postgraduate degree. With regard to personal monthly income, 17.5% earned under US$1000, 24.6% earned US$1001–2000, 15.1% earned US$2001–3000, 6.6% earned US$3001–4000, 2.6% earned US$4001–5000 and 33.6% avoided to answer the question. That among the 378 respondents, 208 (55%) were of western origin (USA — 8.2%, UK — 8.2%, Germany — 6.3%, Australia — 6.1%, France — 6.1%, Italy— 5.0%, Canada — 2.6%, Spain — 3.7%, Holland — 2.9%, Poland — 2.1%, Greece — 2.9%, Hungary — 0.8) and 170 (45%) were of Asian origin (South Korea — 19.8%, Japan — 16.9%, China — 2.6%, Singapore — 2.6%, Egypt— 0.8%, S. Africa — 2.1%).

Respondents' average length of stay in the region was two-and-a-half days. Preferred accommodation types were hotel (74.6%), pension (boardinghouse) (17.7%), motel (2.9%) and backpacker lodgings (4.8%).

Pre-shopping Attitudes

Whereas 63.1% of respondents were first-time travellers to Turkey, 61.6% of the respondents had not purchased Turkish products prior to this trip. Moreover, 70.6% of the respondents indicated that they did not plan to shop before coming on the tour to the region. Although the Grand Bazaar (Istanbul) was reported as the most favourable shopping place, it was followed by Cappadocia, Antalya, Kusadasi and East Anatolia. Although the authors believe that a lack of information about shopping opportunities in the region may be one of the primary reasons, further research is needed to find out the other reasons the majority of respondents had not thought about shopping before purchasing the tour to the region. Knowing facts in this regard has the potential to help tourism stakeholders, particularly shop operators, to design effective and efficient strategies to make the region more attractive for shoppers.

Budget and Payment Methods

Whereas half of the respondents reported that they planned to spend up to US$250 in the region, around 40% planned to spend up to US$250 specifically on shopping. However, 51.1% actually ended up spending less than US$250 on shopping. This may suggest that although some 11% of respondents did not plan to spend money shopping, they did eventually do so. Obviously, it is beyond this study to explain what factors made those respondents spend on unplanned shopping purchases, but these factors should be evaluated since they can be utilised as an instrument to increase the region's attractiveness in shopping terms. For example, respondents might not have had sufficient information about shopping opportunities in the region prior to their visit, and the variety of retail opportunities only became evident only after arriving in the area. Respondents put the payment methods in the order of cash (52.4%), credit cards (48.1%) and cheque (79.6%).

Shopping as a Motivational Factor for Travel

Respondents were asked to state what motivated them to visit the region. They were given 11 factors and were requested to put them in order of importance. The item, 'to experience new cultures and places'

(63.8%) was expressed as the most important motivational factor for visiting. This was followed by meeting new people (31.2%), shopping opportunities (23.3%), tasting local foods (22%), having a holiday romance with a foreign man/woman (18.5%), health/spa (17.7%), business and meetings (15.3%), general touring/sightseeing or driving for pleasure (14.3%), religious purposes (13.8%), and interacting and spending time with travel companions (10.6%).

The above figures suggest that although shopping opportunities were the third most important reason for visiting the region, interacting and spending time with travel companions was the least important. Although there are many religious relics belonging to various faiths, visiting the region for religious purposes was indicated as the second least important motivational factor. These results may be explained by the evolution of the destination. For example, Tosun (2001) asserts that during the initial stage of tourism development, the exploration phase, independent tourists visited Cappadocia for cultural and religious purposes during the 1960s and 1970s. However, the tourism development policies designed by the military-led governments in the early 1980s accelerated the transformation of the region from the exploration stage to Butler's development stage.

Consequently, early on, the region attracted more of Plog's (1973) allocentrics and Cohen's (1972) institutionalised tourists who do not have a genuine interest in cultural and heritage attractions. Allocentrics, in the psychographic typology of Plog (1973), are more willing to take risks and are more adventurous than others. They travel by themselves or in pairs, make their own tour arrangements, avoid heavily developed tourism destinations and are open to spontaneous changes. Cohen's institutionalised tourists are the individuals of mass tourism. These tend to buy package tours with all transportation, attractions, accommodations and meals arranged in advance.

Desired Shopping Items

Respondents were asked to state what items they had actually purchased during their visit. The answers were general souvenirs (78.3%), pottery (53%), clothes (19.8%), carpets (17.7%), jewellery (15.6%) and leather (4.8%). However, in response to one of the open-ended questions, most respondents noted that despite the fact that carpets were the most attractive items to buy, prices were higher than they had expected.

In response to 'what motivated you to shop in Cappadocia', half of the respondents indicated that authenticity of the product was the first factor, followed by efficiency of sales staff (25.7%), the tour itself (24.3%) and quality of products (22.5%).

Tourists' Satisfaction with Attributes of Shops and Staff Service

Respondents were asked to note their satisfaction levels with tangible attributes of shops and the service of staff. Answers were examined by assigning ranks based on the mean (M) scores of each variable from the lowest mean (rank equals to 11) to the highest mean (rank equals to 1). The higher the M score, the higher the level of satisfaction. Variety of products was scored highest, followed by product authenticity. Other variables were ranked in the following order: language ability of sales staff, location of shops, accessibility, choice of payment method, staff knowledge of products, shop hours, attitude of staff, lighting-ambiance, and neatness or cleanliness of shops respectively.

Tourists' Perception of the Shopping Environment

Respondents were asked to state their level of agreement or disagreement on 23 variables representing five different dimensions of shopping including shopping culture, shopping information, product reliability, issues affecting shopping decisions, and trustworthiness. For the purpose of this study, an additional item was included to measure relative shopping experience of respondents abroad. The majority of respondents (64%) had a positive shopping experience. However, 45.8% agreed or strongly agreed that the area was over-commercialised, whereas a much smaller proportion (15.6%) disagreed or strongly disagreed. A majority (51%) reported that sales staff behaved aggressively to capture tourists. Responses to an open-ended question supported this assertion. For example, one participant noted that 'during my vacation most people working in tourism had a clear emphasis on shopping. This over emphasis diminished my satisfaction and enjoyment of my vacation. This bothered me and I may not come back to Turkey'. Another respondent argued that 'This is a cultural thing. Maybe others feel the same way. In many shops the sales people are walking right behind you. It makes you feel very uncomfortable, then you think maybe they think I am guilty of shoplifting'.

Although the majority of respondents (50.8%) stated that they liked the tradition of bargaining, 48.7% of them stated this tradition reduces trust, whereas only 26.2% stated their disagreement or strong disagreement with this item. Interestingly, 36% of the respondents found that the difference in shopping culture was difficult for them whereas 39.4% did not. In general, and as a reflection of the tradition of bargaining, prices are not written on the products—rather, sales staff tell customers when they ask. For the majority of tourists (57.7%), this reduces trust. The vast majority (64%) agreed or strongly agreed on the lack of information about shopping opportunities in the region. Of the respondents, 54.3 and 64.5% were satisfied with product reliability and quality respectively.

A majority of the respondents (54.3%) stated that they visited different shops to compare products and prices, but a larger majority (67.7%) preferred shopping venues where local people shop. Surprisingly, less than one-third of respondents (30.1) stated that low prices were a main reason for their shopping in the region, whereas this was not a major factor for approximately one-fourth. It is interesting to note that a significant portion of the respondents (26.5%) could not decide if low prices were the main factor in their decision to shop. More than half of the respondents (51.6%) stated that they took into account the advice of the tour guide about shopping, whereas less than a quarter (20.6%) did not. Just under half of all respondents (46.8%) preferred shopping alone to shopping with a group, whereas 27.7% of them stated their disagreement or strong disagreement with this item. Moreover, 35% agreed or strongly agreed with the statement 'I prefer shopping centres to individual shops'. Finally, a majority of the respondents (54%) stated that they shopped generally for souvenirs.

Respondents were also asked to compare their overall shopping experience in Cappadocia with their previous shopping experiences abroad. Half of the respondents reported that they were more satisfied with their shopping experience in Cappadocia than their previous shopping experience abroad.

Conclusion

This paper has examined the tourist shopping experience in the Turkish region of Cappadocia. The authors are cognizant that the findings cannot necessarily be generalised to shopping destinations everywhere. However, they provide valuable information for the study region in particular, as well as for similar cultural regions in other parts of the world. In this context, variables representing tourist satisfaction with shopping attributes, features of shops, and the service quality of sales staff, among others, were considered. It was found that although a vast majority of respondents had not previously been to Turkey, had not previously bought Turkish products, and had not planned to shop in the region, more than half of the respondents actually engaged in shopping once there. This may suggest that shopping opportunities in general in Turkey and in particular in the study region have not been promoted sufficiently to the international tourism market. This result is supported by the responses given to the item 'lack of information about shopping opportunities in the region'. It is a fact that shopping is often one of the main appeals of visiting a tourist destination and is among the most pervasive of tourist activities.

Thus, sufficient information should be provided about shopping opportunities in the region through various advertising media to create more enjoyable travel experiences in general and better shopping experiences in particular. This is not only necessary for improving tourist satisfaction; it is also vital for authorities to sustain the region as a competitive tourist destination and increase the area's economic benefits. It may be argued that using every supply component of the tourism destination, including shopping, as a marketing feature has become necessary under fierce competition between many similar 'commodified' tourist destinations. Although the results indicate that shopping is the third most important reason for visiting the region, product authenticity was the most important factor in motivating respondents to shop.

The study also demonstrates that respondents were satisfied with the authenticity of products, although this was not defined in this study, and its meaning in the context of shopping and souvenirs is rather dubious. Surprisingly, although previous research suggests that relative prices between countries are the most important motive for tourists to shop, this study demonstrates that the relatively low prices in the study region were not in fact the most important influence in respondents' decision to purchase. Based on these findings, three main policy recommendations may be suggested to achieve sustained tourism development through shopping.

First, retail venues should be improved. If necessary, new shopping facilities should be established. It is also argued that tourist shopping facilities should not be developed separately from places where local people shop, since the findings here suggest that visitors are interested in shopping where destination residents shop.

Second, in this regard, it is suggested that shopping activities and shopping experience should be presented as a part of local culture since the vast majority of respondents (63%) in this study desired to experience new cultures and places. Clearly, cultural tourism appeals to a larger segment of the international tourism market than shopping tourism alone does. Therefore, retail opportunities should be promoted as part of an augmented product of cultural tourism in the region, rather than a core product itself.

Third, the authenticity of retail merchandise in particular and the region as a local tourist destination in general should be defined, maintained and protected. For example, a participatory tourism development approach can be utilised to maintain and improve product authenticity in terms of souvenirs and handicrafts. To achieve this objective, local people, including indigenous artisans, should be encouraged by receiving financial incentives, free consultancy services in the production of crafts and souvenirs, and training to develop their entrepreneurial skills.

However, Tosun (1998a) argued that highly organised mass tourism limits tourists from experiencing the authenticity of local culture. He asserts that: Tour guides and big hotel companies do not want tourists to visit small shops in the centre of the county. They have often given wrong information to tourists in order to stop them visiting the locally owned small shops... tourists are frequently directed to visit predetermined large shops with which tour guides and hotel companies have made commission contracts. These shops are just outside of the county and many of them are owned and operated by non-local people.

Some hotel companies even provide free accommodations for tourists in order to sell goods from their souvenir shops. In this regard, it is argued that tourists should be left free to visit city centres, and city tours should be encouraged. If necessary, some regulations should be enacted. Professional experience in the tourism sector and personal observations by the authors suggest that without breaking down psychological and commercial barriers built around tourists by well-organised tour guides, travel agencies and large accommodation companies, it may be difficult to create real opportunities for tourists to buy souvenirs and handicrafts at local prices, and to experience the sociocultural shopping environment shared by local residents. Tosun argued that: Consumer rights associations, the Association of Turkish

Travel Agents and Tour Operators, the association of Hoteliers, and various Non-Governmental Organizations (NGOs) should create a local-level mechanism to control tour guides through coordinating and cooperating among local and central organizations. Job-training seminars and courses for tour guides and retail personnel should be organized by the appropriate public and private bodies, and Non-Governmental Organizations. Initially, new regulations should be enacted to protect tourists' statutory rights in the case of mistreatment and unsatisfactory products and services.

As part of the strategy for protecting and maintaining the authenticity of local handicrafts and souvenirs, NGOs and professional tourism and trade associations in cooperation with local authorities should determine standards for authenticity. These standards should be represented and protected by a trademark indicating the authenticity of a product, and must be included in the front page of all tourism and trade-related brochures.

Moreover, some participants reported being highly motivated to buy carpets, but they could not afford them because of high prices. This may suggest that pricing policies should be reconsidered by taking into account the purchasing power of potential visitors and other relevant factors directly related to cost perceptions. On-site observations and communication with tour guides suggest that shop owners tend to follow a market-skim pricing policy due to the short tourism season, which leads to higher prices in relative terms. Thus, through participation by relevant stakeholders in the tourism industry, pricing policies related to tourist merchandise in general, and carpets in particular, ought to be redetermined. It should be kept in mind that price is one of the most important elements of the marketing mix. If this element is not utilised properly, overall marketing strategies may be less efficient and effective. Thus, although stakeholders in the industry should pay careful attention to pricing policies at local, provincial/regional and national levels, they should not ignore pricing strategies at the sectoral level such as shopping, accommodation, and entertainment. Although the study results indicate that respondents were satisfied with various attributes of staff and their services, responses given to open-ended questions suggest that sales staff and retail personnel should be educated about communication skills and relevant cross-cultural issues in the context of shopping. This could increase levels of satisfaction among tourists involved in shopping activities in the region. For example, some respondents noted that the differences in shopping culture between locals and tourists may create misunderstandings. In Turkish culture, for instance, when a shopkeeper trails shoppers through the store, it is an indicator of kindness, paying special attention and high-quality service.

However, for western tourists, this creates an uncomfortable situation, because they feel that the clerks do not trust them or suspect them of shoplifting. Likewise, aggressive selling behaviours (e.g. calling out to passersby), which are normal in Turkish market life, are often perceived by tourists as being bothersome. In brief, it may be argued that an overemphasis on getting visitors to shop and aggressive attitudes among sales staff create resentment and mistrust, resulting in lower levels of satisfaction among tourists for the shopping experience and perhaps the entire trip.

The results derived from this study suggest that although the respondents liked the tradition of bargaining, exaggeration by giving very high prices and then lowering them considerably, and not indicating the prices of products on labels decreases the perceived trustworthiness of sales staff. Thus, educating retailing staff through various job-training courses about consumer psychology, rights and satisfaction is strongly recommended. Shop employees should be strongly advised that tourist satisfaction, which is necessary for them to maintain their own employment, can only be provided by delivering high-quality services and appropriately priced and quality products.

This study and on-site discussions with tour guides about cultural differences between shoppers and shop operators, including sales staff, suggest that there appears to be a cultural backlash and misunderstandings between the sellers and buyers due to lack of cross-cultural understanding of and information in shopping culture by both partners. Consequently, while this may reduce tourists' shopping satisfaction and overall travel experience, it also leads to customer and profit loss for shop operators. In this context, it may be argued that although there is a strong need for disseminating information to visitors about shopping opportunities, including the shopping culture of destinations, shop operators and sales staff should be educated about shopping culture and their potential customers.

The results of this study have significant management and theoretical implications. The practical implications may be that unless sufficient information at the right time and place about shopping opportunities is made available for visitors prior to their visit to a destination, they will not make plans regarding what to buy and how much to spend on shopping. Consequently, this may result in lost profits and loss of competitiveness as a tourist destination. The conceptual implications of this are that cultural differences between buyers and sellers may create significant consequences for tourist shopping experiences and levels of satisfaction, as well as negative relations between residents and visitors. Although cultural differences are desirable, as a reflection of authenticity in a destination, it may be harmful if not managed properly and carefully.

Finally, the authors recommend that more rigorous and systematic studies about the effects of cultural differences between shoppers and shop operators on the overall shopping experience by tourists should be conducted. It is believed that such studies would lead to the establishment and implementation of various strategies to increase tourist satisfaction with the shopping experience.

Limiting Factors for the Development of China's Tourism Shopping and Countermeasures

Proportion of tourism shopping expenditure in total tourism consumption is the dominant index, which reflects whether or not the consumption structure in certain country or area is reasonable, and it is also used to evaluate the depth and maturity of the development of tourism industry in certain country or area. Many countries and areas in the world support tourism shopping, which has become the important support in modern tourism economy.

Currently, tourism shopping expenditure in western countries such as America, etc., covers 30% to 36% in total tourism consumption and the proportion in China is only about 20%. The six essential elements in tourism industry have developed during the development process of China's tourism industry but the relatively undeveloped Purchasing remains the weak link in the industrial structure in China's tourism industry, which limits the effective exertion of the further development of China's tourism industry and its related functions. Tourism shopping is the important tourism requirement of tourists, which is the indispensable link in tourism. To promote the tourism shopping and consumption is favourable for the development of tourism industry with depth and connotation, which has become the consensus in

China's tourism circle. Recently, tourists have strong objections against problems existing in tourism shopping in both domestic tourism and outbound travel and the number of complaints against tourism shopping remains numerous. Information from Quality Supervision Institute of China National Tourism Administration (CNTA) indicates that complaints against tourism shopping increased greatly with many more problems among complaints formally accepted as cases by quality supervision institutes in different levels in 2006.

Recently, some travel agencies, tourist guides or drivers have fully understood the shopping intentions of tourists and exerted immoral black trades, which has disturbed the normal order in China's tourism shopping market and caused enormously negative influences and it has become one of the main non-harmonious performances in the development of tourism development. Therefore, to analyze the limiting factors for the development of China's tourism shopping and to probe into promotion countermeasures for development of tourism shopping from the aspect of tourism economy in order to realize Multiple Winnings among tourism areas, tourism enterprises and tourists have become the research subject with certain realistic meanings.

Analysis of Limiting Factors for the Development of China's Tourism Shopping from Three Levels

Undevelopped tourism commodities: Tourism commodities remain the important precondition and basis of tourism shopping and consumption. In China, there are abundant kinds of tourism commodities. Nevertheless, we also find out that most tourists have the same feeling, that is, the severe phenomenon of monotonous and duplicate commodities such as tourism souvenir and native products, etc., instead of native products with renowned brands, exists in tourism everywhere and there are little purchasing-worthy products, which is unable to effectively satisfy tourism shopping and it just indicates the lagged condition of tourism commodity development. The contradiction between profundity of potentials in the development of tourism commodity and the lagged condition of its practical development remains the principal contradiction in the development of China's tourism commodity development, which is the principal problem in front of us.

Fraudulence in commodities and prices: Recently, many problems, namely, impractical quoted prices, virtual height in prices, replacement of quality goods with fakes, replacement of high-quality goods with goods in bad quality, shortage of marked prices of commodities and great difference in quoted prices among similar commodities, etc., are severe in tourism commodity market, which make tourism commodity market bear the notoriety of selling only the commodities with bad qualities, high prices and faked commodities, influence the construction of harmonious relationship between tourism enterprises and tourists and force most tourists to have risk-preventing conscientiousness.

Misled shopping and forced shopping: Some sales personnel in shops and tourist guides irresponsibly exaggerate in the introduction to tourism commodities, mislead tourists and even force tourists to purchase commodities. According to Investigation on Tourism Service Quality on March 15th released by Ctrip in 2007, Forced Shopping has become the largest Cancer in tourism industry and over 60% consumers list it as the most nauseous thing in tourism. We will find, from the aspect of tourism destinations that the outbound tourism shopping complaints focus on Hong Kong and Macau and domestic tourism shopping complaints centre on Zhuhai and Shenzhen. Prices of guided commodities are higher than market prices with unreliable qualities. Tourists' negative mentality and resistance against guided shopping by tourist guides become more and more intense. Furthermore, problems in some areas, such as imperfect shopping facilities, bad service attitudes of some service personnel, imperfect sale service, shortage of materials in propaganda and introduction to tourism commodities, and severe imbalanced information between suppliers and providers, etc., have also become the limiting factors.

Mediumscopic level: Credibility Crisis in Tourism Industry Limits the Development of Tourism Shopping

Recently, behaviours with the deficiency of credibility in some tourism enterprises such as violation against contracts, discounted service, impractical quoted prices, bad qualities and fakes, misled advertisement and fraudulence in prices, etc., occur, which influenced the entire image of China's tourism industry. The negative influence caused by phenomenon of "Zero tourism group fee" happening in places such as Hainan, etc., that is, tourism group composition in low prices, shopping in high prices, benefits division by three parties (travel agencies, drivers and tourist guides, shopping places), aggravates the credibility crisis in tourism industry. The publication of book titled How can I resist the temptations in killing you written by Guo Jingmin makes people to have further attentions to the problem of credibility in tourism shopping, forces most people to have risk-preventing conscientiousness, which is also the important factor limiting the development of tourism shopping. The author summarizes the main reasons from the following aspects:

China's tourism agencies remain in low level and cut-throat competition of low prices exists among them: The amount of China's tourism agencies increases rapidly, 1063 agencies in 1990, 4986 in 1997 and 18475 in 2006, among which there are only about 100 powerful agencies and most agencies are small in size, weak in power, sporadic in location and bad in quality and the contracting of departments makes scale effects of enterprises become less and less. Tourism agency industry enters the state of purchaser's market and meager profit. Some agencies, pressed by competition and driven by profits, concentrate only on misleading tourists and ignore cost orientation. They sell their products in the way of cutting prices, which makes their profit margin less and less and the phenomenon of zero tourism group fee emerges thereby.

Imbalanced information and limited combat among main bodies of tourism commodities trading: Imbalanced information indicates that one party owns more information in comparison with that of the other one during the trading process owing to the imbalanced information amount, which causes inverse selection and survival of the un-fittest.

Imbalanced information will make tourism commodity suppliers with advantage of information, according to their principle of maximum profits, adopt opportunistic behaviours, namely, enterprises will choose the unfaithful operations when their unfaithful net earnings are larger than their contracted net earnings. Therefore, the deficiency of credibility of tourism commodity suppliers belongs to the market trading behaviour and performance with the target for their own maximum profits under the condition of imbalanced information. The larger the imbalanced information is, the more severe the problem of deficiency of credibility in tourism is. The combat between tourism enterprises and tourists belongs to the limited combat under incomplete information. Imbalanced information puts tourists in disadvantageous position in the combat, which makes them unable to distinguish the fake from the real, good from the bad. The limited times of travelling for tourists in tourism destinations make them unable to punish the immoral behaviours of illegal enterprises. The limited combat makes it easy for some tourism enterprises to pursue the motive for maximum profits in short periods in immoral methods and causes the deficiency of credibility in tourism enterprises.

Declining of moral standard of tourism personnel: Declining of moral standard in management personnel, sales personnel in shops and tourist guides, etc., is obvious, which causes the deficiency of credibility consciousness. The deficiency of tourist guides' payment security and popularly low prices of tourist guides make them depend mainly upon tips and the rake-off in shopping process for their major economic resources. Some tourist guides in the cooperation with drivers work for tourism shops who take back rake-off from purchasing behaviours of clients, which is obliged behaviour to some extent.

Government's Management on Tourism Shopping

Insufficient recognition of its importance: Development of tourism shopping resources has been ignored for a long time and nobody takes shopping as one kind of precious resource. Insufficient development of tourism commodities in depth is related to insufficient leading and support by administrative management departments over development, production and sale of tourism commodities.

Deficiency of information introduction service: Purchasing of tourism commodities belongs to the consumption in different place. Therefore the integrated providing of service information by government is favourable for lowering purchasing risks with governments' credits and reducing imbalanced commodity information. We will find, after we have consulted web pages of tourism bureaus in many provinces and cities, that information on tourism shopping is extremely limited.

Imperfect market administration: Tourism quality supervision institutes in all places often compose of few or over ten people and the costs for execution mainly come from meager interests of quality security earnest money paid by tourism agencies, which determines lower execution amount and frequency in tourism market, causes short-sighted operating behaviours with malignant price declination and common practices of Gresham's Law due to insufficient punishment, makes fakes and commodities of bad qualities flood in the market and damages the general image of tourism commodities. Insufficient joint control conducted by tourism administrative management department and other administrative management departments.

Development of China's Tourism Shopping

He Guangwei, Director of CNTA, once pointed out in the work conference aimed to regulate tourism market orders that the immaturity of tourism consumers fosters unhealthy ways and customs in tourism market. Currently most tourists are unknown of their rights and benefits who indulge the irregularities of tourist guides and tourism agencies. Besides, the deficiency of maturity in purchasing and consumption makes them depend on enthusiasm of tour guides and shop personnel in making purchasing decisions instead of being on their own wills. To strengthen self-protecting consciousness and independent consumption consciousness of tourists plays important role in monitoring and promoting the regulation and control of tourism market order.

Aspect of Tourism Enterprises

Deepen the leading in tourists' requirements: Development of tourism commodities shall be based upon the study on market requirements and insist on tourist oriented development thought, which shall not only provide commodities with obvious characteristics, abundant categories, nice packaging, excellent quality, low price, genuine goods at fair prices, and comfortable shopping environment, but also gradually develop operations such as mail order, consignment and free delivery, etc., which will get rid of tourists' fear of trouble in the rear. Besides, tourism commodity manufacturing enterprises shall strengthen cooperation with dealers and constitute production and marketing alliance, which will better satisfy diversified and individualized shopping requirements of tourists and promote the effective supply of tourism commodities. Strengthen consciousness of brand and establish brands of tourism commodities, which shall be related to uniqueness of tourism destinations and features of tourism resorts, by which it will enable the commodity to become spokes commodity of area image or spokes commodity of tourism resort and improve attractiveness and competitive strength.

Improve sales methods and strategies: Enterprises such as tourism commodity developers and dealers, etc. shall cooperate with administrative departments, make great efforts in promoting sales and improve acquisition capability of tourism shopping information. In the aspect of sales methods, it shall utilize both traditional and modern diversified propaganda methods to increase the transparency of information and improve credibility of information. The only way to form concurrent consumption with preparations is to enable tourists to master full shopping information. Tourism enterprises such as tourism agencies shall carry out differentiated product strategy and brand strategy. The establishment of brand is mainly based upon the differentiation of commodities, which will increases characteristics of commodities and promote competitive strength of enterprises.

Strengthen establishment of its own credibility: Strengthen moral construction and foster credibility culture.

Firstly the idea of credibility must exist in moral thoughts of leaders and the moral philosophy and individual quality of leaders in the enterprises determine the development direction of the enterprises and the credibility of tourism enterprises mainly comes from the operation ideas of enterprise leaders.

Secondly, carry out education training on employees, form active enterprise culture and promote employees to have excellent professional ethics. Tourism enterprise especially tourism agencies and shops shall consciously participate in the establishment of credible tourism, conquer the three deficiencies, that is, centering on profits and ignoring credibility; centering on operations and ignoring management; focusing on immediate profits and ignoring long-term benefits, operate with credibility, provide genuine goods at fair prices, provide excellent service, which will satisfy tourists materially and spiritually.

Rationalization of tourist guides' payment system: Currently the unreasonable tourist guides' payment system largely impacts tour guides' enthusiasm, which makes tour guides providing best service quality become shopping guide in order to make a living. Therefore, the reformation of currently existing tour guides' payment system is imperative. Tourism agency shall establish a kind of payment system, which will not only fully reward responsible tour guides, but also punish those who violate against rules by paying all costs, by which tour guides will put all their minds on how to satisfy tourists instead of how to attract tourists to purchase more commodities and force them to go shopping. They will treat the problem of leading tourists in shopping in a correct and active attitude.

Aspect of Government

As to the aspect of tourism shopping market, we shall, when we let market, the invisible hand give better play in resource distribution, strengthen the dominant function of government to create an excellent tourism shopping environment. Creditable and harmonious tourism shopping environment belong to typical public belong, which possesses obvious positive externality and needs the correct leading by government.

Governments at all levels shall take tourism shopping as the component of tourism industry in developing it: Tourism shopping system is relatively complicated and it is hard to make great achievements relying only on tourism management departments and it is necessary for relative administration departments in governments such as industrial and commercial management department, etc. and all essential elements to cooperate together in joint efforts to propel it. Currently all places shall strengthen the basic construction of tourism commodities, make efforts in the establishment of sales networks of tourism commodities in all places, implement refined product project of tourism commodity, start establishing tourism commodity brand in every place, promote the propaganda and strengthen HR training in tourism commodities. Besides, the realization of brand development of native products in different places shall be emphasized.

It is necessary to constitute organizational and management platform for tourism shopping: Establish management and organizational institute for tourism shopping, for example, strengthen the establishment of tourism commodity associate or tourism shopping associate, try to make tourism commodity development and sales market more normalized and scientific, encourage and regulate research, development and design for innovated tourism commodities, support the sales of tourism commodities and development of service network, and improve the acquiring capability of tourism shopping information.

Strengthen the tourism credibility system establishment and system building, maintain competition orders: It is necessary to strengthen credibility consciousness, improve credibility system in tourism industry and establish relevant local codes, rules and systems, etc., which will be favourable for establishing good social credit and image for enterprise industry, training professional ethics of related personnel and building an equal and fair market competition environment. The basic framework for tourism credibility system includes: the establishment of tourism credibility database, which will publicly open credibility records of tourism enterprises and relative tourism personnel; establishment of credibility evaluation system for tourism enterprises and relative tourism personnel; establishment of credibility awarding and punishing system for relative tourism personnel, etc. Choose through public appraisal model credibility tourism enterprises and excellent tourist guides to establish models for creditable operations of tourism enterprises and relative tourism personnel. Tourism enterprises without credibility shall be punished to avoid the awkward situation, that is, tourists hesitate to purchase.

Implement combining-four supervision system for tourism shopping market: In order to actually maintain legal rights and profits of tourists, it is necessary to constitute the combining-four, namely, centering legal supervision, administrative supervision, social group supervision and supervision by public opinion, and mutually coordinated model tourism enterprises, establish social mechanism for protecting tourists' rights and benefits, create a fair, equal and credible market competition environment, all of which shall play an important and fundamental role in establishing harmonious society and regulating industrial structure in tourism industry. Certainly the development of China's tourism shopping is very complicated with numerous influencing factors. But we firmly believe that China's tourism shopping and consumption market will become more and more prosperous and mature with the joint efforts made by all circles in the society, which will greatly promote more continuous, rapider and healthier development of China's tourism industry.

3

The Influence of Shopping Tourism on Cultural Changes

From the beginning of the sixties on, Yugoslavia differed a great deal from other Eastern European countries. The difference did not only show in the political system but also in the personal standard of living, tourism, travelling, shopping abroad and imitating the western life style. In a addition to that Slovenia had a specific position within Yugoslavia: bordering to Italy and Austria, and with strong national minorities in those countries, it was Yugoslavia's most developed and pro-west oriented region. This allowed Slovenia-with the exception of the first postwar years-to be constantly in touch with the two countries and to make realistic comparisons of the standard of living. Since the mid-fifties the authorities in Slovenia had been striving to approach the level of personal and social standard of living of the neighbouring capitalist countries. However, the system remained a socialist one, despite some capitalist elements it contained.

It was based on egalitarianism, full employment, a high degree of social protection, as well as on the specific socialist ideology and morale. Community (collective), not the individual were given privileged position, although Slovenians are great individuals by nature. A blend of socialist system and capitalist influence from the west created an unusual atmosphere. People did believe in Tito, in self-management, in nonalignment but also in washing machines, refrigerators, TV sets and other postulates of consumer society. Since the laws of market economy and competitiveness were not being fully implemented, the production was unable to comply with the demands of the customers and fashion trends. As a result of that, the only real contact Slovene people had with western type consumerism in the sixties and also in the seventies was through shopping abroad, in which they frequently and readily indulged.

Italy was the first window to the western world for the Slovene (and Yugoslav) people. Incising painfully in the life of people who had until then lived together, first within Austria-Hungary and later, between the two World Wars, under Italy, a new border-to the advantage of Yugoslavia-was set between the two countries in 1957. In some cases the border ran between the houses, crossed gardens, or even-as in the case of village Miren-divided the graveyard into two parts. (At funerals armed border guards are reported to have been present along the provisional demarcation in the graveyard and the coffin was literally pushed from one state to the other by the mourners in order to allow the relatives and friends from both states to take leave from the deceased). In order to preserve a small piece of land for their country, people used to move the provisional demarcation pales until the boundary stones were placed.

The relations with Italy remained tense as long as until 1954 when the so called Trieste question was resolved by the London memorandum (the division of the Free Territory between Yugoslavia and Italy). Border crossings were therefore scarce; only people who lived within the 200 m frontier zone and the so called double owners (i.e. people who possessed land in both states) were entitled to them.

The latter were allowed to take the shortest route to their land in the other state but forbidden to visit bigger villages or towns. In spite of the strict control on both sides of the border they did visit them (on Italian side they were frequently recognised by their "socialist" shoes or by the license plates on their bicycles). As the first buyers of western products people living along the frontier used to smuggle them to Slovenia. The goods were mostly hidden on bicycles or under the garments. One man even built a secret telpher line (lift) across the border to help himself at the smuggling (border guard catched him and he was sent into prison for two years). The most attractive smuggling articles being sugar, coffee, rise, lemons, medications, soap, cameras and other goods lacking in Slovenia (like blue copperas used in wine-growing and even scrubbing brushes and brooms).

The shopping was predominantly based on exchange of goods; in return, meat, brandy, eggs and butter were smuggled to Italy (even today the story about a woman smuggling butter can be heard; hiding it under her blouse it melt and started to trickle exactly when she was at the border crossing). Some smugglers even had an agreement with the police whom they helped to purchase office materials, type writers and similar. In the first half of the fifties foreign fashion articles became an attractive smuggling business; this was especially the case with a sort of raincoats made from synthetic material. The risky smuggling business paid well, and quite some people living along the border made enough money with it to be able to build themselves houses of their own.

In summer 1950 rumours spread along the Yugoslav-Italian border that the residents of the frontier zone from both states were to meet at all major border crossings. Three years after this region was divided by the frontier, the residents from both states were to meet their relatives, renew connections with friends and demonstrate their wish for coexistence. On 6 August, 1950 there was such a meeting at the border crossing Rozna dolina in Gorica and it should be repeated on 13 August, 1950.

On that day thousands of people gathered-predominantly on the Yugoslav side-at the border crossing; they literally pulled it down and scattered subsequently along the streets and shops of Gorica. The unexpected "shopping spree" was described as the "march of the hungry" by the Italian press (although people were mainly buying scrubbing brushes/brooms/, which were lacking in Slovenia), but there was no report about the incident in the Yugoslav press. The press of the Slovene minority in Italy published the following: "On Sunday morning our people pulled down the unjust border at the check-point near Rdeca hisa (red house) and for half a day Gorica regained its position as the centre of Slovene people from the Soca (Isonzo) and Vipava region." The author concluded that sooner or later the artificial frontier would have to be removed; but not just for a few hours.

In his opinion the frontier should be moved to where it belongs, namely to the boundaries of the territory with Slovenian population on the other bank of the river Soea. There were other commentaries, i.e. in the Trieste workers' newspaper Il lavoratore (which supported Kominform-at that time the conflict between Yugoslavia and The Soviet Union was at its height), which wrote: "The Tito government organised jointly with the Italian one a 'legal' crossing of the border to feed its people."

After this unusual incident the border remained tightly closed for the next five years, until the Videm (Udine) agreement was signed. In 1955 Yugoslavia and Italy signed an agreement on the local border (border land) traffic the so called Videm (Udine) agreement. It was the first agreement of its kind to be signed by a capitalist and a socialist state respectively during the period of the cold war. The right to crossing the border was expanded to all the population living along the frontier which resulted in vast increase of border crossings.

People of these regions were particularly keen to visit diverse fairs (i.e. the fair of St. Andrew in Gorica), where they were buying cheap goods. One of the most popular articles was the so called "bambola"- a big baby doll clad in coloured dress; as decoration such dolls were placed on matrimonial beds. Further, people used to buy confetti (for marriages), chewing gum and typical Italian sweets. The goods purchased on Italian stands had a major influence on forming the taste of Slovenian and Yugoslav customers in the fifties, but also later on. Double land owners were not allowed to enter Austria before 1953 when the agreements on frontier traffic and real assets of Austrian double owners on Yugoslav territory were signed. Apart from double land owners, in exceptional cases other residents of the frontier region were granted three-day permits for crossing the border, whereas there were no limitations for doctors, veterinarians and midwives. (In 1958 6000 and 5000 permits for crossing the border were issued on Yugoslav and Austrian side respectively). In 1960 an additional agreement on frontier traffic was signed, according to which residents of the 10 km frontier zone were allowed to enter Austria. These people received permanent permits for crossing the border; they were allowed to go abroad four times a month and stay there up to 60 hours. The same border crossing had to be used upon their return (the regular border crossings between Austria and Yugoslavia totalled 19). A Yugoslav citizen was allowed to take 3500.-dinars (about 12$) abroad every month. However, due to its moderate range of goods available and higher price level, Austria was not as attractive as Italy for Yugoslav shoppers.

People who were not living within the 10 km frontier zone were able to acquire a passport (either a personal, a family or a group passport). Passports were issued by the district departments for internal affairs; application for a passport could be refused without further explanation; further, passports were not issued to men who had not yet served the army.

A visa was necessary for almost all the states; in addition to that, a Yugoslav citizen had to provide a letter of guarantee from the destination state. Until the beginning of the sixties administrative hindrances and also low standard of living prevented Yugoslav citizens from more frequent visits abroad; their travelling was restricted to business trips and visiting relatives. Quite a number of people crossed the border illegally and emigrated afterwards to overseas countries. In the second half of the fifties, however, tourism began to develop which resulted in more frequent visits of foreigners in Yugoslavia.

A lot of them were attracted by diverse trade fairs. A gradual opening towards western culture in the late fifties and in the sixties was also demonstrated by organising fashion shows, song festivals (after San Remo festival in Italy) and miss competitions. In 1958 regular TV broadcast was introduced in Slovenia; in the sixties TV became a mass phenomenon. Its programme (western TV serials, films, music programmes and also commercials) additionally promoted the consumer mentality and affinity for western values; this everything enhanced the wish for travelling abroad. Most Slovenians were able to receive either some Austrian or Italian TV programme; their shopping decisions abroad were therefore frequently based on information gained from commercials. Some Italian and Austrian shop owners (especially those of Slovene origin) gradually started to advertise their products in Slovene newspapers and radio. In the mid-sixties Yugoslavia opened up towards the world and the standard of living increased a great deal.

Passport became available (with hardly any administrative hindrances) to the majority of the citizens; visas for the neighbouring countries were gradually abolished. In 1962 Yugoslav citizens were allowed for the first time to purchase legally foreign currency in the amount of 15 000 dinars (50 US$; a larger sum was only available for the purpose of medical treatment abroad and attending international meeting/conferences).

It was possible to open a bank account for foreign currency. Masses of people went to Austria and Germany to work there; only through employment agencies 62347 Slovenian citizens found work in the west between 1964 and 1969 but there were even more people who moved to the west on their own. For major holidays they were coming back home and bringing products from the west. The western shopping trend gradually moved from jeans (being one of the first citizens of Ljubljana wearing jeans in the fifties, the famous Slovenian actor Janez

Hocevar still bears the nickname Rifle), tennis shoes (in Slovenia they are still called "superge", after the popular Italian trademark), cosmetics and washing powder towards washing machines, vacuum cleaners and other domestic appliances and even cars. I can remember purchasing a washing machine Candy (the most popular Italian make for domestic appliances of that time) in Trbiz (Tarvisio) with our neighbours who had already possessed a car.

My mother possessed only a half of the necessary money, but the Slovenian dealer was willing to grant her a credit, so she could pay it on instalments (six months). During that time the Slovenian production and trade were gradually adapting to the needs of their customers: Gorenje started to produce domestic appliances which became popular in Eastern European countries in the following years; self-service stores and department stores started to emerge. However, the supply of goods in these shops was not as good as in the west and the prices were higher.

Like elsewhere in the world, towards the end of the sixties the teenage generation gradually became a very strong consumer group. The socialist supply of goods was not able to cover their demands for all sorts of notebooks with portraits of film stars, felt-tip pens, school bags, fashionable clothes, records and similar articles. Even if this was not so (like in the case of high-quality skis Elan), they were often considered to be inferior and the parents were forced to buy-with their modest socialist salaries-fashionable foreign makes of skis abroad.

As regards the standard of living, the seventies turned out to be the best postwar years for Yugoslavia (Slovenia). The non-aligned Arab friends had prevented Yugoslavia to suffer from the oil-shock; foreign loans were cheap-due to its specific position, they were literally forced upon Yugoslavia. The official policy had defeated the liberal orientation of the sixties; it wanted to prove that the self-managed socialism was the best system in the world. With the help of cheap loans, a large number of Slovenians were building houses of their own in the seventies. Shopping abroad proved this tendency: building material which was either better in quality, cheaper, or not at all available in Yugoslavia was transported in car boots from abroad. The most popular articles purchased abroad were bathroom tiles, washbasins, water-taps, furniture, diverse (garden) and other tools (even concrete-mixers). There was a great demand for domestic appliances, clothing articles, shoes (Italian shoes have remained to be a byword for quality, despite the good quality of Slovenian products), foodstuffs, spirits and items which were-due to ideological reasons-not available in Slovenia (communion and confirmation clothes, garlands, white shoes and handbags, etc.). Another phenomenon of the seventies was the so called "Ponterosso", where cheap goods and gimcrack were sold. It attracted thousands of Yugoslav buyers who were coming as organised groups by regular trains, buses and cars even from the most distant parts of the country. They were buying everything, even most worthless goods. "Ponterosso" grew into a symbol of consumer mentality, adapted to socialist buyers with little money. Hiding purchases from the customs officers (duty free imports were limited to the value of 100 dinars only) was one of the favourite Yugoslav sports of the seventies, regardless the age or sex of the people involved.

Mass shopping in Italy was also a result of the so called Osimo agreements, which Italy in Yugoslavia-influenced by the spirit of Helsinki-signed in 1975. Yugoslav-Italian border became by far the most open border between a socialist and a capitalist country. In 1978 over 40 million people crossed the border in the Triest region (Trzaska pokrajina); 21 million with passports and 19 million with regular border permits. New border crossing points were opened but there were traffic hold-ups in spite of that, particularly during weekends; a phenomenon which had first started in the sixties.

The frontier zone was increased to 30 km (the residents of Jesenice, a community bordering on Austria and Italy were so entitled to Austrian and Italian regular border permits). The authorities were not enthusiastic about shopping abroad because so much money was spent on it; but on the other hand, foreigners were shopping in Yugoslavia too, particularly petrol, meat and other food which was cheaper in Yugoslavia. Even more important was the ideological reason: how is it possible that people living "under the best system in the world" go shopping to Italy? From time to time therefore articles criticising shopping abroad appeared in newspapers, often with the comment that Yugoslav shoppers were being exploited by the capitalist traders. Particularly communists and public officials/civil servants were advised not to succumb to that shopping fever, but there were no sanctions and no other efforts to reduce shopping abroad (except for customs measures). The third phenomenon of the seventies was the expansion of agency tourism/ organised tourism. From the beginning of the seventies on, Yugoslav travel agencies had been organising holidays abroad, particularly in

Spain, Italy and Tunisia; further, they organised shopping trips to the main European capitals and even USA (especially New York). Organised shopping tours focused on consumer electronics/audio systems (Munich was considered to be the best place to buy these products), or clothes and leather products (Istambul).

In the eighties Yugoslavia glided into a crisis. The standard of living fell to the level of the mid-sixties. A number of products were rationed or not available at all (petrol, oil, washing powder, citrus fruits). Shopping abroad concentrated therefore on buying foodstuffs; and anyway, due to the growing inflation rate which in the mid-eighties grew to hyperinflation Yugoslav citizens were hardly able to afford to buy anything else. The geographic position of Slovenia allowed its citizens to compensate the shortage by weekly shopping trips abroad (and besides, the supply in Slovenia was better than elsewhere in Yugoslavia). The buying power improved in 1990 when the Yugoslav Prime Minister Ante Markoviæ froze the exchange rate of the national currency dinar in relation 1: 7 to German mark. For a period of a few months Slovenian salaries have reached the level of Italian and Austrian ones, which had an immediate effect on shopping across the border. After the crisis, which led to disintegration of Yugoslavia and consequently to independence of Slovenia, shopping abroad gradually normalised. Goods are abundantly available in shops at home, therefore shopping abroad is not a consequence of insufficient supply anymore; it is rather a matter of lower prices and (or) of prestige.

Border crossings, shopping abroad and travelling have importantly influenced the life style of Slovene people in the postwar decades. They sharpened their sense of quality and influenced domestic production and trade which made effort to reach the western standards. Shopping abroad further exerted indirect pressure on politics, which was-at least to some extend-forced to take account of the demands of consumers and act accordingly. It has to be mentioned however, that shopping was limited-particularly in the fifties and in the first half of the sixties-by the low standard of living. In the course of time a specific consumer ritual was established, a sort of shopping fever to which the majority of Slovenians (and even more Yugoslavs) succumbed. A typical feature of that attitude was that people did not only buy products they really needed. When abroad they had to "take the opportunity" to make the journey "worth the money and time" it took and therefore used to buy everything that came to their hands. This philosophy was in perfect agreement with the belief that saving and rational spending of money made no sense, since in socialism the state was believed to be responsible for providing housing, regular income and solving other problems of the citizens (however, not everything could be implemented and especially Slovenians tended to be more economical; a lot of them bought flats or built houses on their own).

Shopping tourism was only one of the influences that formed the postwar socialist consumer mentality in Slovenia. Its impact has to be seen within a broader context, together with films, music, television, mass motorization, expanding of foreign tourism in Slovenia and economic emigration. Everything this led to the fact, that Slovenians accepted western standards and behaviour patterns as regards the style of home decor, clothing and spending leisure time as early as in the "liberal" sixties (in the second half of the seventies, for example, the more affluent citizens already had access to international credit cards, including American Express). People took from socialism what was of use to them (free schooling, good health services, full employment), whereas ideology that filled political speeches, newspaper articles and TV news was perceived as the necessary evil. During the last two decades, the self-managed socialism was hardly taken seriously by anyone. This was probably also due to the fact, that both, regime critics and party officials met on their shopping tours across the border.

Draft: National Tourism Policy of India

Tourism emerged as the largest global industry of the 20th century and is projected to grow even faster in the 21st century. India has immense possibilities of growth in the tourism sector with vast cultural and religious heritage, varied natural attractions, but a comparatively small role in the world tourism scene. A New Tourism Policy, which builds on the strength of the national Tourism Policy of 1982, but which envisages new initiatives towards making tourism the catalyst in employment generation, environmental regeneration, development of remote areas and development of women and other disadvantaged groups in the country, besides promoting social integration is, therefore, vital to our economy. It would lead to larger foreign exchange earnings and create conditions for more Foreign Direct Investment.

The Mission

Our mission is to promote sustainable tourism as a means of

economic growth and social integration and to promote the image of India abroad as a country with a glorious past, a vibrant present and a bright future. Policies to achieve this will be evolved around six broad areas such as Welcome (Swagat), Information (Suchana), Facilitation (Suvidha), Safety (Suraksha), Cooperation (Sahyog) and Infrastructure Development (Samrachana). Conservation of heritage, natural environments, etc. and development and promotion of tourist products would also be given importance.

Objectives

The objectives of tourism development are to foster understanding between people, to create employment opportunities and bring about socioeconomic benefits to the community, particularly in the interior and remote areas and to strive towards balanced and sustainable development and preserve, enrich and promote India's cultural heritage. One of the major objectives is the preservation and protection of natural resources and environment to achieve sustainable development. Given the low cost of employment creation in the tourism sector and the low level of exploitation of India's tourism potential, the new tourism policy seeks to expand foreign tourist arrivals and facilitate domestic tourism in a manner that is sustainable by ensuring that possible adverse effects such as cultural pollution and degradation of environment are minimised. The New Tourism Policy also aims at making the stay of foreign tourists in India, a memorable and pleasant one with reliable services at predictable costs, so that they are encouraged to undertake repeated visits to India, as friends. This would be in tune with India's traditional philosophy of giving the highest honour to a guest (Atithi debo bhava).

Tourism a Multi-Dimensional Activity

(a) The Government will aim to achieve necessary linkages and synergies in the policies and programs of all concerned Departments/agencies by establishing effective coordination mechanisms at Central, State and District levels. The focus of national policy, therefore, will also be to develop tourism as a common endeavour of all the agencies vitally concerned with it at the Central and State levels, public sector undertakings and the private sector.

(b) It will be the policy of government to encourage people's participation in tourism development including Panchayati Raj institutions, local bodies, Co-operatives, non-governmental organisations and enterprising local youth to create public awareness and to achieve a wider spread of tourist facilities. However, focused attention will be given for the integrated development of identified centres with well directed public participation.

(c) Public and Private Sector Partnership: A constructive and mutually beneficial partnership between the public and the private sectors through all feasible means is an absolute necessity for the sustained growth of tourism. It is, therefore, the policy of the Government to encourage emergence of such a partnership. This will be achieved by creating a Tourism Development Authority consisting of senior officials of the Government and tourism experts and professionals from the private sector.

(d) Role of the Government: Tourism is a multi-sectoral activity and the industry is affected by many other sectors of the national economy. The State has to, therefore, ensure intergovernmental linkages and coordination. It also has to play a pivotal role in tourism management and promotion. The specific role of the Government will be to:

i. Provide basic infrastructural facilities including local planning and zoning arrangements.
ii. Plan tourism development as a part of the over all area development strategy.
iii. Create nucleus infrastructure in the initial stages of development to demonstrate the potential of the area.
iv. Provide the required support facilities and incentives to both domestic and foreign investors to encourage private investment in the tourism sector.
v. Rationalise taxation and land policies in the tourism sector in all the States and Union Territories and in respect of land owned by Government agencies like Railways.
vi. Introduce regulatory measures to ensure social, cultural and environmental sustainability as well as safety and security of tourists.

vii. Ensure that the type and scale of tourism development is compatible with the environment and sociocultural milieu of the area.

viii. Ensure that the local community is fully involved and the benefits of tourism accrue to them.

ix. Facilitate availability of trained manpower particularly from amongst the local population jointly with the industry.

x. Undertake research, prepare master plans, and facilitate formulation of marketing strategies.

xi. Organise overseas promotion and marketing jointly with the industry.

xii. Initiate specific measures to ensure safety and security of tourists and efficient facilitation services.

xiii. Facilitate the growth of a dynamic tourism sector.

(e) Role of Private Sector: Tourism has emerged as the largest export industry globally and all over the globe private sector has played the lead role in this growth. The private sector has to consider investment in tourism from a long term perspective and create the required facilities including accommodation, time share, restaurants, entertainment facilities, shopping complexes, etc. in areas identified for tourism development. Non-core activities in all airports, major stations and interstate bus terminus such as cleanliness and maintenance, luggage transportation, vehicles parking facilities, etc. should be opened up to private operators to increase efficiency and profitability. The specific role of the Private Sector will be to:

i. Build and manage the required tourist facilities in all places of tourist interest.

ii. Assume collective responsibility for laying down industry standards, ethics and fair practices.

iii. Ensure preservation and protection of tourist attractions and give lead in green practices.

iv. Sponsor maintenance of monuments, museums and parks and provision of public conveniences and facilities.

v. Involve the local community in tourism projects and ensure that the benefits of tourism accrue to them in right measure.

vi. Undertake industry training and manpower development to achieve excellence in quality of services.

vii. Participate in the preparation of investment guidelines and marketing strategies and assist in database creation and research.

viii. Facilitate safety and security of tourists.

ix. Endeavour to promote tourism on a sustained and long term perspective.

x. Collaborate with Govt. in the promotion and marketing of destinations.

(f) Role of voluntary efforts: Voluntary agencies and volunteers have to contribute their expertise and understanding of local ethos to supplement the efforts of other sectors to provide the human touch to tourism and foster local initiatives. All such efforts shall be encouraged.

Tourism Development Fund and Resources for Development

It would be the policy of the Government to facilitate larger flow of funds to tourism infrastructure and to create a Tourism Development Fund to bridge critical infrastructural gaps.

Priority would be given for development of tourist infrastructure in selected areas of tourist importance and for those products which are considered to be in demand in the existing and future markets so that limited resources are put to the best use.

Foreign Investments and Incentives and Rationalization of Taxes

i. In view of large investment requirements in the tourism sector and the need for maintaining high quality standards in services, hotels and tourism related industries will continue to be in the priority list of industries for foreign investment. Export-house status has been accorded to Hotels, Travel Agents, Tour Operators and Tourist Transport Operators vide Notification No.33(RE-98)1997-2002 dated 26.11.98 of the Ministry of Commerce. The status needs to be extended to all tourism units irrespective of the annual turnover.

ii. In order to offset the specific constraints of tourism industry and to put in place the required infrastructure as quickly as possible, particularly in less developed areas, appropriate incentive schemes would be considered. It would also be the endeavour of the Government to persuade the State/UT Governments to rationalise taxes, to put a cap of 20% on all taxes taken together on the accommodation and hospitality units, to allocate suitable land for tourism purposes at reasonable prices, harmonize movement of tourist transport across State borders, etc.

Adoption of New Technologies

a. Efforts will be made to adopt the technological advances in the tourism sector to provide better facilities to tourists and to market the tourism product, to the benefit of all concerned.

b. Information technology shall be given the pride of place in the efforts to promote Indian tourism. Every endeavour in this regard would increasingly rely on optimising the use of e-commerce/m-commerce, use of internet for dissemination of tourism related information, increasing use of portals as gateway to accessibility to tourism information, development of Handy Audio Reach Kit (HARK) Tourist Guidance System at important monuments and heritage sites, networking of States, setting of tourist information Kiosks, encouragement to information technology and eco-friendly practices by the private industries and above all keeping abreast with the global technologies for promoting and facilitating tourism. It shall be ensured that Information Technology (IT) and Indian Tourism (IT) become synonymous.

c. The Central Government will set up a Paryatan Bhawan in New Delhi as a modern Tourist Interpretation Centre to cater to various needs of travellers, foreign as well as domestic and to offer facilities for air and train reservation, money changing counters and information about all tourist centres in the country. The Centre will be equipped with e-connectivity and networking facility to all state tourist offices. Efforts will be made to have similar state level Paryatan Bhawans in state Capitals.

The economic and social benefits of tourism and its importance as an instrument of economic growth have to be fully recognised by all sections of the society. It would, therefore, be the endeavour of the Government to bridge the information gap through proper statistical documentation of the impact of tourism and its wide publicity to create awareness so that the economic and social significance of tourism is well recognised and tourism is given due attention and national priority.

Tourism Economic Zone, Tourist Circuits, Special Tourism Area and Areas of Special Interests

1. Tourism Economic Zones will be created with private participation based on the intrinsic attractions, potential for development and availability of resources in these zones. Air, road and rail connectivity to these areas will be established to facilitate direct and easy access to these zones from international and domestic destinations. Adequate backward and forward linkages will also be established to ensure flow of benefits to the local community. The development of such zones will be guided by well conceived Master Plans and executed by specific Tourism Development Authorities which will be created by the Government involving senior officers from the Department of Tourism, and other relevant Ministries/Departments of the Govt. of India, professionals from tourism industry and representatives of Industry & Trade Associations.
2. India with vast cultural and religious heritage and varied natural attractions has immensed potential of growth in the tourism sector. 25 travel circuits and destinations have already been identified for development through joint efforts of the Central Govt., the State Governments and the private sector. State Governments of Kerala, Tamil Nadu, Orissa and Maharashtra and Union Territory Administration of Daman & Diu have also declared Bekal Beach, Puri-Konark, Sindhudurg, Muttakadu-Mamallapuram and Diu as Special Tourism Area for integrated development. Steps will be taken to work towards the integrated development of all the tourist circuits of the country with the involvement of all the infrastructural departments, State Governments and the private sector.
3. Areas of Special Interest: Government would initiate and support special programmes and schemes for the development of tourism in North Eastern States, Himalayan region and island States/U.Ts with a view to achieve overall economic development of the regions, and as part of the strategy for removing regional imbalances.

Sustainable Development and Perspective Plans

The principle of sustainable development stipulates that the level of development does not exceed the carrying capacity of the area. It will be governments' policy to ensure adherence to such limits through appropriate planning instruments, guidelines and enabling regulations and their enforcement. Efforts will be made to diversify the tourism products in such a way that it supplements the main stream of cultural tourism. Comprehensive perspective plans for developing sustainable tourism by assessing the existing tourism scenario in each State/Union Territory with respect to availability of natural resources, heritage and other sociocultural assets, quantitative/demographic factors like population, employment, occupation, income levels etc., services and infrastructure will be developed by initiating immediate action in this direction.

Conservation and Development : Tourism development needs to be properly guided and regulated to avoid adverse impact on the natural environment and cultural heritage which constitute the tourist attraction. A judicious balance needs to be maintained between conservation and development. Government will continue its policy of trying to maintain balance through planning restrictions and by educating the people in appreciating their rich heritage and by eliciting their cooperation in preserving and protecting it.

Promotion and Marketing : Promotion and marketing is an important component of tourism development and needs to be undertaken along with product development in conformity with consumer profiles and product characteristics. The policy of the Government therefore will be to develop and implement cost effective marketing strategies based on market research and segmentation analysis in each of the tourist generating countries.

International Cooperation : Tourism is a global industry requiring inputs from various international agencies and collaborations with other countries. The policy of the Government therefore will be to foster positive win – win partnership with all the international agencies and other countries.

Professional Excellence : Tourism being a service industry it is necessary to enhance its service efficiency. The new policy will strive towards excellence by introducing professionalism through training and re-training of human resources and providing memorable visitor experience to both domestic and international tourists.

4

Shopping in Recreation Tourism at the Venetian Resort

Introduction

Today's competitive environment encourages retailers to provide a product or service and create unique consumer experiences. Experiential retailing focuses on the complete shopping experience required to meet consumers' total functional and emotional needs and symbolic consumption, and entertainment retailing. This paper offers a practical understanding of experiential retailing and examines its' application by an existing tourism destination complex, the Venetian in Las Vegas. The Venetian's use of specific experiential retailing strategies, branding, thematic/entertainment retailing, lifestyle retailing, and brand extension, and their value also are discussed.

Las Vegas Tourism and Related Retail

Traditionally, most tourists to Las Vegas were male visiting there to gamble. Las Vegas' visitor demographic profiles have changed significantly and now are 53% female and 47% male. While gambling still generates the greatest revenue in Las Vegas, non-gambling entertainment generated revenues of more than $4.8 billion in 2001. About 69% of Las Vegas tourists gamble, while 63% shop. In 2003 about $2.9 billion retail dollars were spent n Las Vegas, supporting the argument shopping is an important part of tourism.

The Las Vegas Venetian

The Venetian, a Venice-themed retail and entertainment complex located in Las Vegas, operates a hotel and casino, and houses a shopping mall, restaurants, theatres, and museum. It mixes retail with tourism features like the Grand Canal Shopping Centre, gondolas and singing gondoliers, and Canyon Ranch Spa Club.

Venetian stores generated sales of over $900 per square foot in 2004 which was almost triple the U.S. national average of $350 and regarded as a highly profitable retail establishment. Compared with the previous year same quarter results, the parent company of the Venetian posted a 72% increase in pre-tax earnings. First quarter 2004 Venetian average available room occupancy rates were 98.9%, increased from 97.4% in first quarter 2003. The Venetian's growth in revenues and occupancy rates crossed all business segments with increases in hotel revenues (49%), food and beverage (67%), casino revenues (29%) and table volumes (17.5%) (Smith, 2004A). Revenue per available room had an annual growth rate of eight per cent.

Major Competitor

The Venetian competes with similar Las Vegas entertainment complex retailers, such as Forum Shops, MGM, Mandalay, and Harrah's. The Forum Shops at Caesars is a Roman-themed retail and entertainment complex that opened in 1992 as a 510,000 square foot mall. The mall leases to upscale shops such as Versace, and Armani, and houses other restaurants and stores. In 2004 Forum Shops retail sales per square foot were $1,400 per square foot and represented revenues four times the U.S. national average. The Forum Shops raised the bar for retail sales in Las Vegas and challenges it competitors.

Experiential Retail Marketing

Experiential retail considers demand and supply side factors existing in the current retail market. The objective of experiential retail is to create a differentiated experience that provides consumers with the products, services, and experiences that satisfy their needs, both tangible and intangible. Experiential retail marketing strategies include branding, thematic/entertainment retailing, lifestyle retailing, and brand extension.

Branding

Branding creates a strong and positive reputation of a company's image for consumers. Traditionally, brand marketing focuses on an individual's preference for certain products such as Coca-Cola, Sony, and Nike. Changes in consumer behaviour require retailers to place more emphasis on brand communities that reflect social culture and are obtained from shared consumer experiences. The Venetian creates a brand with a unique image of recreation of Renaissance-era Venice through use of Italian architecture.

Thematic/Entertainment Retailing

The Venetian offers its customers a themed and experiential shopping environment through several entertainment features inspired by tourist destinations. A gondola ride, one of the Venetian's most popular attractions, gives consumers a change to see the sights of the Grand Canon Shopping centre or outside the resort. Spacious walkways and a gondola-laden canal encourage consumers to shop the 500.000 square foot upscale shopping complex. Strolling juggler and opera trio, dressed in regal opulence entertain shoppers. Singers and actors perform in the Venetian's St. Mark Square.

Brand Extension

The Venetian expanded its brand with a 1,000 room hotel tower and casino in 1999. Other brand extensions include multi-channel resort forms, such as Grand Canon Shoppers and Canyon Ranch SpaClub. The Venetian is the one of largest hotel and convention complexes in the U.S, with 4,049 hotel suites, 120,000 square feet of gaming floor, approximately 500,000 square feet of retail, and approximately 500,000 square foot of meeting space. Also, The Venetian has formed a strategic alliance with another high end firm, London-based Le Meridian and a global hotel group, planning luxury operations in 57 countries.

Lifestyle Retailing

Consumption reflects consumers' lifestyles and meets their desire for functional and emotional value. The Venetian targets a high-end fashion customer. Retail operations respond to customers' needs through excellent customer services, consumer loyalty programs, and with technology which allows customization by tracking customer patterns and preferences. The Venetian uses an internet based customer relation management system.

Symbolic/Experiential Retail Value for Tourists

Symbolic reflects a consumers' perception towards a certain object, a sign or symbol, and utility gained from its purchase. The total tourist environment at the Venetian creates symbolic value for tourists. For example, the Venetian will have a triplex wedding chapel complex offering unique wedding events and experiences. The Venetian is selling Venetian romance in Las Vegas.

Statistics indicate shopping is an important part of Las Vegas tourism. The Venetian provides favourable shopping environments via product assortments, shopping atmosphere, and entertainment. The retail mix saves customers time and stimulates cross-selling that add to their bottom lines.

According to the Las Vegas Review Journal, people spend $500 to $700 at the Grand Canal Shops, while they spend $200 to $300 on the average shopping trip. Retail enables gambling gain to remain in the resort. New technology provides retailers with additional opportunities to tourists through the internet, Television, telephone, and catalog. This multi-channel retailing helps create lasting customer relationships that save consumers time, energy and money when searching for information and purchasing and increase revenue per person.

Conclusions

The Venetian uses experiential retail strategies that create differentiation in a competitive market. Unique consumer experiences help increase consumer loyalty and revenues. The Venetian has built a strong brand image by replicating the romance of Venice and providing a differentiated shopping experience with unmatched customer services. These are strategies can help other tourism related retailers create customer value, encourage repeat tourism, and increase per person spending.

Events Tourism: Potential to Build a Brand Destination

A destination is a town, city or a place which has one or more attractions for tourists. These attractions may be in the form of scenic sights, culture, leisure activities, shopping rebates, food, and excursion. Those attractions are used to accruing revenues from tourists. A tourist has some pre conceived notions about a destination which he might have heard from his surroundings sources like ads, internet and word of mouth from a friend or family member or may be read in a travel book. A destination image can be positive or negative and is considered an important part of the decision making process of consumers when they consider their destination alternatives. As many of the researcher has explained destination image as is an important determinant and also plays an important role in destination selection process. In the context of the previously discussed point that there are certain attributes to attract tourists to a destination, EVENTS are the emerging sign of success in the list of these attractions. Events can be defined as a package carried out with a perceived concept, and then customized or modified to achieving the aim of organizing that event. In the new millennium the targeted tourists are attracted. The key elements of an event can be considered as venue, target audience, media, and event infrastructure. The above diagram shows how an event involves different attributes with one action. Here venue and infrastructure are directly related to the DESTINATION where an event takes place. Events are capable of delivering:

1) Key messages about destination.
2) Community's positive image to the world.

With growing technologies and advertising scenario, events also include media coverage. This is how the event and destination are two different entities but yet serving each other in a manner. Destination gets a vide media coverage as well as advertising. The participants of the events and the attendances of events visit the destination to take part in the event which brings lots of foreign currency to the particular destination to entire nation of the event is huge.

Thus an event can be a most powerful way to attract tourists to the destination. The events may be in the form of MICE (meetings, incentives, convections and exhibitions), sporting event, and cultural event or may be award functions like Oscar etc. This is how word Event tourism came into being. Although it is a newer concept but is now widely recognized, having a potential significant contribution to local economies. In simple terms, an event acts as an attraction for people from outside the local community to visit the location and spend money on accommodation, food and leisure activities at the destination. Events also help to build an image into the minds of tourists who have never visited the place definitely grabs their attention to the destination through media coverage. The tourists have several options and the first thing comes in the mind is the brand names which emerges out of the level of satisfaction.

Key issues

The goal of this conceptual paper is to enlighten the new horizons of tourism by concept of events tourism. This paper will mainly concentrate on benefits of hosting events:

- Events tourism is useful to attract tourists whether a first time visitor or a repeater.
- How an event and destination are co-brands.
- To show positive effects of events on a destination.

The anticipated outcomes of this paper are showcasing:

- understanding events portfolio.
- growing magnitude of hosting an event in tourism at a destination.
- positive effects of co-branding by image transfer.
- strategies to host an event.

However there are arguments about the image and brand perceptions. Some argue that destination branding is intensely associated with destination image. According to others, image is very different from branding; yet the brand is created through the image.

Brand vs. Image

Image and Brand are interrelated attributes. Image plays a vital role to develop brand identity and brand is said to have certain images and believes in the mind sets of tourists (Jenson and Kotler). In tourist destination context, there are several different definitions of image. Hunt defined country image as people's impressions of countries that they do not reside in. Millman and Pizam calls image as the sum of tourism experience-related attributes.

Image transfer between events and destination:

The image transfer is considered when any benefit that tourist recognise in events becomes benefit for host destination. The co-branding of two brands namely destination and events is very sensitive in nature. They share image transfer (use uni assignment govers). The can be positive image transfer or negative image transfer. The mere pairing of events and destination is not important rather it is important that which destination is paired with which event. It is essential to explore the events brand relation with the destination brand to acquire desired results; Van Auken and Adams (1999) The image of both brand whilst event and destination play important role while they are paired together; Van Auken and Adams (1999); Koernig and Page (2002); McDaniel (1999); Till and Busler (2000).

The poor match of events and destination may lead to negative brand building and may cause transfer of negative image. But if a destination losses a customized event then it can probably be used as brand extensions. In recent years some vents have been developed which are closely related to their destinations' brand and are recognised by their hosting destinations as to name some Dubai's duty free shopping festival etc. These events often bear the name of their host destination's name to be more associated with the destination brand. However the literature on branding suggests that it is not that an event should always possess a brand name. It can contribute to the host destination as a feature to make the destination unique in nature and more popular place to visit; Ahang and Markman (2001)). By increasing the frequency of organising events, the drawback of short term impact of events can be nullified.

There are different themes and strategies to use events as effective tools to building a brand destination. There should be community support cooperative planning and media support to make most of organising at a destination. This transfer image between the two. The favourability towards closing a destination increases visitation aspect. Events bring pleasantness and excitement for travellers to return to the destination in future.

Building Destination Brand

The ideation of destination branding is although a newer concept but any of the resources and industry experts has been interests towards destination brand management. Branding is a major issue in product strategy. There is hardly anything that goes unbranded. A brand is a complex symbol that can convey up to six levels of meaning i.e. attributes, benefits, values, values, personality and user (Jennifer) A destination therefore is product which depends on brand recognition, perceived, brand quality, strong mental and emotional associations and other assets Consequently, branding focuses on marketing of a product in terms of degree which increases brand equity. As cited by Maureen Atkinson, an eminent industry agent "A brand is a type of shorthand for a product with city branding, what you try to do is create that shorthand so that when people think of your city, they automatically think of what is best about it."

Thus, a destination brand not only executes name, logo, reputation or status symbol but also the destination's physical attributes, experience, quality of services provided, attractions. While branding a city or a region one needs to identify the attractions and activities to associate them with the destination to build a brand image. In terms of destination's brand equity if a tourist shows inclination towards one destination than the other, it is considered that the brand acceptability of the brand of higher brand equity is more. Researches in this field prove that image is a key factor in tourism development. When a tourist plans a holiday it is expected that the tourist will have an initial image of the destination that might not be visited or might have already been visited. The destination's image plays a vital role because the level of visitation goes down when the same destination is visited frequently that effects the destination branding. Several methods have been used to identify the relevant dimensions of destination image including multidimensional scaling, repertory grid. The brand image closely relates to the branding of a destination as it represents the attractions, cultural and benefits to tourists expectations delivering total customer satisfaction. The brand makes use of and coordinates a full repertoire of marketing activities to build equity.

Branding strategies can vary depending on what kind of a brand is. A functional brand is that brand which involves functions of product. An image brand that involves celebrity associated with a brand. An experimental brand that involves people and place. The empirical research by many quantitative research experts acknowledge that the brand perception of tourists to destination is three dimensional namely sincerity, excitement and conviviality that there is a positive impact on perceived destination image. Therefore a strong brand adds unique features to products or services to impart perceptions of quality and value which cultivates market share and customer loyalty. There are various tools for brand-building public relation, sponsorship clubs and consume communities, trade shows, event marketing etc.

Co-branding: (Event vs. Destination)

Co-branding is an effective way to reinforce or change a brand image; Simonin and Ruth(1998)). In the view of a destination co-branding, the aim objective is to transfer the desired portion of the other brand to destination features. This will require the tow brands to be jointly advertised and promoted. The pairing of two or more brands in a composite brand should match and is paired in such a way that each one of it is perceived when they are paired.

Out of all the brands an event can be the most effective one as it involves the study of brand prints, understanding what the brand stands for, its positioning and values, identifying the target audience and liaisons with the creative conceptualization to create an event for a perfect mesh with brands personality. Event involves 5 c's namely conceptualization of creative idea and ambience, costing which calculates the margins, canvassing for sponsors, customers and networking components, customization of the event according to brand personality, budgets.

Thus events help in creating awareness about the brand highlighting the added features, image building and associating brand personality to target market. In standpoint of destination branding events deliver destination's culture, attractions, quality services provided and a long term impact to visit the destination again to explore it more. Events and Festivals have a significant economic impact Community events are expected to increase the number of tourists and the amount of expenditures.. They are believed to bring social benefits towards community and last but not the least they lengthen the life cycle of destination.

The enhancement of community and creation of positive images improve destination's image. Several researches verified that image improvement is associated with hosting different events.

The basic technique in co-branding a destination with an event is to identify the associating network of competitive destinations and then hosting an event that can reinforce, change or add desirable associations. (Laurence Chalip and Carla A-Costa,). It is important to spot an appropriate events portfolio for a destination that can foster the process of destination branding. As the effects of co-branding depends on the associate event brand with destination brand. By pairing of event's brand with destination brand, it is expected that the elements of event brand will transfer to destinations brand.

Destination marketers can not ignore the pitfalls of co-branding too. If an event, which is well established brand can hamper the host destination's brand image which can result in a reverse or negative effect. The empirical research by Boo and Busser (Event gt.) proved that tourist images after visit was not impacted positively. Moreover festivals participants' images were not changed favourably when compared those of non-participants' image.

Thus, dissimilarity between the event brand and destination brand would render a poor match and would therefore have a negative consequence for the intended transfer of brand image. But despite of all these destination marketers seek to host events. The only need is to plan a managed event communications that can render a change in destination image. The main objective is not that the event includes the host destination's name rather how consistency is maintained between concepts and features represented by the destination brand extensions and are accepted favourably. If such events are received open handed by market, then the brand equity of the destination should increase as a consequence of tourists' enhanced perceptions. The core focus should be consistency with the benefits to destination. As events grow, destination marketers need to bulk them into their marketing strategies and they need to take tactical advantages of events when planning the destination's marketing communications campaign. Every possible precaution should be taken while pairing of events with the destination, so that the strong image of the event may not hamper the destination image.

Mega events are short term events with long term consequences that attract large numbers of international tourists. On the other hand the fact states that mega events have negative impacts like housing evictions. Although, these mega events can increase an artificial or temporary spike of accommodation, transport or hospitality while the preceding benefits of mega events might be short lived.

Therefore, destination marketers who seek to use events to build their brands must construct a portfolio of events (Jago et al.). A single event with a high profile has only a passing effect on the destination brand but if tourism authorities want it to be long lasting then it is much beneficial to host smaller events through out the year.

Cultural events featuring music, dance, food, shopping, art or any other cultural activities can be supportive to build up a brand image. The effect of events on a destination's brand depends substantially on the reach and the frequency of event mentions and visuals. An event portfolio should appeal to attract tourists of each age group having different interests in different. Since an event portfolio delivers a destination's image, on grounds like the attractions, services, accessibility, community festivals and the touring experience. Only those events should be included in portfolio that can successfully reinforce the destination's brand. The elevation of destination's brand is by the impact of effective hosting at the destination.

Event and Destination; A Case Review: Quantitative study by Xiaoyan Xing and Laurence Chalip:

> *There are arguments that events can hamper the destinations image if not paired well with destination. Here is a case to prove this argument worth noticing.*

It is within the discussed context Xiaoyan Xing and Laurence Chalip investigate the interaction of both event and destination attributes on a person's intention to visit the destination. An individual's awareness of a destination made up of the cognitive evaluation of experiences, learning, emotions and perceptions related to the destination's image. An event can be defined as something that happens at a given place and time.

Amongst a variety of alternatives, the authors utilized quantitative methods to conclude that how a destination's rating raises when paired with a suitable event or alternatively how an event's rating slows down when not paired with a suitable destination. This article particularly discusses that how an image is transferred or shared by two brands, a destination (i.e. city) and an event. The research also investigates how the image transfer affects the intension to visit the destination.

There is a debate in past researches about destination image and destination brand. According to Asli D. A. Tasci and Metin Kozak in the revised form of March 2006 argue that destination branding is overwhelmingly associated with destination image and also image is very different from branding; yet the latter is created through the former. This matter is untouched in the article. Although the research goes along the hypothesis considered but the study seems to be complicated due to many considerations at one instance. Also the researcher may have included an events portfolio rather than a single event. This might have justified the bias towards sporting events.

Methods: Overview

The research stands out in terms of its validity and reliability where in an effort to identify possible mismatches between events and their host communities, a quasi-experimental design was utilized. Two cities and two events were identified to the extreme ends of the active-leisurely continuum. Chicago and a NASCAR motor sport event were selected to represent an active city and an active event respectively. The city of Des Monies and a Masters Golf tournament were represented the leisurely end of the continuum. The design also provided for a no event and a no city option, meaning that nine sets of conditions were possible, but the cell for no city and no event was omitted from the study. These eight conditions were assigned randomly to the participants. Eight mock advertisements were created. In four of these advertisements, the destination was central and in the remaining four, the event was central. This alternation of centrality was an important part of the experimental design because this would identify the image transfer effects. That is to evaluate that to what extend the brands pairing help the two brands to be paired together.

Method: Participants

The 317 participants were undergraduate, social science university students. They aged in range from 18 to 41 years. This selection can be biased as their mind sets are much intellectual than the general public. They see very thing critically than in a way like a general traveller may not do. The sample here does not seem to be justified. The tourists have different age groups and different interests. They have different interests towards sports. The selection of the sample group is clearly based on convenience and future research should seek to overcome this important limitation. This could be achieved by sample that more accurately reflects the diversity in the wider community.

Method: Instruments

Participants were exposed to the mock advertisements and were then invited to proceed to the questionnaire. According to the centeredness of the questionnaire were prepared. The condition where the destination was centred the participants had to rate the destination only and the ads where events were centred they had to rate the destinations also. The ratings were on the image scales identified in earlier phase of study mentioned in previous paragraphs. The study does not show any specific questionnaire which makes it difficult for a reader to understand the question line.

Method: Procedures

The three key constructs measured in this study were 1) image transfer between events and destination; 2) intentions to visit; and, 3) involvement in sports.

Image transfer between events and destination was measured using obligatory study to find scales for measuring image transfer by brain storming of various literatures on semantic differential items on brand image, destinations image and general semantic differential model that were relevant to the study. The common identifiers or adjectives used for the destinations and events were selected under three categories whilst evaluation, activities and potency. There were five dimensions for evaluation and four dimensions for activities. The dimensions for potency were multi-loaded therefore it was eliminated. These dimensions were identified through tests and were proved by a replicate test.

As an argument the events and destination image transfer can be affected on political grounds too which are related with the destination. The recent example can be Beijing Olympics and the Tibet issue. Although the sporting event has nothing to do with the political issue but the whole world has been prompted and allegedly forced to speak because of the upcoming Olympics, where more than 157 Countries and 646 Athletes are participating. Intention to visit was measured by Willingness to Buy scale. The participants rated the destinations on nine pointer scale, which calculate their intentions to visit. This will help to compare the results obtained by the further image transfer scale.

Involvement in sports was measured by Orlick's SSI (Secondary Sport involvement) scale. The participants had to report the frequency at which they watch sports on television. This was considered an important factor to measure because their level of interests towards sports would affect their willingness to visit a destination to where sporting events is on. The sport-events consideration shows only a category from a population who likes sports but researcher would have used other cultural events to see the effects of image transfer in holistic terms of events. Events can't be generally categorized in sports event only. On the other hand, simply keeping a track of how much they read news about sports does not proves their involvement in sports. That can be just out of the fact that one wants to be informed about happenings around.

Analysis

The data analysis was done through various statistical equations namely MANOVA, this analysis can detect mean differences among a number of different groups on several different measures, while holding one or more variables constant. The method is useful for research studies where there are a variety of segments being assessed on a number of different measures, where one or more variables needs to be controlled for that may potentially bias the results To evaluate the image transfer city to event {3 (city) * 2 (event) * 2 (gender)} MANCOVA model and to evaluate event to destination {2 (city) * 3(event) * 2 (gender)} MANCOVA model was used. The two-way three-way and four way interactions analysis was done by multi-variate Roy's largest Root for all the eight conditions. This included gender, city and destination. The use of statistical method for analyzing the data is strong point for this article to prove its hypothesis but at the same time this massive calculation has made it more complex. The study could have been divided into different research, studying co-branding effect of destination and events one for positive and the other for negative. This could have reduced the complexity of the article.

Results

The results emerged out of the study was interesting to know and might be basis for further studies in effects of sporting events on destination. Out of all the interactions, the four ways and three way interactions had no significant result meaning that the holistic effect of gender, sport involvement, city and event was found less significant while two-way interaction was more significant. In the case of where destination was centred, it was found that city when paired with an event had better ratings while involvement of females and males affect the intention to visit. In the case where events were centred, a remarkable result emerged. The event when paired with destination had no significant effect on ratings but it had a significant effect on males and females intentions to visit which was out of the fact that they were more involved with the sporting event than the destination. This proved that nothing matters more than event if event interests people. In other findings it was employed that the ads do not have any direct effects on intension to visit meaning that perceived image plays an important role while planning a trip to destination. The other findings suggests although the ratings of both the destinations improved when paired with events but the ratings were categorized on two dimensions evaluation and activities.

The sport-events consideration shows only a category from a population who likes sports but researcher would have used other cultural events to see the effects of image transfer in holistic terms of events. Events can't be generally categorized in sports event only.

Conclusions

The research has proved that mere association of an event with destination had transferred some image as an affect of co-branding. The pairing of brands depends on match up. This match can be in terms of product attributes or interests towards brands. This study suggest that a less active destination provides less activities to tourists but when paired with a sport which is liked by people will definitely improve the destination's perceived image. The researcher further has discussed the co-branding effects with literature. It can be added to this research that ways that pairings of event and destination are interpreted matter.

Events into Building Brand Destination

Events can prove to be as USP for the destination brand. Benchmarking in tourism is characterised by emphasis on improving performance across tourist destinations. Frederic Dimanche put up an idea International Conference of strategic development of tourism by creating awareness, quality management for the benefit of the tourism authorities. This study will look into the deeper effects of events to create a brand equity of destination as events represent the image of cultural and social backgrounds of a destination (Liping A CAI; Bihu, Billy bai) in their research article have presented that the level of the visitation to a destination goes down when the same destination is visited frequently. The proposed research will give DMO's an outline to create an event which can fill the gap of satisfaction levels of visitors and will give newer ideas to attract tourists in off seasons too gave a new concept of benchmarking for tourists satisfaction which depends upon quality provided to the tourists.

If planned effectively and used strategically, such events can create economic as well as social benefits for the host community. If events are poorly understood (and planned) communities run the risk of missing an important economic opportunity, while at worst they may even experience some degradation in quality of life and economic costs. Governments have been fast to see the potential of large sporting events to generate economic benefits media attention and the raising of a local area's profile; adding animation and life to existing facilities; encouraging repeat visits; and assisting economic regeneration. The majority of the reports trace the flow of spending associated with the event in the host community and identify resultant changes in sales, tax revenues, income and jobs. A point of contention in these studies has been the ability to separate between the short-term economic impact of the event (i.e. visitors attending the event) and so-called destination branding events which in turn are assumed to lead to increased tourism in the long—term. Whilst the 'holy grail' appears to be measuring the level of increased tourism to a destination that occurs because of an event, the proposed study seeks to a more modest outcome of determining the ability of an event portfolio to influence the decision of a tourist to visit a destination. If this can be established it provides impetus to the argument that events are able to induce tourism beyond the timing of the event itself.Sport tourism is one of the fastest growing domains of the leisure tourism market. Like wise there can be other cultural events too that can be developed considering different interests and different age groups. Events also bring immense benefits to the local community if they are included in strategic planning of an events tourism.

Events Portfolio

An event portfolio consists of hosting city/cities and event/events. A marketer should always prepare an events portfolio for a destination while seeking to use events as brand building tool. A mega event may not have long lasting effect on destination but heaps of small events all round the year might increase the interest of people towards a destination. This will lead to focus on different age groups, different interests like cultural, sports, music etc.Since events cater those tourists who have interests in entertainment and activities, a marketer or events portfolio desinger should have a target tourist segment. This may consist of families, groups, adventure sporties, individuals, newly wed couples, back paker etc. Events portfolio may contain sporting events, cultural events, business meetings, family festival etc. Thus, the reach of events portfolio depends on targeted tourists. An events portfolio should reinforce the brand image of destination.

Conclusion: Event Related Marketing Strategies

Past researches prove that there is synergy between a place and its marketing tool. Here destination being a place and events are being a marketing tool. Events are covered by media and the information about the destination where is the event is being hosted automatically market the key features of that destination. The events have the capacity to spread a positive image of a destination. This theory can be said from a range of marketing theories, concepts and strategies.

Media

The brand is affected by advertisement. It increases awareness and may change attitudes towards perceived image of a brand. Promotion for an event as well as destination is required to approach the targeted tourists. This requires adequate planned publicity campaign by the event marketer to balance the theme and advertisements well between destination and event. The print media, radio, internet and television outdoor media should prepare a well organized time and minutes of advertising and their schedules as to when and where the promotions will take place.

Public Relations

Unlike paid advertising for a destination, reporting about an event and a city or a country hosting that event is a purely journalistic activity in terms of coverage. It is absolutely essential that the events are covered for its pre activities, then during the event as well as after event effects. If a large event is covered then it is needless to say that media persons should be invited but when it comes to organize an event with intention to promote a destination then it should be pre decided that who will cover the event and how the event and destination will be covered to balance the effect of image transfer. It is thus necessary that PR activities be well planned. Press conferences, press releases, invites to events for impresarios are some means of networking for good public relations. PR personnel have the responsibility to identify and create rapport with press reporters and networking with influences so as to maintain a positive image of the event and destination.

Merchandising

Events have a capability of physical manifestation of destination. Most popular attributes of a destination can be used to be printed on products and the materials which are used for events marketing. The products may bear the destination's name promoting the key features of the host destination. Sports based events have traditionally shown the best example of merchandising the destination and event promotion.

Infrastructure

It is thoughtful that does the destination contain a proper infrastructure to hold a big event or there is there a need to develop a new infrastructure to meet such need. It includes proper accessibility to destination via airport, trains or other transfers. High quality hotels should be available for tourists for every class that may at least stand for hygiene and services.

Other Consideration

Hosting an event at a destination may include considerations like institutional or organizational framework. Different permissions from different institutional and tourism bodies like local government and Ministry of Tourism. The laws related to investment and community safety. Hosting an event also involves the social aspects because tourists may be from different cultures and there may be culture shock for the local community. To protect such odd situations the local tourism ministry should set up a body that may keep an eye for any such mishaps that can ruin the sporting spirits of event hosting.

Benefits of Events

It provides off-season benefits to the economy. The tourist may visit the destination if any event is on at the destination. It also adds to increase demand of local business weather hotel bookings, food restaurants, transportation. Events also encourage tourists to stay for a longer time at the destination. Events are also a tool to reach specific target market or a wider market both. They reinforce the destination's image. They help in promotion, positioning and branding a destination. The events help to communicate the destination's awareness. They build brand equity. The long term advantages of hosting an event may be referred as improvement in infrastructure, attractive investment by big companies, quality of life for locals and amazing experience for travellers, destination's brand building and an added value to the city's identity It can be added further to this research that the co-branding of events with destination or vice-versa can be positive or negative. A huge event may hamper the destination's image as the tourist will be more involved with the event than the destination which will not have a long lasting effect whilst a huge event may not have good response if the destination is not well known. Further study can be on terms of that what kind of events can cater the positive impacts on destination. Overall this article puts an undoubted study in terms of co-branding effects of destination and events.

5

Economic Development, Retail and Tourism

The Regional Economic Strategy *('East of England 2010 – Prosperity and Opportunity for All')* (RES) was published by the East of England Development Agency (EEDA) in June 2001. It sets out how sustainable economic growth can be achieved throughout the East of England. Government guidance states that RSS should assist the implementation of Regional Economic Strategy (RES) and that the RES must sit within the spatial planning framework provided by RSS. In effect the two regional strategies must be complementary.

EEDA is currently reviewing the RES, with a consultation draft published in Autumn 2004. The synergy between the two documents is based on work undertaken to align the draft regional spatial strategy with the regional economic strategy 2001: "prosperity and opportunity for all". This work developed to give a spatial distribution of job growth required to achieve the regional economic strategy and other spatial policy objectives, such as directing growth to deprived areas in order to facilitate regeneration. As a result of this work, RSS proposes total job growth across the region, for the period 2001 to 2021, of 421,500. The RES shares this proposition.

EERA and EEDA have jointly researched the land use implications of the RES. This concluded that some growth could be achieved in the Region through gains in productivity and policies such as promoting skills development and innovation, overcoming key transport bottlenecks and facilitating higher participation rates within the Region's existing population. However, to achieve the RES objectives, additional employment growth would also be needed, in particular to support the

Region's key economic sectors and clusters. Much of this growth is forecast to be concentrated mainly where these sectors and clusters already exist, i.e. Hertfordshire, the Cambridge sub-region and parts of west Essex. This concentration remains true whether the target is to achieve the Enhanced Growth by 2010 scenario required by RES or by 2021. The additional employment growth implies higher rates of population and housing growth than currently planned for in existing RSS.

The economic forecasting research essentially provided a statistical assessment of the means of achieving the RES aspirations for the region, and were not specifically driven by spatial policy. When comparing the relationship between the forecast and the emerging RSS spatial strategy, it became clear that it could not fit with policy. For example, it did not fit with a number of policy-led priorities:

- Thames Gateway regeneration priority;
- Milton Keynes South Midlands growth priority;
- Stansted/M11 growth priority (Sustainable Communities Plan).

The effect of this was that while the forecast indicated the required rates of employment creation/replacement needed to meet the RES target, it did not give a workable spatial distribution, with some areas under-allocated. Hence the figures in Policy E2 of this chapter represent an 'EG2021 plus' policy-led approach.

Policy E1: Human Resource Development

Local development plan documents will include policies that ensure sufficient and accessible premises are available (taking into account the availability of services/facilities in more rural areas) for training and education purposes to suit the requirements identified through the relevant strategies, including the Regional Economic Strategy, the Framework for Regional Employment and Skills Action (FRESA) and those drawn up by Learning and Skills Councils and Lifelong Learning Partnerships.

Supporting Text

Human resource development is central to harnessing and promoting future economic success and social opportunities in the Region, in enhancing access to jobs, and providing opportunities for those currently disadvantaged in the labour market.

Skills are a key driver of productivity. The rise of the knowledge economy is causing increased demand for skills, particularly higher-level skills. The East of England is in line with England's NVQ average at level 2 but falls behind at levels 3 and 4. The current supply of higher-level skills amongst the East of England work force will be inadequate to meet the future needs of the region's economy. FRESA identifies key priorities for action to secure the necessary skills. Top priorities include increasing participation rates in higher education, response to redundancies, skills for employability, work force development and young people and career choices.

The Learning and Skills Councils, local learning partnerships and local employers play an important role in enhancing skills and opportunities in the Region. Further and higher educational establishments are also vital to the success of training and education strategies. Local authorities and other partners will support similar measures to those already employed by the best universities and colleges in establishing effective links with knowledge based industries. The scope for provision of training and childcare facilities in association with development should also be explored through the use of planning obligations, in order to assist access to job opportunities.

The requirement for "accessible" premises is intended to allow innovative solutions to access to reflect the Region's diversity. For example, in rural areas this might mean mobile facilities. Accessibility also encompasses the mode of travel to facilities, as dealt with in the policies in the Regional Transport Strategy.

Several of the sub-regions in Chapter 5 set out specific aspirations and policies for the improvement of Higher Education, particularly as a catalyst for regeneration.

Policy E2: Job Growth

Supporting Text

Policy SS10 sets out the overall strategic approach to the regional economy. This Policy E2 sets out the distribution of economic growth.

The distribution of projected job growth targets across the Region is based upon an analysis by Bone Wells Associates (BWA) of what is required to achieve the RES Enhanced Growth scenario by 2021 and adjusted by reference to a number of subsequent policy initiatives and research studies.

The key influencing factors are:

- the Government's Sustainable Communities Plan and its requirements for the Region's 'Growth Areas', namely Milton Keynes South Midlands (Luton and Bedford in the East of England), London-Stansted-Cambridge-Peterborough and the Thames Gateway;
- the potential for indirect and catalytic impacts of airport expansion, particularly associated with Stansted and Luton Airports, and port expansion, particularly at Tilbury, London Gateway (Shellhaven), and Haven Gateway;
- the regeneration needs and opportunities across the Region;
- the provision of land to meet the needs of emerging and maturing key sectors and clusters in situ, as well enabling growth to occur along development corridors;
- the potential of key cities and towns to support economic development in a sustainable way (the agglomeration approach); and
- the potential of transport interchange centres and other strategic centres to act as focus points for sustainable mixed-use economic development.

Policy E2, together with policies E3 and E4, aim to secure an appropriate and effective distribution of job growth, particularly in the Sustainable Communities Plan Growth Areas. At the regional level, the employment growth figures are broadly aligned with the housing provisions in Policy H1, and create a more sustainable relationship between workers and jobs. It is more difficult to assess alignment at the sub-regional level, because of the nature of the data involved and local commuting across boundaries. In some cases a deliberate 'misalignment' is proposed to address existing deficits (e.g. provision of additional jobs in regeneration areas).

Given the dynamics of economic growth, the varying assumptions about density, vacancy rates and 'churn' in the market (take up of employment sites in the market place), policies must allow some flexibility and not be prescriptive. Proposals in local development plan documents for employment land supply need to be indicative and allow some 'spaceless growth' (job growth without the need for land allocations). Such flexibility needs to be accompanied by clear monitoring procedures and targets. Within this context EERA will work with EEDA and local partners to produce guidance on the production of 'indicative' district-level targets for job growth, and will also apply the 'plan, monitor and manage' approach to identify any required changes in policy or targets.

Further work is also to be carried out to look at the delivery of job growth in Norfolk, in particular to desegregate the figures for the Norwich and Great Yarmouth/Lowestoft sub-regions. This may have implications for the Norwich sub-region boundary.

It is important to note that Policy E2 provides only for the net increase in employment growth. It does not take account of the need to provide supply to allow for 'churn' in the employment land market and maintaining a vacancy or availability rate to allow choice and flexibility. It is important to promote a range of sites to meet employment and investment opportunities particularly in areas of high economic pressure, and provide an improved offer in regeneration areas, contribute to dispersal of pressure, accord with agglomeration principles and provide for expansion and employment churn, within the overall urban renaissance strategy.

The delivery of employment is influenced by the delivery of infrastructure and housing. EERA will closely monitor job creation, infrastructure delivery and housing completions through its annual monitoring arrangements as describe.

Policy E3 – Approach To Employment Land Allocation

Local development plan documents will allocate employment land to provide a range of sites and premises to meet the quantitative and qualitative needs of business within the sequential approach of the core spatial strategy, and job growth targets of Policy E2, enabling urban renaissance, economic regeneration, social inclusion and rural diversification.

Where development proposals and issues cross local authority boundaries this approach will be developed and applied across the whole urban or development area.

Efficient use will be made of existing employment land resources. Sites for industry and commerce will be provided in:

- urban areas and key market towns;
- locations that minimise commuting, and promote more sustainable communities, and a closer relationship between jobs and existing *or* proposed labour supply;

- locations where the maximum use of sustainable (public) transport can be made;
- locations and ways that minimise loss or damage to environmental and social capital, and so far as possible substitute for losses and secure positive enhancements. This will often mean giving precedence to the re-use of previously developed land and, wherever possible, the intensification of use on existing sites over the release of greenfield land;
- locations which meet the needs of the region's significant clusters as set out in the Regional Economic Strategy.

Land in employment use will be considered for alternative uses only where a completed employment land assessment demonstrates that sufficient land is available, of an appropriate type, range, quality and quantity, to ensure that the Regional Economic Strategy's objectives are achievable.

Supporting Text

The availability of sites or premises is only one influence on business locations. Other factors, such as the availability and skills of the labour force, supply chain issues, the availability of funding support and housing and lifestyle choices all play a part in making location decisions. The quality of land to meet the needs of business is critical to ensuring success and attracting inward investment. Local development plan documents will ensure that there is a high quality offer of employment land, taking account of the contribution that can be made by strategic and sub-regional employment sites and ability to meet the levels of job growth identified in Policy E2. Phasing and review of policy to accommodate economic potential and demand over the plan period, will also be considered. Allocations can help to promote more sustainable communities directly by redressing an imbalance between the availability of local workers and local jobs (and hence helping to reduce the need to travel) or more indirectly such as town centre office development supporting town centre shops and leisure economy, or through townscape improvements that contribute to perceptions of local quality of life.

Policy E4: Provision of Strategic Employment Sites

Local development plan documents will provide strategic employment sites of the appropriate quality and quantity are required, particularly in the following locations, to meet the needs of business: Harlow, development linked to the expansion of Stansted, Thames Gateway (linked to the Basildon, Southend-on-Sea and Thurrock Zones of Change), Cambridge Sub-region, Peterborough, Norwich, Ipswich, Great Yarmouth, Harwich and sites in Hertfordshire supporting key clusters and regeneration needs.

Local development plan documents will identify further sites to take account of opportunities in other areas in accordance with the core spatial strategy.

Supporting Text

Research has been carried out on the quality and quantity of sub-regional and strategic sites within the East of England and the categorisation of strategic and sub-regional employment sites (the strategic sites study).

The research highlights the changing role of strategic sites and suggests site-specific criteria against which to assess the market suitability of sites. Within each of the sub-regions, local development plan documents should provide for at least one readily available serviced strategic employment site and two sub-regional employment sites for general employment land use (B Class). Local development plan documents will propose serviced strategic employment sites solely for 'high technology' users in parts of the East of England where there is an identified need to develop significant clusters and sectors, including the Cambridge Sub-region. Where a need is identified, readily available serviced strategic employment sites solely for warehousing and distribution will also be proposed. Strategic sites are needed for the following reasons:

- Harlow – to achieve regeneration needs, ensure growth in key sectors and clusters, and ensure a balance to housing growth;
- Harlow and Stansted-development linked to the expansion of Stansted;
- Thames Gateway – to support the role of Thurrock as a sustainable European Logistics Hub, to support the role of Basildon as a business hub and strategic centre and to promote sustainable economic regeneration in Southend-on-Sea and its role as a strategic cultural and intellectual centre;
- Cambridge Sub-region – to secure its full potential as a centre for world-class research and development;

- Peterborough – to achieve regeneration, attract business activities and key sectors and clusters including environmental services;
- Norwich – to support regeneration and its role in bio technology;
- Ipswich – to support regeneration and its role in ICT as exemplified by Suffolk Innovation Park and Adastral Park;
- Harwich, Great Yarmouth and Felixstowe-development associated with port expansion; and
- Hertfordshire-at locations that support strong, continued growth of mature and emerging clusters and sectors and to support regeneration in the Lee Valley corridor and at Stevenage.

Policy E5: Supporting Economic Diversity and Business Development

Economic diversity and business development will be encouraged to facilitate small and medium enterprises, together with local economic strengths, support the growth of a variety of economic sectors, urban regeneration and growth, and to address rural isolation and rural diversification. Local development plan documents will assess the requirements of the various sectors of the local economy, including tourism and culture, and formulate policies and proposals to support their sustainable development. Local development plan documents will ensure that sufficient range, quantity and quality of land to meet the needs of business, including the provision of smaller units, is provided and safeguarded for a balanced economy in both urban and rural areas.

Supporting Text

It is important to encourage all aspects of the economy and ensure it is broadly based. This will increase its resilience to external changes and pressures, including geo-political changes to the global economy and the impact of climate change. A balanced economy requires a range of types of employment space in terms of size, location and cost. Tourism and culture are significant elements of the region's economy and are likely to be major growth sectors. In addition to the growth sectors, it is important to retain sectors such as manufacturing which are not expected to provide large-scale additional employment.

Assessing the requirements of the local economy is likely to also involve an assessment of the availability of local labour and potential skills fit with new jobs (refer also to Policy E1).

Policy E6: Information Communications Technology (ICT)

Local authorities and EEDA will work with telecommunication companies and private sector bodies to:

- improve the regional coverage of broadband infrastructure, particularly in rural areas;
- improve the level of service from existing broadband infrastructure; and
- promote the use of information communications technologies by businesses and the public and voluntary sector.

Local development plan documents seek to ensure that acceptable provision can be made for information communications technology, taking into account environmental constraints.

Supporting Text

Information and communication technology (ICT) is an essential component and feature of a world-class economy and an inclusive society. It can overcome obstacles to access in rural and peripheral areas, enable businesses to participate in e-commerce and operate in a global market, reduce the need to travel through the encouragement of flexible and remote working, encourage flexibility in business location decisions and encourage business start-ups in areas of need of regeneration, deliver training and learning opportunities and promote social inclusion by enabling internet access for all.

But current access to this technology varies across the East of England with private sector investment in broadband so far focused on the major centres of population. The Government's target is for all communities to have access to broadband by the end of 2005. Local authorities will work with private sector providers to ensure that the benefits of ICT are spread wider.

Policy E7: Supporting Cluster Development

Clusters are an important feature of regional economic growth and prosperity. Local development plan document will support those regionally significantly clusters identified by the East of England Development Agency (EEDA) and locally significant clusters defined by local economic partnerships in collaboration with local authorities and EEDA. Local development plan documents will:

- support the sustainable and dynamic growth of inter-regional and intra-regional business clusters identified by the above process;

- ensure there is sufficient quantity, quality, choice of range of sites including provision for incubator units, grow on space and larger facilities for established business clusters;
- address the need for accommodation and allocation of sites immediately adjacent to or close to key institutions including higher education and university facilities; and
- address the need for user restrictions to secure land use for specific activities.

Supporting Text

Clusters are defined as 'concentrations of companies in related activities, specialised suppliers, service providers and institutions, which are co-operating, competing and collaborating to build competitive advantage, often across traditional sector boundaries'. Such concentrations often depend on access to specialist skills and infrastructure within a specific area. The Government's competitiveness white paper and the DTI's 'biotechnology clusters' report (DTI August 1999) emphasises that the clustering of businesses operating in the same or complementary sectors can benefit the local, regional and national economy.

The Regional Economic Strategy states that business growth is likely to be concentrated in the key sectors and clusters. Several of these, such as biotechnology and research and development, are based upon the strengths of the Cambridge Sub-region. This will be supported and enhanced and, where possible, harnessed to benefit other parts of the region. For example the interaction between London and Cambridge is stimulating activity in the biotechnology sector at intervening locations, especially along the M11 and A1 corridors. There is potential for economic links to be strengthened between Cambridge and Ipswich and westwards through Bedfordshire to Milton Keynes and Oxford (Oxford to Cambridge Arc). Other opportunities within the region also merit further analysis, for example linking Cambridge to Norwich, Stevenage and Peterborough.

A study of economic sub-regions and clusters in the East of England identifies the land use and other requirements of each of the regionally significant clusters. Cluster development requirements include quality infrastructure, availability of land and premises, access to housing and appropriate social facilities and a suitably qualified labour force. Infrastructure requirements include freedom from of congestion, fast and reliable public transport and broadband communications. In some cases there is a need for specialist property (e.g. laboratory space for bio tech firms), while in others the requirement is related to quantity and location. If a cluster is to flourish, the institutions and resources which underpin it must be protected or supported. This will mean that sites need to be close to research establishments, research hospitals, institutes and campus.

Access to housing is a particular issue in the East of England, and inevitably tends to be more problematic for the lower value support activities within a cluster rather than the high value core.

There are opportunities to develop 'green business' clusters based on environmental industries (for example those specialising in recycling or exchange of materials) that will support the RES and other regional strategies. As an example, the Greater Peterborough sub-region has specific policies to build upon its environmental business sector.

Local development plan documents will consider the opportunity to provide specific guidance for strategic and locally important clusters. Where a key resource is critical to a cluster/sector reaching its full potential, specific sites will be identified.

There are areas where intense development pressures are focussed on a single location and where capacity and environmental constraints require the selective management of uses. Guidance on high technology clusters and the management of the economy in the Cambridge sub-region is set out in the sub-regions chapter. Local authorities will work together to ensure that existing businesses or new investment displaced by this policy are assisted to find alternative suitable sites within the region.

Policy E8: Simplified Planning Zones

Local development plan documents may propose simplified planning zones where such proposals will complement the regional or sub-regional economic strategy, particularly to assist areas for regeneration by means of an accelerated rate of inward investment, and support regionally or subregionally important clusters and sectors while protecting local environmental, heritage and cultural interests from adverse development impacts.

Supporting Text

Simplified planning zones (SPZ), if adopted through statute, should be of high quality and should be of low environmental impact, and will set the parameters of development tightly to ensure that high quality environments are created. This is not only for the protection of those in the vicinity of the new SPZs but to enable companies operating within the zones to be guaranteed that they will have good neighbours. An environmental impact assessment will be required before a SPZ can be designated. SPZs offer a speedier development control process whilst maintaining sufficient overall control to provide necessary security for potential investors.

Policy E9: Regional Structure of Retail Centres

The regional structure of retail centres is:

- major regional centres: Basildon, Cambridge, Colchester, Chelmsford, Ipswich, Norwich, Peterborough, Southend, and Watford;
- regional centres: Bedford, Bury St. Edmunds, Great Yarmouth, Harlow, Hemel Hempstead, King's Lynn, Lowestoft, Luton, St Albans, Stevenage and Welwyn Garden City;
- other towns and market towns. Local development plan documents will define the towns and market towns that comprise the structure of main retail centres within their area; and
- villages and local centres. Local development plan documents will define the villages and local centres that complete the structure of retail provision within their area.

Supporting Text

The retail sector is an important driver of the regional economy. Policy SS4 'town centres' in the core spatial strategy chapter sets the wider context for town centres, whilst Policy E10 considers the role of retail centres (not all of which are located in town centres) based on a national ranking of retail centres.

The East of England has an established structure of retail centres ranging from major regional centres to smaller market towns and villages, all of which play a key role in meeting the needs of their catchment areas. In the north of the Region retail centres tend to be more widely dispersed with relatively discrete catchments, while in the south the larger centres are closer with more complex, overlapping catchments. The south of the Region is also more strongly influenced by London.

The region is not dominated by any one retail centre although Thurrock Lakeside has the largest concentration of retail floorspace. Lakeside is not listed in Policy E9; it is a regional out of town retail centre and does not have the range of functions of a town centre.

For retail, leisure and some other services the East of England competes with surrounding national centres, particularly in London, but also with Milton Keynes, the Bluewater shopping centre and, to a more limited degree, Nottingham and Leicester in the East Midlands. During the plan period Milton Keynes is likely to continue to grow in significance and town centres in Bedfordshire will need to respond to this impact by raising and upgrading their offer.

Policy E10: Retail Strategy

In accordance with the regional structure in Policy E9:

- new retail development will be located in existing centres and will be consistent in scale with the size and character of the centre and its role in the regional structure;
- local development plan documents will propose higher order provision only where a need is clearly established, it would result in a more sustainable pattern of development and movement, including a reduction in the need to travel, there would be no significant detrimental impact on other centres or the transport network, and there is environmental capacity. Any new regional centres will be subject to similar considerations, and will be brought forward only as part of a review of this RSS;
- in the Sustainable Communities Plan Growth Areas, local development plan documents will propose development of retail and services in new and existing centres in accordance with sub-regional strategies and policies; and
- local development plan documents will consider the role of retail within Priority Areas for Regeneration and propose development and enhancement to implement regeneration strategies.

Supporting Text

Research undertaken within the region did not identify any need for major change to the retail structure to meet existing need. However, where there is significant growth within the region's Sustainable Community Plan Growth Areas and Priority Areas for Regeneration retail growth will be essential to meet new needs. The advancement of Harlow to the status of a sub-regional centre will be sought, while expansion of Stevenage's retail and services offer should also be sought in association with its regeneration. EERA and local authorities need to plan more positively for retail in order to:

- maintain and enhance the viability and vitality of retail centres; and
- make proper provision for new forms of retail distribution.

All local development plan documents will address retail needs and present an analysis of their area designed to produce a coherent retail strategy in relation to their existing town centres, edge-of-town centre and out-of-town centre retail sites, and E-tailing growth. These strategies should be prepared from robust data and analysis and make provision for new retail development whilst ensuring the viability and vitality of existing centres.

Generally new development needs to be of a scale appropriate for the centre to promote internal competition and linked trips and to ensure consistency with transport networks.

Retail centres should aim to support and enhance their existing functions and absorb expenditure growth through higher quality development without changing the centre's position in the regional structure. However, major retail development can be a driver of growth and regeneration, so in the Sustainable Communities Plan Growth Areas and the regional growth areas significant planned retail and associated services growth will be needed to deliver sustainable communities. The implications of this growth will need to be carefully considered at the sub-regional level and planned for through the development plan process.

Policy E11: Retail Distribution

Strategic retail distribution centres will only be permitted in locations with good rail and road access and, where available, waterway access. Local development plan documents will consider the needs of distribution arising from increased use of internet retailing and will implement policies to ensure that development is in accordance with the sequential test, and with good public transport, rail and road access.

Local development plan documents will consider how development supporting the local sourcing of products can be encouraged.

Supporting Text

There is potential for radical change in retail technology in the plan period as evidenced by increased use of internet retailing. The key impact of this is likely to be on the need for distribution centres and on existing town centre retailing functions. Policy needs to provide for strategic development in sustainable locations and to focus new development on existing town centres wherever possible in accordance with the sequential test. The local sourcing of products can help to reduce 'food-miles' or distance travelled by products. Whilst it is recognised that in many cases local availability is not feasible, local development plan documents should consider how this can be encouraged for those products that are.

Policy E12: Out-of-town Retail

It is considered that there is no need for any additional regional out-of-town shopping centres in the plan period.

Local development plan documents will define the current and future role of existing out of town centre retail sites in relation to existing town centres, in particular to determine whether:

- out-of-town centre sites should remain purely retail centres; or
- they should be developed into town centres with a full range of service provision.

Out-of-town centres will only be developed into town centres where it will:

- improve social, environmental and economic sustainability; and
- deliver improved sustainable transport accessibility, particularly improved public transport access.

Supporting Text

There are some significant out of town centre retail sites within the East of England most notably Thurrock Lakeside, but also the

Brookfield Centre in Broxbourne, Hatfield Gallerias, and London Colney. Local development plan documents will set policy for such centres, to indicate the role they should fulfil within the retail structure.

Policy E13: Tourism

Local planning authorities, in liaison with the East of England Tourist Board, will ensure that local development plan documents:

- include policies to encourage investment in the maintenance, improvement and appropriate diversification of the region's tourist industry. This investment should be based on maximising the benefits to, and minimising negative effects on, the natural and built environment, local distinctiveness and host communities;
- integrate with the range of tools in use for managing tourism, particularly local and regional tourism strategies and visitor management plans, and secure policy compatibility with neighbouring authorities. In drafting locational policies authorities must recognise that some forms of tourism development are not footloose;
- promote development that encourages more sustainable tourism including: the coordination of activities and accommodation to minimise the need to travel; enhancing existing facilities and/or re-using existing buildings; the regeneration of seaside resorts; extending employment outside the normal tourist season; regeneration (rural and urban); or urban renaissance; and
- encourage new development where it would add to the tourist product being offered, attract additional visitors and be based on realistic projections of demand.

Supporting Text

Tourism is one of the East of England's key economic sectors and, with leisure and heritage, is projected to make among the highest contributions to absolute increase in the Region's Gross Domestic Product. A Regional Tourism Strategy is in preparation and will assist the preparation of local development plan documents and development proposals.

Careful management and sustainable development of tourism can create opportunities to boost local economies, enhance the natural and built environment and contribute to the social well-being of an area. Tourism can be a catalyst to stimulate investment, revitalise deprived areas and encourage growth in other employment sectors. Particular attention should be given to tourism development in environmentally sensitive areas, e.g. Areas of Outstanding Natural Beauty (AONBs), Sites of Special Scientific Interest (SSSIs) and conservation sites.

These may include some 'honeypot' tourist areas. Such areas often attract large numbers of visitors due to their unique appeal as visitor destinations and it is important that these qualities are protected for future generations to enjoy. Significant growth in visitor numbers in such areas can have lasting effects on the natural and historic environment and it is in the interests of tourism developers to conserve the environment upon which they rely.

This can be particularly important in locations such as the Heritage Coast and the Broads. Measures to disperse visitors away from sensitive tourist hotspots to areas that have the capacity to cope with larger visitor numbers can often be used as an effective tool for sustainable visitor management.

It is also important to consider the impact of tourism on areas that do not have the capacity or suitable infrastructure to accommodate large numbers of visitors such as some popular historic towns and villages and coastal resorts. Effective visitor management strategies are crucial to their sustainability.

Tourism has traditionally been focused on a limited season leading to potential for excessive pressures on the environment, host communities and seasonal employment. Reducing seasonality through the development of off-peak tourism can help to provide year-round employment, provide businesses with an incentive for retaining staff and spread visitor numbers.

Improved facilities to cope with increased visitor numbers at existing highly utilised tourist sites, concentration of visitors in special areas to make better use of visitor management resources and enhancing host community relationships should be encouraged. Proposals for strategic tourism facilities will need to comply with the requirements of Policy C2.

Tourism development can contribute to finding new uses for existing buildings whether in rural or urban locations, and so can help stimulate regeneration and investment. Sensitive adaptation of historic or locally distinctive buildings can capitalise on the region's unique qualities. Although new development is required to extend the tourism infrastructure, priority should also be given to investment by existing businesses to ensure that the quality of tourism products is maintained.

Regional flagship tourism projects have the potential to both boost the profile of the region in terms of attracting new visitors and to stimulate further growth and investment in tourism and related sectors. Thorough commercial assessments should be required for such projects, particularly where projects are dependent on public grant aid.

A sustainable approach to tourism development needs to reflect not only the physical impact of tourism on an area but also its potential economic and social value. Integration of tourism planning policies is vital between neighbouring authorities as destination areas and visitor movements rarely follow administrative boundaries.

The East of England Tourist Board (EETB) identifies five key principles of development: Partnership, Quality, Sustainability, Competitiveness and Accessibility and Inclusion. It is important to ensure that new tourism development meets the broad objectives of EETB along with the specific requirements of strategic and local planning policies.

Effective tourism development should not focus solely on destinations but should exploit opportunities from a range of tourism initiatives, including events, specialist activities, food and drink, shopping, leisure and recreation, not necessarily linked to places of interest.

Policy E14 Regional Airports

Airports have an important and strategic role as drivers in the regional economy and local economy as well as having significant potential to contribute to meeting regeneration needs. Airport growth is supported to the maximum capacity of the existing runways in the case of Luton and Stansted and modest expansion to meet local market demand in the case of Norwich and Southend.

It is vital that the future growth of airports in the region achieves an acceptable balance between economic, employment and other benefits and environmental and other considerations. The support of the Regional Assembly for appropriate growth at each regional airport is subject to:

- a surface access strategy for each airport being prepared, agreed and implemented;

- effective and timely implementation of other necessary infrastructure requirements;
- safeguarding of the amenity, character and appearance of the environment and communities in proximity to and affected by airport operations;
- minimising noise and air pollution. Levels must be monitored against national and local targets. Energy and resource conservation measures need to be introduced as appropriate to achieve pollution reduction;
- ensuring best practice in air and ground safety provision;
- airport development not leading to consequential pressures to exceed levels of planned growth, infrastructure and service provision beyond that provided for in local development plan documents; and
- the completion and regular review by airport operators of their airport master plans (5 yearly) and review no less frequently of their operating procedures.

Supporting Text

Studies of Stansted and Luton Airports have highlighted the important role that airports perform in their local and in the regional economy. They provide a range of employment opportunities with a significant proportion of jobs that do not rely on high skill and educational attainment levels and can attract firms that value proximity to airport services. Airports can provide a useful catalyst for economic regeneration, which is likely to be a positive outcome for local communities resulting from the growth of Luton, Norwich and Southend Airports. Local planning authorities will need to make appropriate provision to meet the employment needs of airports operating in their area or nearby.

Airports give rise to serious environmental impacts on surrounding areas and overall increases in air transport usage contribute to global warming. EERA has weighed economic and employment benefits with environmental and other consequences and, in consequence, supports growth at Stansted and Luton Airports being restricted to the existing runways as built (2160 metres long in the case of Luton). It also supports modest expansion of Norwich and Southend airports to meet local market demand.

Airport operators are required to update or prepare master plans for their airports by 2005, to review these five yearly thereafter, and to engage the local community in their preparation. They will be a valuable informative for local development plan documents.

This policy lists areas that require special consideration by airport operators. These need to be addressed satisfactorily if airport growth is to occur without undue adverse consequences for the local and wider community.

Transport choice and adequate provision are essential to airport growth and to minimising congestion and related problems for local communities so a surface access strategy will need to be prepared by each airport operator, agreed by the relevant local planning and highway authority(ies) and implemented within an agreed timescale. Progress will need to be monitored and reviewed. The strategy will include proposed measures to achieve a progressive increase in the proportion of employees and passengers travelling to an airport by modes other than the car and to minimise congestion, particularly at peak times. The strategy will also need to cover car parking both on and off airport and its management.

It is imperative that airport operators ensure adequate and timely provision of all essential infrastructure in advance of need, in particular the implementation of key items of infrastructure, including enhanced public transport service provision, by key date(s) including schemes listed in the Regional Transportation Strategy and/or as required by local development plan documents.

A major objective of strategic planning policy is safeguarding the amenity, character and appearance of the environment and communities in proximity to and affected by airport operations. This includes minimising noise and air pollution. Both day and night noise cause concern but night noise is particularly problematic. Levels must be monitored against national and local targets with energy and resource conservation measures introduced whenever appropriate. At all times best practicable means should be used to achieve pollution reduction.

6

Economic Development, Employment and Tourism

Introduction

County Louth has a tradition of entrepreneurial flair and industrial innovation. Over the course of the *County Development Plan 2003 – 2009*, the county shared in the benefits associated with the Celtic Tiger and has become well positioned as a major manufacturing, commercial and service centre catering for both domestic and international markets. Louth Local Authorities have proactively engaged with the private sector and other agencies to create strong economic partnerships.

This has been coupled with the development of a holistic approach to economic development which involves educational institutions, cross border engagement and the establishment of concrete targets for job creation and economic development. The key economic strengths and drivers in County Louth include, inter alia, its strategic location, high quality infrastructure, people resources, education and skills of its work force and the high quality of life available to its residents.

Louth enjoys a very favourable location along the Dublin-Belfast corridor with close proximity to Dublin and the related advantages of easy access to Dublin Airport, Dublin Port, third and fourth level educational institutions and domestic and international markets. It is also very accessible to Belfast and the highly urbanised north east including proximity to Belfast International and City Airports and the sea ports in Belfast and Larne. The A1/M1 motorway linking Dublin and Belfast runs through the heart of the county providing high quality access to national roads and motorway infrastructure. The improved level of rail infrastructure and services provide an alternative and sustainable transportation option for both goods and passenger traffic.

Louth is highly urbanised and has a high density of population compared to other rural counties. This is primarily as a result of having within its boundaries two of the largest provincial towns in the country, namely Dundalk and Drogheda. This generates critical mass and a large and well educated labour force pool, which is an essential resource for economic activity and expansion.

The high quality of life enjoyed by the residents of County Louth and which is available to potential investors is regarded as a major economic strength of the county.

County Louth Economic Development Strategy 2009-2015

This report presents an economic development strategy for County Louth for the period between 2009 and 2015, which coincides with the timeframe for the Plan. It focuses on the following:

- Assessment of the economic strengths and weakness of Louth.
- Identification and making of recommendations on economic opportunities that can be successfully delivered.
- Identification of current and future challenges and threats facing the county.
- Making of proposals for a unique County Louth brand and a supporting marketing strategy.
- Identification of potential funding sources and mechanisms.

Whilst it is accepted that the majority of employment growth will be focused on the two principal urban areas of Dundalk and Drogheda, the Strategy also recognises that there is considerable scope for new economic opportunities in rural County Louth.

Key Development Opportunities for Louth as identified by County Louth Economic Development Strategy

Location

Louth is ideally placed to capitalize on the advantages afforded to the county arising from its approximate location to Dublin along the Dublin Belfast economic corridor.

People Resources

The significant commuter population in County Louth points to an opportunity to leverage the high skilled labour pool to market Louth as a location for future investment.

Economic Sectors

Existing and emerging strengths would suggest that there are potential significant development opportunities for Louth in foreign owned and domestic owned high value industry and internationally traded services, including high end, specialised manufacturing, financial and business services and other commercial activities, including retail.

Louth has particular advantages such as high quality visitor attractions, easy access to Dublin Airport and accommodation which indicate significant opportunities to further develop the county as a high quality destination for overseas and domestic holiday and business visitors.

The following recommendations for the promotion of economic development of the county are contained within the Strategy.

1. The county development plan should target an increase in the population of the county and its main towns to approach 150,000 persons in the county and around 190,000 persons in the wider economic area surrounding the county by 2020.
2. The county development plan should facilitate commercial and other development to provide additional employment of between 17,000 and 22,000 jobs in the administrative and economic areas respectively, to support the targeted expansion in population.
3. County Louth should develop a diversified economic base to reduce its vulnerability to any one sector or a limited number of potentially vulnerable sectors.
4. A labour and skills strategy should be implemented which supports the required growth in the work force while addressing the specific skills required to support the sectoral economic strategy.
5. Continued and intensified efforts should be directed as a priority at addressing specific challenges faced by the county in the areas of unemployment and social exclusion.
6. Deficits in important key infrastructure, such as high quality broadband availability should be addressed in the county to facilitate economic and population growth.

7. Town centre development should continue to focus on ensuring the development of attractive centres for the county's main towns,
8. A marketing and branding strategy should be implemented which capitalises on the strengths of Louth and its constituent main towns as locations for investment and tourism.
9. A coordinated and consistent approach to the implementation and delivery of the development strategy is required, supported by appropriate structures at local authority and agency level.
10. A range of public, private and public private partnerships (PPP) funding options should be explored to support the delivery of infrastructure and other priorities. Economic development strategies have also been prepared for the towns of Dundalk, Drogheda and Ardee. The Plan will support the implementation of these in addition to the economic development strategy for the county.

Policy

To capitalise on the location, natural and people resources of County Louth in the pursuit of the economic development priorities identified in the *County Louth Economic Development Strategy 2009-2015* and *Economic Development of Ardee 2009-2015* and support the implementation of similar strategies for Dundalk and Drogheda.

Employment Opportunities in smaller Towns and Villages

The main centres for employment within county Louth are Dundalk, Drogheda, Ardee and Dunleer and the council supports the role of these towns as the primary locations for employment generating activities within the county. However, the council also acknowledges the need for greater employment opportunities in smaller settlements and in rural areas. The spread of employment opportunities throughout the county is considered necessary in order to revitalise and sustain rural communities where traditional employment sources, such as agriculture, are in decline.

The following settlements are identified as suitable for small scale businesses and enterprise and it is proposed that lands for employment activities will be identified and zoned in the review of the local area plans.

- Clogherhead

- Castlebellingham/Kilsaran
- Greenore
- Louth Village
- Collon.

Policy

To protect and enhance the status of Dundalk, Drogheda, Ardee and Dunleer as the principles centres of employment, industrial and commercial activity within the county.

To secure a spread of employment opportunities at key strategic locations throughout the county and facilitate the development of local based micro and start –up enterprises. To identify and zone additional lands, if required, for employment activities in the review of the local area plans for Clogherhead, Castlebellingham/Kilsaran, Greenore, Louth Village and Collon.

It should be noted however that the above policies do not preclude the location of industrial and commercial activity elsewhere in the county, where consideration will be given on the merits of each individual proposal.

Development at Motorway Interchanges

The M1 has the potential to act as a major stimulant of economic development and activity by providing high quality road infrastructure and connectivity to air and sea ports and thereby to domestic and international markets. Motorway interchanges are strategic locations much sought after by developers due to the desirability and benefits of having immediate access to the primary road network.

However, uncontrolled and poorly regulated development at interchanges can often be problematical. This can be due to such development being solely dependent on roads transport, the possibility of traffic congestion on national routes, the impact on rural landscapes and environments and the costs involved in the provision of other infrastructure such as piped services, electricity and gas. Such development can also detract investment from existing towns and settlements that are badly in need of renewal and development.

In order to maximise the benefits accruing to the county from the motorway and to regulate development in a sustainable and appropriate manner along its route, the following policies will be applied.

Policy

To promote and facilitate development at urban–related* interchanges in accordance with the zoning provisions of the *Dundalk and Environs Plan* and the *North Drogheda Environs Local Area Plan 2004*.

To resist development at rural-related** motorway interchanges.

Urban –related interchanges are Ballymascanlon, Castleblayney Road, Dundalk South interchange and Drogheda North.

Rural –related interchanges are Carrickcarron junction, Drumleck, Charleville, Mooremount and Woodlands.

Cross Border Economic Co-Operation

The emergence of a lasting peace in Northern Ireland presents significant opportunities for cooperation between local authorities, community groups and the private sector in the promotion and development of the region on a cross border basis for the mutual benefit of both.

To this end, the International Centre for Local and Regional Development (ICLRD) has developed a number of concepts which include the Newry-Dundalk Twin-City Region and a Newry-Dundalk International Services Zone. It is considered that a twin-city region would have the capacity to facilitate an integrated approach to the strategic planning and special needs of the area and to promote a sustainable central corridor strategy on the eastern seaboard. The International Service Zone concept is based on the Derry-Letterkenny modal. Newry-Dundalk is considered a prime location as a centre for internationally traded services due to its location at the centre of the Dublin-Belfast economic corridor.

Consideration will also be given to the carrying out of an economic analysis and development strategy focusing on the M1 corridor extending into Northern Ireland and to the counties of Meath and Fingal.

Policy

EDE 7: To support joint initiatives between local authorities, community groups and private sector for cooperation and promotion of the region on a cross border basis for the mutual benefit of both.

Adoption of a Partnership Approach

A key facet of the economy in County Louth has been the adoption of a partnership approach towards growing the economy. This is manifested in the work of organisations such the County Development Board, Louth County Enterprise Board, DKIT, Fas, the Chambers of Commerce and Louth Leader Partnership, Enterprise Ireland, the IDA, and the Newry-Dundalk Business Linkage Programme. The partnership approach has been most successful in the work undertaken by the Dundalk Economic Development Group. The DEDG was established by the Louth Local Authorities in 2006, as a partnership initiative bringing private and public sector leaders together to promote Dundalk as an ideal place to live, invest or visit. Its work has been recognised at a national level.

Policy

EDE 8: To work in partnership with development agencies within the county to promote economic development, enterprise and employment.

Employment Trends and Opportunities

County Louth has traditionally had a strong employment and industrial base centred primarily on the towns of Dundalk, Drogheda, Ardee and Dunleer. The significant foreign direct investment in new enterprises supported by the Industrial Development Authority (IDA) has taken place in county Louth in more recent years and this has made a very valuable contribution to economic development and employment opportunities.

The Dundalk Institute of Technology (DKiT) provides a range of high quality third level diploma and degree courses in the sciences, engineering, building and construction and the number of highly qualified graduates passing through the college each year is a major strength and opportunity for the county. The changing employment profile of Ireland has been manifested locally in a shift towards information, communications and technology (ICT) based industries, specialised engineering and food processing. Today, the county is rapidly becoming one of Ireland's principal industrial centres and has attracted new growth in the engineering and IT sectors, principally to the two major towns.

The quality of infrastructure in terms of road, rail and access to sea and air ports in addition to the high quality of the environment and quality of life, makes the county an attractive location for investment and as a place to live.

Employment Sectors

The breakdown of sectoral employment within the county is set out. Currently the majority of employment in Louth is in commerce (31.1%), education, health and social work (22.3%) and manufacturing (17.9%). A relatively low proportion of the county is involved in farming or agricultural activities, reflecting the highly urbanised nature of the county and the general decline in agricultural employment in recent years. As might be expected, the economic boom of the past decade has resulted in significant increase in employment opportunities within the county and a corresponding decrease in the unemployment rate from a peak of 22.3% in 1996 to 11.1% in 2006 (*CSO 1996 and 2006*). However the 2006 figure of 11.1% is significantly higher than the national average of 8.5%, which is reflective of the existence of high social exclusion and high unemployment within the RAPID areas of the towns of Dundalk and Drogheda. The deteriorating economic climate that has emerged in late 2008 and is continuing, could have serious implications for employment in county Louth and it is likely that the unemployment rate will increase, if temporarily, until such time as there is a sustained economic upturn.

Policy

To work in partnership with national and local economic development and employment promoting agencies to support employment generating initiatives within the county.

Development Management Standards for Industrial and Commercial Developments

The council will require that industrial and commercial lands be developed to a very high standard in campus style settings combining aesthetics with enterprise and attracting high calibre business occupiers. In spatial terms this will mean the development of a series of innovative landmark buildings set in attractive landscaped grounds. New development proposals should aim to provide design excellence realised within a hierarchal road structure and a hard and soft landscaping framework.

Landscaping and Amenity

Commercial and industrial development should present a pleasant aspect, aided by a high quality of landscape design, including tree planting, within both public and private domains. The existing landscape framework and its associated topography should be respected. Landscaping should be such as to ensure that the buildings will not be dominated by extensive areas of parking, hard standing and roads, thereby detracting from the quality of the environment. A detailed, high quality landscape plan, planting schedule and planting programme will be required with all applications. Planting shall include semi-mature trees in order to reduce the visual impact of structures on surrounding areas.

The provision of a buffer zone of not less than fifteen metres in width will be required where industrial and other land uses adjoin to ensure amenities of adjacent properties are not adversely affected. There should be no significant amenity loss (by way of noise, smell or other nuisance) to immediate neighbours or the area in general resulting from the nature of the proposed business, the amount of traffic generated or the servicing arrangement.

Surface Water Drainage

Adequate measures should be taken by commercial/industrial users and developers in the treatment and disposal of surface water to prevent pollution, including the adoption of the principles of sustainable urban drainage systems (SUDS) in designing surface water management arrangements.

Sustainable Design

All commercial and Industrial development should adopt a sustainable approach to design and building methods including passive design, use of solar energy, low energy performance buildings and the use of renewable energy supplies, in association with Sustainable Energy Ireland and having regard to the Guidelines for Sustainable Design and Energy Efficiency in Buildings as set out in paragraph 9.7 of the Plan..

Car Parking, Loading and Unloading Provision

All surface car parking areas should preferably be located behind the building line, out of view of the general public. Where this is not practical, parking areas should be suitably screened and landscaped. All car parking areas should be suitably surfaced and illuminated. Individual parking spaces should be permanently marked and shall not be less than 5.0m X 2.5m in dimension and shall have appropriate access and circulation aisles.

Sufficient loading and unloading bays should be provided. These should be of sufficient size to accommodate loading and unloading operations without encroachment onto any public road, footpath or interfere with the safety and free flow of vehicular traffic or pedestrians.

Design

Where two or more commercial or industrial buildings are being developed, a uniform design for boundary treatments, roof profiles and building lines is recommended. The scale and design of proposed development should be in keeping with the surrounding area and adjoining developments.

Site Coverage and Plot Ratios

The maximum site coverage permitted in industrial areas shall be 50% and the maximum plot ratio shall be 2:1.

Open Storage

Any open storage areas shall be located behind the building line and be adequately screened from public view.

Roads and Footpaths

The width of all internal industrial estate roads shall, generally, not be less than 7.3 metres with minimum radii of 10.5 metres at junctions. Visibility splays shall not be less than 70m x 4.5m x 1.05m within speed control zones and 160m x 4.5m x 1.05m elsewhere. Footpaths shall not be less than 1.8 metres in width.

Nuisance

The 'good neighbour' principle should be applied in respect of all industrial and commercial developments where possible conflict could arise with other established uses. In particular, noise emissions, whether from plant, machinery or traffic, shall comply with the provisions of Noise Regulations (S.I. No. 140 of 2006).

Foul Sewerage

All discharges of trade effluents to sewerage networks or receiving waters shall be subject to a Water Pollution Act Discharge Licence. Specified appropriate pre-treatment of trade effluents shall be required prior to discharge to council sewers.

Public Water Supplies

All supplies to industrial developments shall be metered and consumers shall be charged on basis of usage in accordance with guidelines set out in the *Water Services Pricing Policy.*

Fire Prevention

Adequate storage and hydrant capacity should be provided in consultation with the fire department of the council.

Building Regulations

Designers, developers and owners should ensure that all buildings and structures comply with the requirements of the *Building Regulations 1990*.

Signage

Signage shall be kept to a minimum. In order to ensure high quality signage and to safeguard the amenities of the area, a uniform signage scheme should be devised and submitted as part of the planning application for the development to which it relates. Billboards or free standing signage will not normally be permitted.

Public Artwork

Public art should be provided within an open space or focal point within new development schemes, through the *Percent for Arts Scheme* administered by the Department of the Environment, Heritage and Local Government. The council should be consulted on opportunities for permanent art.

Commerce and Retail

The level of commerce and retail activity is reflective of the overall economic well being of the economy. County Louth, by reason of its border location, has suffered as a result of different pricing structures, monetary and taxation regimes, north and south of the border. This is particularly evident in recent months and is being further exacerbated by the current economic downturn. The importance of commerce and retail in County Louth is evident from the proportion of the total labour force, some 31.1%, employed in the sector.

Traditionally, the main destination for shopping has been town and village centres. These also acted as the focus for a variety of other activities including business, social, leisure and residential uses.

Recent trends have seen the decline of small independent grocers and the emergence of larger supermarkets, franchise based local convenience stores, discount food stores and retail warehouses at out-of-town locations. These emerging trends in the retail sector have increasingly influenced shopping patterns and have created a demand for large shopping centres at locations where extensive car parking facilities are available. The council recognises the importance of retaining the primary role of town centres for commercial and retail activity. Therefore, the retail policies outlined in the Plan aim to preserve the viability and vitality of the town and village centres of the county whilst also recognising the need to provide for new retailing formats to meet consumer demands.

Louth Retail Strategy 2009

The *Retail Planning Guidelines for Planning Authorities 2000* were issued under the provisions of *Section 28 of the Planning and Development Act 2000* and were subsequently revised in 2005. The purpose of these guidelines is to:

- Promote a healthy competitive retail environment.
- Promote forms of retail development which are easily assessable by public transport.
- Protect the role of town centres and resist large scale out of centre shopping malls.
- Resist large retail centres close to national roads or motorway interchanges.
- Assist local authorities in the preparation of retail policies for incorporation into development plans.

In order to comply with the guidelines planning authorities are required to prepare retail strategies.

The *Louth Retail Strategy* was prepared and adopted in 2002 and subsequently reviewed in 2009. The 2009 Strategy has informed the retail policies of this development plan. The purpose of the *Louth Retail Strategy 2009* is to:

- Promote a healthy, vibrant and competitive retail environment within County Louth.
- Identify the core shopping areas in Dundalk, Drogheda and Ardee.
- Formulate policies to protect the vitality and viability of existing town and village centres.
- Ensure the provision of appropriately scaled convenience retail outlets in new residential areas.
- Establish a county retail hierarchy.

- Define criteria for the assessment of future significant retail developments.

The Strategy has confirmed that there has been a 127% increase in the retail floor space available within the county since the previous strategy was completed in 2002, with increases of 170% in Drogheda, 108% in Dundalk and 49.2% in Ardee. This represents a very significant increase and is reflective of the progressive development of the county over that period. One of the important functions of the retail strategy was to establish a county retail hierarchy which is set out. The primary positions of Dundalk and Drogheda at level one is recognised whilst the local importance of Ardee places it at level 2. Other important local centres of Blackrock, Dunleer, Collon and Carlingford are included at level 3 and all other villages are at level 4.

In terms of retail warehouses and retail parks the strategy suggests that there is considerable existing floor space and that there is unlikely to be any additional need or demand over the period of the Plan. The also concludes that Ardee should continue to develop its convenience retail offer in tandem with its expanding population and that there is a current need for an additional convenience retail store up to 2500 square metres.

However, it considers that there is no justifiable need for retail park development. Furthermore, the development of Ardee's retail comparison offer should be closely linked to the evolution of the town's untapped tourism potential.

In the other towns and villages, the priority is to cater sufficiently for the basic convenience and lower order comparison requirements of their existing populations, and the aim is to facilitate retail development commensurate with their population sizes, location and traditional built environment.

The retail policies as set out below are inclusive of those recommended in the retail study.

Policy

To promote a healthy competitive retail environment within County Louth and to maintain the vitality and viability of town and village centres and their role as primary retail core areas. To ensure that applications for retail development comply with the provisions of the *Retail Planning Guidelines 2005* and the *Louth Retail Strategy 2009.*

To support the development of Dundalk and Drogheda as important regional shopping centres and to maintain the role of Ardee as a sub county retail centre and the retail function of all other settlements, commensurate with locally generated needs.

To resist the provision of large scale retail developments outside town centres subject to the application of the sequential test and demonstration that the existing town centre will not be adversely affected.

To promote the provision of local retail centres serving small, localised catchment populations in new residential areas, commensurate with locally generated needs.

To generally discourage permission for change of use from retail or service (including banks and similar institutions with over the counter services) to non-retail or non service uses at ground-floor level.

Town and Village Centres

Rural town and village centres have traditionally been at the heart of the economic commercial, social and cultural heart of rural communities. They were bustling centres of activity which had a complex mix of uses including residential, retail, professional and other services, leisure and cultural activities. The advent of the motor car and changing consumer demands have resulted in a decline of the role of town and village centres as both the residential and commercial functions sought to relocate to more desirable and accessible out of town locations. This has had a negative impact on the fabric and environment of many towns and villages, resulting in a loss of vibrancy and activity particularly outside of business hours.

The council recognises the important role that rural town and villages play in the social and economic life and therefore considers it necessary to devise policies that will protect the vitality and viability of these settlements. The retail policies outlined above which are derived from the *Retail Planning Guidelines 2005* and the *Louth Retail Strategy 2009* seek to preserve the retail function of town and village centres. It is considered that, though important, retail policies alone will not be sufficient to protect the broader range of essential town and village centre uses.

Town and Village Centre Environments

It is important that town and village centres are attractive, safe and easily accessible to all. A number of town and village improvement schemes have been carried out during the period of the last plan, in cooperation with local Tidy Towns Committees. The success of Louth's towns and villages in the Bord Failte sponsored Tidy Towns Competition bears testimony to the improvements made.

Improvements to footpaths, street lighting, street furniture and landscaping make a valuable contribution to the attractiveness of the environments of town and village centres. The council will continue to cooperate with local groups towards further improvement in towns and villages throughout the county.

Policy

To promote the improvement of the environment of town and village centres through good design in all development, landscaping, street furniture and public art works.

To improve traffic mobility through traffic management, improvements to pavements, provision of access for mobility impaired and public transport waiting facilities.

To cooperate with local Tidy Towns Committees and other community groups in the implementation of environmental improvement schemes.

Architectural Conservation Areas and Protected Structures

Many of the towns and villages within the county have designated architectural conservation areas (ACA) and a number of protected structures. Any proposed developments within an ACA or involving modifications to a protected structure shall comply with the requirements.

Living over the Shop

The council will promote the provision and modernisation of residential accommodation over commercial premises in towns and villages in order to improve the vibrancy of their centres. This will be subject to the provision of good quality accommodation with separate and safe access from the street and the protection of residential amenities from any possible conflict with other uses.

Policy

To promote the provision and modernisation of residential accommodation over commercial premises in towns and villages in order to improve the vibrancy of their centres.

Shopfronts

The towns and villages of County Louth contain numerous examples of traditional shopfront design together with large numbers of more modern design, much of which reflects a certain amount of corporate harmonisation. The council will encourage the preservation of authentic, traditional shopfronts and the provision of good quality contemporary designs. Design criteria for shopfronts should ensure that:

- Entrances are fully accessible to all people with mobility difficulties.
- Where a shopfront involves two or more units, that it is divided with separate fascias and columns to reflect the separate units.
- The shopfront respects the building's elevation and architectural details. Period shopfronts on protected structures and in ACAs should be retained.
- The design takes into account adjacent shopfronts where they make a positive contribution to the streetscape.

Policy

To encourage the preservation of authentic, tradition shopfronts and good quality contemporary designs.

Security Shutters

Whilst the council recognises the need for the sufficient security for commercial premises the installation of security shutters can detract from the appearance, visual amenity and safety of town and village centres particularly at night and weekends. The council will discourage the mounting or location of rollers on the exterior of shop premises where such shutters would detract from the streetscape and ambience of the town. However innovative solutions involving tradition wrought iron window guards or shutters which provide a high degree of transparency which allows the window display to be visible will be considered.

Policy

To discourage the mounting or location of rollers on the exterior of shop premises where such shutters would detract from the streetscape and ambience of the town or village.

To consider innovative solutions including tradition wrought iron window guards or security shutters which provide a high degree of transparency which allows the window display to be visible.

Canopies and Blinds

Blinds were traditionally incorporated into the shop front fascia and designed be retracted into it when not in use. This is still the best way to handle a blind where one is required. Curved and Dutch style canopies are unsympathetic to the traditional streetscape will be discouraged.

Policy

To encourage the incorporation of blinds, where required, into the shopfront fascia so that they are capable of being retracted when not in use. Curved and Dutch canopies will be discouraged.

Signage

The size, shape and position of signs should reflect the scale and facade of the building on which they are located. Hand painted signs or illumination by bracket or wash lighting are preferred to internally illuminated fascia signs. In general signs should not be located above fascia level.

Signage forms an integral part of most shop fronts and commercial areas. However, the proliferation of insensitive displays of advertisements can seriously detract from the visual quality of the area and have implications for public safety. The following guidelines should be applied in the design of town and village centre signage:

- Signage should be kept to a minimum and be of a size, design, scale and degree of illumination which is compatible with the surrounding area.
- Signage above fascia level, free standing signage and billboards will not normally be permitted.
- Only one projecting sign per unit will be permitted at fascia level.
- Signs should not adversely affect the safety or free flow of traffic, including pedestrian traffic.
- The location of free standing advertisements and other objects shall be discouraged in the interest of pedestrian safety. Any such objects shall be subject to licence under Section 254 of the *Planning and Development Act, 2000.*
- In new development a uniform signage scheme should be prepared and submitted with the planning application for the relevant development.

Policy

EDE 24: To discourage a proliferation of signs within town and village centres which would detract from the visual amenities of the streetscape and which would interfere with the free flow and safety of vehicular and pedestrian traffic movements.

Site Coverage

Site coverage shall not exceed 80%.

Height

The height of proposed buildings should respect the height of adjoining structures on either side. Normally buildings in excess of four storeys in height will be discouraged except at key locations or landmark sites where taller buildings might be acceptable. The height of new developments should not detract from views of existing protected structures and landmark buildings.

Overshadowing and Overlooking

Where three or four storey buildings are proposed adjoining lower buildings, the council will require that the developer submit daylight and shadow projection diagrams and demonstrate that the adjoining properties will not be unduly affected by the proposed development.

Windows and balconies of new building should avoid overlooking of adjoining property, particularly residential property.

Tourism

The *Economic Development Strategy for County Louth 2008* identifies the potential of tourism to contribute significantly to the economic development of the county. The attractions of County Louth as a tourist destination include an unspoilt natural landscape, areas of outstanding natural beauty, clean uncluttered beaches, a pollution free environment, a wealth of historical and architectural heritage and a range of high quality tourist attractions and facilities.

The county is conveniently located to the heavily populated areas of Greater Dublin and the north east of the island, centred on Belfast, which provides a large population mass within a one hour drive of the county. The improved road and rail infrastructure which has been put in place, both north and south of the border in recent years and accessibility to east coast air and passenger ferry ports makes the county very accessible to the international tourism market.

Tourist Attractions

The broad range of tourist facilities and attractions of County Louth include, inter alia, the following:

- Historic towns of Dundalk, Drogheda, Ardee and Carlingford,
- Areas of Outstanding Natural Beauty,
- 120 kilometres of clean coastline and blue flag beaches,
- Marina, sailing and sea adventure centres,
- Clean air and water,
- A large number of archaeological sites and monument,
- Historic Boyne Valley and Battle of the Boyne Site,
- A large number of historic houses and landscaped gardens,
- Equestrian based activity,
- High quality golf courses,
- Identified cycling and walking routes,
- Cultural based activities,
- High quality hotels and other accommodation,
- Places of recreation including theatres, cinemas, pubs and restaurants,
- All weather racing track and international standard ice rink.

Regional Tourism Policy

Failte Ireland East and Midlands Regional Tourism Plan 2008-2010 provides a road map for both national and local agencies, local authorities and other public bodies to contribute to the sustainable development of tourism in the region.

Louth is one of eight counties included in the remit of this plan which aims to deliver increased tourism benefits to the region by providing better hospitality, greater appeal and an improved quality of visitor experience. It notes that visitors are attracted to the region because of the diversity of tourist attractions. Within County Louth the Cooley Peninsula has proved attractive as a natural base for outdoor pursuits, whilst the major heritage and historic sites such as those at Monasterboice, Mellifont and the historic towns of Dundalk, Drogheda, Ardee and Carlingford combine to provide a rich heritage menu.

Tourism Plan 2008-2012

Louth Hospitality, which is a local authority supported partnership with the private tourism sector in the county, recently published the *Tourism Plan 2008-2012*. The mission statement of this action plan is *'to attract tourists to County Louth by providing a quality experience'*. It aims to offer compelling reasons to motivate tourists to visit Louth and to make attractions more accessible and tangible. To facilitate the development of Louth's heritage sites as top class visitor attractions, it is an objective of the action plan to provide the necessary infrastructure, visitor services and promotional material to market the sites.

Policy

To support the implementation of the *Tourism Plan 2008-2012* and the *Failte Ireland East and Midlands Regional Plan 2008 – 2010*.

To promote the sustainable development of Louth as a quality tourist destination themed on heritage, culture and an unspoilt natural environment.

To assist in the development and marketing of County Louth in conjunction with the local authorities north and south of the border.

To support the development of community festivals, cultural activities and other outdoor activities.

Co-Operation with other Bodies

The council is aware that the development of tourism in County Louth would benefit greatly from a cooperative approach with other local authorities and relevant agencies both north and south of the border. Such initiatives could involve the co-funding of tourism infrastructure, product development and marketing. Cooperation on a number of projects has already taken place and it is proposed to pursue and bring to fruitation these initiatives during the course of the Plan.

Cross Border Ecologically Themed Project

During the period of the Plan, the council will explore with the relevant authorities north of the border the development of an integrated themed cross border project based around the common themes of a high quality landscape and natural heritage. This is most strongly manifested in the geological underpinnings which characterize the Cooley Peninsula, Mourne Mountains and Slieve Gullion. This common bond has left a legacy of great beauty and economic potential which can be harnessed to greatest effect by the respective local authorities adopting a collaborative approach to the development of the regions natural wealth.

Much of Cooley, the Mournes and Slieve Gullion comprise of dramatic mountainous areas where the visual impact is increased by proximity to both the open sea and Carlingford Lough. The open moorland of the higher areas has a variety of undisturbed flora and fauna together with large pockets of coniferous forest In human terms, the area is rich in archaeological items and renowned in legend and folklore. These factors together with the isolation and tranquillity combine to give a very broad appeal for visitors and locals alike.

Policy

To pursue the development of an integrated themed cross border tourism project including joint marketing, promotion and where appropriate and viable, infrastructure provision.

Narrow Water Bridge

The provision of a road link through the construction of a bridge between the Cooley Peninsula in County Louth and the southern portion of the Mourne Mountains in County Down at Narrow Water would make a valuable contribution to the development of tourism in Louth and the Mournes. Initial funding for the project has been provided in the *National Development Plan 2007-2013* and preliminary design work commenced.

Policy

To cooperate with the authorities in Northern Ireland in the provision of a road bridge between Cooley and south County Down.

Oriel 2012

Oriel 2012 aims to promote the Newry and Mourne and the Louth region as a base for pre-games training camps for participants in the 2012 London Olympic Games. Given the region's proximity to London, the cluster will also put in place strategies to attract teams and spectators to the region in their pursuit of leisure and recreational activities. Membership of the Oriel 2012 cluster is open to businesses, sporting organisations, schools and support organisations that are keen to tap into the opportunities that will inevitably arise from the training camps. The council is fully supportive of this initiative.

Policy

To support the Oriel 2012 project and cooperate with relative authorities, business interests and stakeholders north and south to advance its implementation.

Boyne Valley

The historic Boyne Valley, Bru Na Boinne, is a world heritage site. It also contains the site of the historic Battle of the Boyne. The Boyne Valley falls partially within the functional area of Louth County Council, Meath County Council and Drogheda Borough Council. The heritage town of Drogheda which is located on the Boyne Estuary is the gateway to the historic Boyne Valley.

The council recognises the significant contribution and potential of the Boyne Valley for the development of tourism in County Louth and is keen to participate in a joint approach with Meath County Council and Drogheda Borough Council in its protection, development and promotion.

Therefore it is proposed to cooperate with Meath County Council and Drogheda Borough Council in the preparation of a strategy for the protection, development and promotion of this important heritage site.

Policy

To cooperate with Meath County Council and Drogheda Borough Council in the preparation of a strategy for the protection, development and promotion of the Boyne Valley heritage site.

Tourist Accommodation

Growth in the tourism sector will result in a corresponding need for more visitor accommodation and facilities across the county. The council is keen to ensure that there is a range of high quality and affordable accommodation provided in order to meet the needs of visitors and tourists to the county. However, care will be needed to ensure that the unspoilt natural environment and landscapes of the county which have been identified as a major reason why tourists come to County Louth are not compromised by inappropriate tourist accommodation development.

Hotel, Guest House and Bed and Breakfast Accommodation

The number of hotel beds within the county has increased significantly over the period of the last county development plan as a result of the construction of new hotels in Carlingford, Drogheda and two in Dundalk. The council will encourage the provision of additional hotels including leisure and conference facilities, within the county in order to attract more visitors and to boast employment. Custom built guest houses should be located within existing towns and villages to avail of and support existing services. Bed and breakfast accommodation is normally provided within existing dwellings and can be accommodated in both urban and rural areas. Low cost, high quality guest houses and bed and breakfast accommodation are an important component in the range of accommodation choice required for a vibrant tourism industry.

Policy

To encourage the provision of additional hotel, guest house bed spaces and bed and breakfast accommodation in County Louth in conjunction with leisure, conferencing and other associated facilities and amenities, subject to the protection of the unspoilt natural environment and landscapes of the county.

Holiday Homes and Self-Catering Accommodation

Holiday homes are defined as '*purpose built self-contained residential units, which provide accommodation on a short term basis for visitors to the area*'. The council will resist the proliferation of holiday home developments in rural areas except where the development would involve the conversion or restoration of existing vernacular buildings and derelict dwellings.

In order to manage the provision of tourist accommodation in a manner that meets the needs of the tourist while at the same time supports the local economy, it is considered important that the provision of holiday homes and self catering accommodation should, by and large, be provided within the network of existing settlements and be of a scale that the settlement can sustain. Therefore the council will resist proposals for the development of holiday homes and self catering accommodation in the countryside, except where existing stone buildings of character are to be converted or where the restoration of vernacular dwellings is proposed.

Policy

To facilitate the limited provision of holiday homes and self-catering accommodation in locations within existing towns and villages, of a scale that the settlement can sustain. To resist proposals for the development of holiday homes and self catering accommodation in the countryside except where existing stone buildings of character are to be converted or where the restoration of vernacular dwellings is proposed. To limit the floor area of all holiday homes and self catering accommodation to a maximum of a 100 square metres.

Caravan Parks

The provision of caravan parks which are popular, particularly in coastal locations, can have a serious detrimental impact on the amenities of the coast unless they are sensitively located and properly managed and maintained. Proposals for new caravan parks will only be favourably considered where they are located within a secluded and a mature landscaped setting and where there is an adequate road network to serve the development. The focus of the council's policy in relation to caravan parks will be to secure the upgrading of existing parks particularly in relation to wastewater treatment, general facilities and amenities.

Policy

To permit new caravan parks only where they are located within a secluded and a mature landscaped setting and where there is an adequate road network to serve the development. To encourage the upgrading of existing caravan parks in approved locations.

Budget Hostels

Hostel accommodation, catering primarily for those travelling on a limited budget, occupies an important niche within the tourist accommodation market. Whilst the individual spend on accommodation is by definition, low, there can be considerable ancillary spending by such tourists on local services.

Policy

To facilitate the provision of budget hostels within existing urban centres or close to public transport facilities.

Tourism Related Signage

The provision of directional and promotional signage is important in facilitating tourists and enhancing their overall experience and enjoyment of their visit. The provision of finger posts and other directional signs is a function of the local authority and is provided under the roads capital budget. Significant improvements in this area have taken place in recent years and the council will continue to improve road signage where required and subject to the availability of adequate funding. In addition to the road signs provided by the council, Section 254 of the *Planning and Development Act, 2000*, makes provision, under license from the planning authority, for additional road signage to facilitate existing significant activities including tourist related attractions and amenities. The council will favourably consider the granting of licenses for Failte Ireland approved finger post signage where appropriate. However, it should be recognised that excessive numbers of signs is counter productive as it leads to clutter and confusion which detracts from the appearance of buildings and rural landscapes and may conflict with essential local authority directional and safety signage. Such a proliferation of signage will be resisted by the council. Tourism related promotional and advertisement signs are also important for the industry. Such signs should be suitably designed and appropriately located on the building or within the curtilage as appropriate so that they do not detract form the visual amenities of the area.

Policy .

To continue to improve local authority directional road signage to facilitate visitors to the county. To facilitate the licensing of Failte Ireland approved tourism related signage subject to a demonstrate need and the avoidance of clutter and confusion with existing road signage. To ensure that tourism related promotional and advertisement signs are suitably designed and appropriately located so that they do not detract from the visual amenities of the area.

7

The Retailing and Tourism Relationship

What is the relationship between retailing and tourism? How might the relationship be developed to the mutual benefit of Australian domestic and international tourism, and Australian retailers?

Executive Summary

At the very top level retailing and tourism are related since both are about selling. They share a mutual interdependence whereby one will drive the growth of the other. Through the multiplier effect the relationship between both industries will generate further growth in the Australian economy.

Using in-depth insight this essay identifies five fundamental relationships between the two industries:-

1. Revenue Generation and Growth,
2. Similarities Between the Two Industries,
3. Tourism Advances the Way Retailers Do Business,
4. Airports,
5. Ownership and Co-location.

Recommendations are also made on development of these relationships. These will benefit each industry and Australia as a nation.

The strength of their relationship is seen on all scales; locally airports exhibit advanced engineering of the retailing and tourism strategy, regionally the Sydney 2000 Olympics highlighted some spectacular results and collectively these and other examples contribute to the tourism and retail relationship nationwide since Australia itself is a marketable tourism/retail "product" on the global scale. Although retailing and tourism have shared a long and successful journey, often known only by those who are intimately familiar with both or either industry, their relationship is still one which has not been developed to its full potential in Australia. Despite past success Australia still faces a major challenge in its positioning on the world stage as a retailing and tourism destination. The world community presents aggressive competition on many fronts.

Given that we live in times of constant and consistent change and where survival in the commercial world is of the absolute fittest, we need to step beyond our immediate industries and look further than our own professional domain to find partnerships which transcend any conceptual "boundaries".

With the growing need for alliances and synergies, what could be better than partnering with an industry which we have always shared an intrinsic relationship with and which consists of equally passionate individuals united by a common cause of improving one's industry and in the interest of our nation?

Introduction

The relationship between retailing and tourism must not be underestimated. Up to 81% of visitors to Australia consider shopping as one of their primary leisure activities. Tourism generated $77 billion in consumption in one year in Australia. Total retailing expenditure by domestic and international tourists was $17.7 billion or 23% of total tourist expenditure.

As more people travel and per capita disposable income rises, we would expect this relationship between tourism and retailing to evolve into something phenomenal. However, despite the compelling evidence, this remains a relationship which is yet to be further developed. Australia still lacks an international image as a major tourism shopping destination due to aggressive competition from countries such as Hong Kong and Singapore which have successfully positioned themselves as shopping and retail destinations. Globalisation has made the same products available in most countries at the same time. Shopping is becoming less differentiated on a locality basis. Consequently the challenge for Australian retailers is to find ways to innovate so that tourists may be offered a more unique shopping experience.

The following profiles the retailing and tourism industries' relationship at top level, then identifies five further pivotal relationships where specific development may be undertaken to combat any challenges. Success will not only benefit both industries but contribute to a brilliant and exciting future for Australia.

Setting the Scene-The Retailing and Tourism Relationship at Top Level

Tourism comprises the activities of persons travelling to and staying in places outside their usual environment for not more than one consecutive year for leisure, business and other purposes not related to the exercise of an activity remunerated from within the place visited. Retailing is the sale of goods or products for personal consumption, occurring primarily from fixed locations or online using the internet. Tourism operators are retailers in their own right, selling package tours, experiences, holidays, conferences or adventure. At the very top level the key relationship is that retailing and tourism are both about selling. The strength of their relationship can be seen on a varying scale, starting with airports (localized), to the Sydney 2000 Olympics (regional), all of which contribute to the selling of Australia itself as a retail and tourism destination (national).

How Much was Spent

What Tourists Bought from Retailers

Tourists bought from retailers all forms of goods and merchandise; particularly gifts and souvenirs. Food and beverage products were of high importance. This trend is evident in the growth of food and tourism industry products combined, e.g. gourmet food tours that promote quality local produce; wines from Margaret River, Barossa and Hunter Valleys or cheese from King Island.

Who Were our Tourists & Shoppers

In terms of demographics, the key groups of shoppers were:-

1. Young/middle-aged couples, with no children;
2. Families with children over 15 years of age;
3. Older individuals who were still working.

Those least likely to shop included:-

1. Young singles;
2. Older non-working individuals.

Relationship 1– Revenue Generation and Growth

At a commercial level there is a mutual interdependence that is fundamental to both industries for revenue generation and growth.

Tourism and retailing contribute significantly to Australia's economy both directly and via the multiplier effect which is concerned with the amount of income generated in an area by each additional unit of tourist spending. Expenditure in both industries filter throughout the economy and stimulate other sectors in the process.

Tourism Drives Growth and Development in Retailing

In Australia, retail districts have always been places of special significance in the urban setting. Historically, one of the main driving forces in the regeneration of retail areas is tourism. Tourist expenditure can represent a source of funding and justification for private and public sector redevelopment and growth of a retail area, or conversely it may be the successful re-development of an area that encourages increased leisure shopping by tourists. To develop this relationship Australian urban planning may take potential benefits for both industries into account.

Tourism also has a role in generating growth in employment in the retail industry. In 2005 the number of tourism-employed persons in Australia was 550,100 and the retail industry's share of this total was 142,600. This means the largest number of persons in tourism-generated employment was in retail. Training of Australian retail and tourism employees in customer service, language and cultural-knowledge skills will benefit both industries.

Retailing Drives Growth and Development in Tourism

The importance of retailing in tourism growth has long been recognized by the government.

Tourism Australia is the Federal Government's destination marketing agency and its creation – "Brand Australia" is a marketing tool available to retailers to promote the Australian authenticity of their products. This development was designed to enable retailers to incorporate tourism into their on-going business strategy and deliver a more uniquely Australian retail experience targeting tourists.

On a national scale Australia itself is marketed as a tourism product and retailing is an important feature of this offering. Retailers may strengthen perception of Australia as a shopping destination via product ranging and development based on the needs of the travel market, improved understanding of market segmentation, ensuring sales staff provide high quality service, accessibility of store location and clustering with a wide variety of other shops and attractions, availability during leisure time and extended hours of operation, continuous reinvention and innovation, using marketing and advertising to target visitor expenditure, focus on length of stay in shop (service and store layout) and repeat visitation (variety and value for money).

Tourists need to be treated in a fair and equitable manner. Although many economic factors beyond a retailer's control (such as world commodity prices and exchange rates) will affect their ability to compete on price, our retailers may still compete on quality and strengths such as premium grade Australian produce (wine, food, wool, souvenirs, opals and pearls) and take advantage of their store location in natural or cultural Australian settings.

An Example

On a regional scale the Sydney 2000 Olympics illustrates the interdependence of retail and tourism in revenue generation and growth.

The retail sector received a significant boost during the Games. Sales in tourist locations increased by 40-80%. It is estimated that the Games resulted in a net increase of $164 million in retail turnover (September alone).

Average retail spending in the CBD increased to $109 per person, with the average spend for international tourists $176, interstate tourists $73 and locals $68. Major spending was in clothing, souvenirs and takeaway food. Turnover for retailers of these goods increased by $152 million in NSW.

Darling Harbour achieved a 209% increase in sales and a 292% increase in visitors from the previous year during the Games. The Olympic Concept stores alone sold $54 million worth of merchandise in the three week period. The value of retail merchandise spread well beyond the Olympic Concept stores with total retail sales of licensed merchandise estimated at $1 billion.

In order to benefit Australian tourism and retailers, we may focus on bidding for future opportunities to host international conferences and major sporting events. Australia's fine reputation achieved through these events will generate more tourism and retail spend.

Relationship 2-Similarities Between Industries

Tourism and retail industries share many fascinating similarities. This provides many opportunities for their relationship to be developed, to build on common strengths and mitigate any weaknesses. Successful development and management of this relationship will help achieve the common objectives of cost reduction, profitability, increased competitiveness and future growth; clearly a win-win opportunity for all.

Similarity 1-Manpower and Labour

The labour force of both industries share the common characteristics of being on average young, characterized by part time and casual employment, requiring relatively low-skilled work in some cases, possibly unsociable hours of work, has high turn over rates and generally low levels of formal educational qualifications. Many operations are also highly labour intensive (e.g. in large supermarkets or at airports) and this means it can be challenging to find efficient ways of utilising costly resources and manpower while maintaining the goals of cost reduction, cost containment and profit maximization.

Development & Benefits

Both industries may invest in jointly developing information technology systems which offer powerful manpower and roster planning optimisation tools with common core functionality. Although it is likely that bespoke developments of systems would be required to adapt such applications for each specific work environment, joint investment of funding and intellectual capital may bring cost savings to both industries.

Radio Frequency Identification (RFID) technology can be used not just for managing inventory in a retail distribution centre, but also for locating and monitoring movement of staff for the purposes of manpower planning optimization or security in large facilities. Hand-held communication devices may direct staff to the "next task". Provided that there are no industrial relation issues, this work force management development will deliver cost efficiencies.

Effective use of manpower and training creates qualitative benefits for Australia since these will improve customer service standards for tourists. Quantitative benefits may also arise due to the more efficient use of costly manpower. Cost savings will lead to more competitive pricing of tourism/retail products; making Australia attractive to tourists.

Similarity 2– Government Regulations and Policies

Retail and tourism industries both need to comply with some common government policies and regulations. Examples of government responsibilities affecting these industries include land zoning or road and transport infrastructure, health and quarantine, food standards, industry research, legal frameworks, consumer affairs (trade practices, ACCC) and work force management laws. The government's policies on visitor entry (ease of attaining visas and passports) will directly impact the number of inbound visitors and ultimately sales levels in both industries.

Development & Benefits

Joint lobbying by both industries and cooperation with the government for common goals will benefit all parties. The Tourist Refund Scheme would be of common interest to both tourism and retailing operators. The simplification of such systems by the government will benefit retailers and contribute to increasing the ease of purchase and travel experienced by tourists when they shop in Australia.

In states such as Western Australia, retailers are still facing restricted trading hours. In Perth's tourism precincts shops are restricted to open from noon to 6pm on Sundays. This sort of restriction makes it hard for Australian retailers to be globally competitive. Improvement will require government cooperation with councils and the community in examining deregulation of trading hours and district classification as tourism precincts.

Similarity 3 – Marketing and Brand Management of Products

Tourism and retail are similar in that they are commonly marketing and managing the brand of their products. In the case of retail the products are tangible goods and merchandise whereas tourism industry products may be package tours with focus on special interests such as shopping. Both industries manage their brand via product, pricing, positioning and promotion. The effectiveness of their brand management will jointly contribute to the selling of Australia as a brand.

Development & Benefits

Companies with a strong Australian brand may conduct joint marketing campaigns in order to attract tourists, enhance their customer and travel experience in Australia and make participating retailers a key point of interest in their itinerary, especially during the seasonal peaks and troughs both industries are affected by. The future will require a greater understanding of market segmentation in product development. Food retailers may consider innovative packaging which focuses on portability and shelf-life; making it attractive for tourists to take products home. Marketing communication and strategies may be designed for growing new markets and targeting existing ones which have a high propensity to shop. As the needs, demographics and expectations of the customer base change, products which target specific age groups, special interests, health and fitness, budget and luxury, ethnic and cultural backgrounds may apply to customers of both industries.

Similarity 4-Yield Objective

Both industries aim for yield maximisation. Retailers range products in a way to maximize return on investment per unit of valuable floor and shelf space. Similarly tourism industry operators target high yielding markets, and particularly in the case of airlines, yield maximization is important in managing inventory (aircraft seats) per revenue passenger kilometre flown.

Development & Benefits

Use of strategic "Yield Management" IT applications and work practices will develop this relationship. Both industries may leverage each other's expertise in maximizing yield with the optimum mix of pricing and product (fare levels available on a flight, product mix and ranging in a store) within constrained parameters (limited aircraft seats per flight, limited shelf space). Inventory in both cases is "perishable" (selling ends upon flight departure, food items have shelf-life).

Similarity 5 – People Focus

Tourism and retail are highly "People" oriented industries where the growth of customer relationships is of paramount importance. The two industries use strategic customer loyalty programs and relationship marketing in order to grow their customer base and aim for repeat business. Supermarket chain and petrol retailer alliances offer discounted fuel to customers. Airlines and hotels have many well established frequent flyer programs, prestigious club membership facilities or services available exclusively to "loyal" customers.

Development & Benefits

Given this common approach to relationship marketing and emphasis on customer loyalty, further programs which provide customers with far reaching benefits to be redeemed in both industries may be possible. Although current programs such as "Fly Buys" are already offering this type of benefit to customers, such schemes may be refined and the means of earning and accruing loyalty points can be enhanced.

One possibility can be seen in some Asian countries; it is the use of a "smartcard" where the customer is rewarded in a seamless and simple transaction of swiping a smartcard at the point of purchase and this records the number of points accumulated by the customer. Points may be used like a single form of "currency" at any participating vendor in either industry. This also means an attractive network and alliance of reputable retailers and tourism operators will develop to take advantage of this synergy and the prospect of access to a strong client base. Reward programs will drive growth in retail and tourism since these inspire consumers to "spend" points or make further purchases in either industry.

Similarity 6 – Information Technology

Use of information technology in addition to the possibilities previously discussed is widely seen in both industries. Airlines' self service check-in kiosks at airports and larger retailers' self service check-out machines are appearing in Australia, yet overseas countries have reached more advanced stages in this technology.

The internet used for e-commerce creates a cheaper and more efficient distribution channel, providing a virtual "one stop" shopping facility online any time and from anywhere in the world. This is convenient and cost effective for retail, tourism and customers.

Development & Benefits

IT development can be costly investments which require time, funding and capital. Systems also require updating and on-going refinement in order to move with changing commercial needs and to ensure that a leading competitive edge is maintained. This is another opportunity for joint investment. Applications which interface with customers may also improve the customer experience.

Relationship 3-Tourism Advances the Way Retailers Do Business

Tourism promotes understanding and learning which can enhance the way retailers do business. In travelling the world, individuals gain insight and exposure to new ideas, knowledge of advancements in retail overseas, cultural appreciation and vision of the changing needs of the market and emerging trends. Study tours or personal travel by members of the retail industry also exposes them to other countries' strengths in production, in manufacturing or commodity output. This leads to development of new networks, potential for global sourcing and outsourcing of functional parts of the business for cost efficiency. Current retail developments include for example:-

1. Innovation at Walmart, Dallas Texas, where store layout now resembles a department store, is designed to best suit the demographics of its location, refresh the customer experience and maximize dwell time;
2. USA Target stores are beautifully laid out and contain product ranges that exude brand credibility. Target sales per square metre of floor space is 15% higher than Walmart's;
3. Microsoft is pioneering technology which enables customers to navigate stores with mobile phones, check stock availability and even be offered specials on products previously bought;
4. Harrods has reinvented the retailing of food by turning its legendary department store food hall into a 21st century stand-alone convenience format. It caters to a range of customer needs including packaged food basics, fresh items, health focused products or even Krispy Kreme doughnuts.

Some key learnings for retailers from tourism include:-

1. Innovation needs to be customer-centric. Innovation is vital since there is increasing evidence of category convergence and consolidation resulting in little choice and differentiation;
2. Give customers control over where, when and how they interact with the retailer with customized product solutions, extensive after sales service and use of IT and customer data;
3. Ensure sales people are engaged;
4. Provide a retail experience where focus is not just on price but on quality, brand value and excellent customer service. Quality is of paramount importance.

Development & Benefits

Tourism is vital for the learning and development of Australian retailers. Since Australia is competing globally as a tourism and retail destination, the retail industry must, as a minimum, meet the standards set by overseas retailers which international visitors will already be accustomed to. Further refinement to not only match but exceed overseas developments while adding a point of difference that is uniquely Australian will be essential. Retailers may leverage product and cost efficiencies worldwide via international trade and global sourcing. Reverse auctions where international supplier networks participate will also help Australian retailers lower their cost of doing business and be globally competitive. Deeper understanding of foreign culture will inspire retailers and tourism operators to tailor products more suited to the needs and expectation of tourists.

Relationship 4-Airports

Airports are a microcosm where the tourism and retail relationship is being strategically engineered. Retail attractions are positioned to maximise tourist exposure and increase their likelihood of spending. Although shopping is not the prime driver of facility visitation and retail is not necessarily core business for airport owners, there is increasing emphasis on including a retail experience for tourists. Retail is a growing source of revenue for airports.

Development & Benefits

Some key retail principles airports and retailers may apply to develop their relationship and attain mutual benefits include:-

1. Retail consideration to be made upfront in the terminal planning stages in order to capture more tourist spend. These include the amount of sustainable retail floor space, optimal location integration into flow and dwell areas, space by precinct (arrivals, departures, lounges), costing of developments and understanding tourists' retail requirements;
2. Airport management may optimise revenue by focusing on retailer selection, retail performance, rent setting policies, service levels, merchandise mix, location of precincts, footfall, retail dwell, sight density and transaction values;
3. Management of brands and signage belonging to retailers in airports is essential as this contributes to visitors' impression of Australia as a brand in itself.

Relationship 5–Ownership and Co-location

Highly topical in the Australian media is the interest of private equity consortiums in retailers, tourism related industries and airlines. Depending on the entities in the consortium, there may be possibility in the future that there is common ownership, control and financial support for some operations in the retail and tourism industries.

Another example of common ownership can be seen in Woolworths Ltd's acquisition of the Taverner Group which includes tourism industry operations such as hotels, hospitality and gaming facilities. This synergy for tourism and retailing will bring:-

1. cost savings in combining facilities and overheads;
2. better buying terms from greater combined volumes of liquor and food;
3. marketing and branding integration;
4. insurance savings (cost of doing business);
5. operational efficiencies, restructuring and rationalizing of support offices.

Development & Benefits

In further development of this relationship the NSW government will allow clubs to build adjacent shopping centres of less than 40 shops, under the Registered Clubs Amendment Act 2006. For the industry this will mean growth as clubs and hotel operators extend into retail. Balmain Leagues Club in Sydney plans to build a supermarket, cafes, apartments and Revesby Workers Club will incorporate a supermarket, aquatic centre and motel.

Such developments will enable co-location of facilities which provide retailers with greater foot traffic and convenience for locals and tourists. The clustering of these facilities may evolve in the future into major one-stop entertainment, leisure and retail super-centres where many Australian brand names in retailing will be prominent.

Discussion and Implications/Benefits for the Industry

It is clear that tourism and retailing share a multidimensional relationship. Identifying the fundamental elements underlying their relationship means that effective strategies may be developed to enable both industries to contain costs, maximize profit and sales, compete on a global scale, have greater influence and positioning as industries and achieve sustainable future growth. These benefits will improve Australia's economic development (eg tourism export earnings, employment rates). Industry similarities highlight the potential for more alliances, sharing of intellectual capital and resources or joint investment in IT, marketing and customer loyalty programs. These synergies and partnerships will result in industry-wide cost savings and subsequently tourism/retail products may become more competitively priced.

Continuous improvement and innovation are essential if Australian businesses are to flourish. Employees in tourism or retail with a genuine passion for what they do will discover, through travel, new opportunities in the achievements of international counterparts. However, the further challenge is to find ways to implement such ideas back home, to add an authentic Australian uniqueness and to attain capital and funding to turn such concepts into a reality that tourists find compelling.

Both industries need to invest in developing their people and future executives. Tourism is one key way for staff to learn from world leaders in each field.

Airports are a focal point for both industries simultaneously. Retail is also a direct source of revenue for airports and this relationship is only set to increase in importance in the future. Once again, the implication is that there is benefit for both industries to engage in closely planning strategies. Urban developers may adopt similar strategic thinking behind airport planning. Airports are a crucial part of "Brand Australia". Common ownership brings the two industries even closer than ever as a return on investment will be a core focus of private equity investors. This change in ownership will mean the way in which business is conducted will come under more scrutiny from investment consortiums which will also offer new sources of funding for growth and investment and commercial insight from their involvement in vast ranging industries worldwide.

Changes in ownership locally with acquisitions across industries within Australia will bring new synergies in buying, cost reductions and greater future growth potential.

Government support of such developments in review of legislation has implications for not just these industries but also the Australian community. Industries may be in a position to jointly influence the government in bringing about any future adjustments to regulations and review.

Conclusion

In the current times of accelerated change there is challenge yet opportunity for any business to compete for sales and revenue.

There is still work required to develop the relationship between retailing and tourism and to heighten its maturity on a global scale. With the intelligent use of strategic development recommendations discussed, Australia may be poised to achieve an explosion of retail expenditure by tourists above $20 billion; and beyond our imagination.

Australia is gifted with attributes such as climate, unique natural heritage, natural resources and abundant produce. It is renowned for its high quality of life, political stability, friendliness, clean environment, natural and urban landscapes, developed transportation network and infrastructure, ease of visitor entry, multi-cultural diversity and close proximity to emerging Asian markets. Successful development of the relationship between retailing and tourism will bring great benefits and prosperity at the industry level and pride to every Australian as we show the world the very best of what our magnificent nation has to offer.

Enhancing the Role of Tourism SMEs in Global Value Chain

Popular questions being raised today are: Will there be travel intermediaries in the future? Will the Internet result in the demise of the travel intermediaries? The questions are being raised because of the Internet, commission caps, commission cuts, and the changing world of travel. The tourism industry is largely dominated by small and medium sized enterprises (SMEs). To survive in an increasingly competitive and global environment, tourism enterprises have to achieve economies of scale and scope in order to reduce transaction costs, increase productivity and gain market power (OECD, 2004). For tourism businesses, the Internet offers the potential to make information and booking facilities available to large numbers of tourists at relatively low costs. It also provides a tool for communication between tourism suppliers, intermediaries, as well as end-consumers. OECD (2000) revealed that the advent of Internet-based electronic commerce offers considerable opportunities for enterprises to expand their customer base, enter new product markets and rationalise their business. WTO (2001) also indicated that electronic business offers SMEs the opportunity to undertake their business in new and more cost-effective ways.

According to WTO report (2001), the Internet is revolutionising the distribution of tourism information and sales. An increasing proportion of Internet users are buying on–line and tourism will gain a larger and larger share of the online commerce market. Obviously, the Internet is having a major impact as a source of information for tourism. The SMTEs, however, are facing more serious obstacles to the adoption of e-business. The main reason has derived from the scale and affordability of information technology. Additionally, possible solutions designed for large, stable, and internationally-oriented enterprises do not fit well for small and locally-based tourism enterprises (WTO 2001).

Despite these challenges, SMTEs with well-developed and innovative Web sites can now have "equal Internet access" to international tourism markets (APEC 2002). This implies equal access to telecom infrastructure, as well as to marketing management and education. According to a UN report (2001), "it is not the cost of being there, on the online market place, which must be reckoned with, but the cost of not being there." It is certain that embracing digital communication and information technology is no longer an option, but a necessity. Thus, one of the most important characteristics of electronic commerce is the opportunity and promise it holds for SMTEs to extend their capabilities and grow with competitive advantage (APEC 2002). The Internet has radically transformed the way people communicate, the way information is distributed, and the way businesses conduct their transactions. It provides a new distribution channel for industries and facilitates the development of a virtual value chain. However, the development of the Internet and in particular its application to the industry distribution chain thus raises two critical questions. "Will the Internet lead to mass disintermediation? Secondly, will the Internet lead to many small intermediaries, or a few powerful ones that control the channel?".

Internet developments illustrate two major trends: on the one hand, tour operators aim to disintermediate travel agencies, and on the other, tour operators are threatened with disintermediation themselves. Ultimately, the more players in the distribution channel, the more commissions and fees need to be generated, increasing the price of the final product.

The Internet provides the tools for tour operators to communicate directly with consumers and to target specific specialized and niche markets. This allows tour operators to bypass travel agencies and to promote holidays directly to consumers, making significant savings on commissions paid to travel agencies (which tend to vary between 10 and 18 percent), as well as reducing the costs of incentives, bonus and educational trips for retailers. Tour operators are also threatened with disintermediation, as the Internet enables consumers and travel agencies to build their own personalized packages and purchase them online. This paper shall attempt to answer these questions, while exploring the impact of the Internet on the value chain of the travel intermediaries. The discussion will commence with an overview of a brief outline of the value proposition and the intermediaries of the tourism value chain. An analysis of two cases in the Korean travel intermediaries shall follow, as well as a discussion on strategic implications affecting the value proposition for this industry.

Global Value Chain for Travel Intermediaries

Value Chain

The value proposition, commonly known as the value chain, is a "model that describes a series of activities connecting a company's supply side (raw materials, inbound logistics, and production processes) with its demand side (outbound logistics, marketing and sales)". Analysing the value chain enables managers to reformulate their internal and external processes to improve efficiency and effectiveness. In the traditional value chain system, information is treated as a supporting element. Rayport *et al* (1994a) provide the example that managers often use information that they capture on inventory, production, or logistics to help monitor or control those processes, but they rarely use information itself to create new value for the customer.

"Because every activity involves the creation, processing, and communication of information, technology has a pervasive influence on the value chain".. "Value is created by all the intermediaries involved in a particular 'vertical market chain'. It is consistent with traditional strategic network theory which states that the locus of value creation may be the network rather than the firm. Brandenburger and Stuart Jr. (1996) distinguish between the concepts of creation and appropriation of value. They analyze how different stakeholders along a market chain create value, and define value creation as the difference between the value of the product and its cost. As the value of the product or service depends upon buyers' perception, they perceive value creation as the difference between buyer's willingness–to–pay and suppliers' opportunity costs. In a result, value creation is an outcome of the efforts carried on by all the intermediaries involved in a transaction. This argument may be more obvious in cyberspace where enterprises' limits are more difficult to draw since many intermediaries have to join together their interests and efforts in order to make a particular transaction. This is the case of an online travel agency, which could be thought as a network that creates value for the end customer based on a joint effort of many intermediaries. For example, in order to help the traveller to find the best fares of a domestic flight, (and, therefore, creating value through 'efficiency') a start–up needs to have access to airfare databases, and may want to sign a contract with the owners of those databases (e.g., Sabre). Similarly, if the virtual travel agency wants to create value through 'complementarities', it may need to sign contract with car rental enterprises (e.g. AVIS). Clearly, taking advantage of the value creation potential of the Internet implies broadening enterprises' boundaries by signing alliances with parties needed to provide the service, which might not necessarily be the case for physical enterprises.

The networking era and the proliferation of the Internet are a challenge to most organizations as they threaten traditional value chain models. However, even though value creation in cyberspace is an outcome of the efforts of the intermediaries that enable an online transaction, each agent looks for its own benefit as regards value appropriation. Since one of the effects of the Internet and related technologies in the overall business landscape is that it changes the bargaining power of the intermediaries, it is particularly important to analyze online value appropriation because, as previously explained, when the bargaining power of a player changes, its ability to capture value changes as well. For example, as customers have more access to relevant information about prices, delivery and brands, they can search for and find the cheapest 'Efficiency' is one of the four e–commerce value drivers suggested in Amit and Zott (2001)." The above paragraph is quoted from *Noboa, F (2003): E-business: Examining creation and* appropriation of value".

Thus, the shape of value chains in the tourism industry is changing in a fundamental way (WTO, 2002). The following "traditional" value chain activities can now be performed on the Internet:

- Travel services, which consist of many types of online reservation/booking systems for travel services, hotel accommodation, tour, air tickets, car rentals, entertainment and E-shopping;

- Online Booking Systems, which are provided for specific travel products and services, such as hotel and package tours;
- Multilingual support. Moving onto the market space system supports all languages. One can have a web site in multiple languages;
- Secure payment system. Secure technology allows payments to be made online using wire transfer methods;
- Reservation tracking systems enable tourists to track the status of their reservations, while the tourist company can edit and update transaction records.

Benjamin *et al*, (1995:69) identify the following benefits of bypassing each element of the industry value chain:

- Delivery costs would be reduced, (as information will be transmitted electronically) resulting in lower overall distribution costs.
- Lower coordination costs throughout the industry value chain. Electronically linked producers and retailers will be able to lower their costs by reducing intermediary transactions and unneeded coordination because of electronic transactions directly with the consumer.
- The consumer will have maximum choice at the lowest price, as well as free market access to all tourism information.

The situation, however, is now changing, as the overall structure moves towards an innovative Value Net (or Value Star).

Innovation in tourism brings new ideas, services and products to the marketplace. Encompassing the whole tourism value chain, innovation does not only mean adapting the tourism industry to the changing tourism patterns with new marketing strategies, but also fostering new and innovative services, products and processes. Innovation in tourism is to be seen as permanent, global and dynamic process (OECD, 2004).

Restructuring and cooperation mechanisms help tourism enterprises to adapt to changes and increase their competitiveness. The forms of restructuring in tourism are very diverse. They include horizontal and vertical integration, but also many flexible structures that encourage product, marketing and organizational innovation.

The emergence of the Value Net tends to raise the questions: if stakeholders can communicate easily with the end consumers, what is the role for intermediaries, including travel agencies as well as travel operators?

Firstly, they minimize distribution costs through routinising and standardizing transactions. Secondly they adjust the discrepancy of assortment, and thirdly, they facilitate the searching process of both buyers and sellers by providing a place for both parties to meet each other. Benjamin, Robert, Wigand, and Rolf (1995) point out that the Internet will give consumers increased access to a vast selection of goods but will cause a restructuring and redistribution of profits among the stakeholders along the chain. The Internet is seen as a new distribution channel, and it is likely that all virtual activities will move to it. The provision of information, the arranging of reservations and searching for destinations are all activities that can be done far more efficiently on the internet than through printed brochures and current intermediaries.

A study of whether or not the Internet is capable of "pirating" the value chain, and resulting in disintermediation shall follow. Free information will reduce the power of current intermediaries, and as argued by Benjamin *et al,* (1995:62) "all intermediaries between the manufacturer and the consumer may be threatened as the Information Superhighway reaches out to the consumer". Referring back to the question in the introduction to this paper, it is implied that the Internet has the ability to cause mass disintermediation in the tourism value chain. Likewise, Pitt, P Berthon and J Berton (1999) additionally state that due to continual technological enhancements, intermediaries such as travel agents may be bypassed, and the Internet can shorten the value chain.

Bloch *et al* (1996:7) identify the following business drivers and new technologies affecting the distribution of travel products. Suppliers are airlines, hotels, rental cars, cruise and countries, regions or cities. The distributors are usually travel agencies, although direct distribution networks (e.g., telephone, kiosks) have been in use for some time now. Process facilitators are typically CRS (Computer Reservation Systems, also called now GDSes, Global Distribution Systems, and the companies owning the databases where airlines, hotel and car rentals fares and timetables are stored. Below is a diagram depicting the business drivers.

Conditions for Re-intermediation are: 1) Imitation and Weak Appropriability-Reintermediation is likely to occur when an EC innovation can be readily imitated by traditional members. Thanks to the openness of EC solutions, technological switching cost is almost zero; 2) Co-specialized Assets-E-commerce-only intermediaries can't easily acquire the necessary industrial network-based co-specialized assets. Traditional intermediaries still lack their ability related to the development of e-commerce applications; 3) Economies of Scale-E-commerce-only intermediaries will not succeed if they do not achieve economies of scale. Many traditional intermediaries have already achieved economies of scale in traditional markets.

Buhalis (2003) stated developments and trends in the marketplace affecting travel agencies.

* Tourism principals and suppliers are anxious to control distribution costs as well as to improve their communication function & therefore attempt to bypass travel agencies by developing internet-based interfaces with consumers.
* Commission capping or termination by airlines around the world.
* Development of no-frills airlines that perform most of their reservation online.
* The majority of the consumers that are capable & able of travelling gradually become computer-literate, set up connections with the internet, and feel empowered to search & amalgamate their tourism products themselves.
* Availability of net rates/fares on the Internet.
* Publication of contact details & internet sites on tour operators' brochures.
* Emergence & rapid development of electronic intermediaries (e.g. Expedia, Travelocity).
* Development of new business models, including auctions (e.g. qxl.com) & and you're your prices sites (e.g. priceline.com).
* Expansion of customer relationship management systems & their gradual integration with loyalty schemes.
* Principals use a wide range of consumer incentives through relationship marketing, aiming to establish a direct partnership with consumers.

* Ticketing eventually will enable he entire process of making reservation & purchasing tourism process paperless.
* Traditional intermediaries (such as Thomas Cook) re-engineering their processes in order to update their offering, improve customer satisfaction & remain competitive.
* Tourism destinations develop regional systems to enhance their representation, boost their image & attract direct bookings.

Case Analysis for Korean Travel Intermediaries Experiences Experiencing the Global Value Chain

Hanatour, which used to be an off-line travel agency, became one of the biggest travel agencies in Korea with the introduction of e-commerce. Hanatour started as Kookjin travel agency in 1993 and in 1997, when Korea was under the IMF bailout, was renamed Hanatour and started wholesale and constructed IT, using the CEO's strong determination and a strategic plan for information technology. Based on that, Hanatour has defended its highest market share since 1999, and became the first tourism company listed in KOSDAG in 2001. No other tourism company has been listed even to this date. For reference, there are approximately 8,300 travel agencies in Korea. With the goal of entering into the Global Top 10 this year, it plans to achieve 300 million dollars of sales, 60 million dollars of gross income, and serve 4.49 million outbound travellers in 2010. Hanatour started its business with $350,000 in capital, but now has $4.1 million in capital due to the rapid growth after the 1997 IT infrastructure construction.

It has also seen the rapid growth of its work force since 2000, and now pulled itself out of SMTE. Target market share for 2004 was 11%, and Hanatour attained that goal without much difficulty. Sales volume last year was $60 million, with $10 million growth each year since the introduction of IT. Hanatour has entered into an agreement with 4,500 agencies out of 8,300 agencies, has nineteen domestic branches, twelve overseas branches, and eight subsidiaries. The twelve overseas branches conduct local tours for outbound tourists from Korea to countries where the branches are located. Forty-five hundred agencies sell Hanatour's products and provide all services to customers on behalf of Hanatour. It made a GSA agreement with eleven foreign companies including Trek America, Amtrek, Star Cruise, Royal Caribbean Cruise, Eurailpass, JR pass, and Alamo Rent-a-Car. It also made strategic partnerships with thirty domestic companies, including BC Card,

Samsung Card, Hana Bank, LG Eshop, Hanson CSN, Emart, etc. It cooperates with other companies through system linkage and joint development, and makes reference to certain companies such as Alamo Rent-a-Car before it changes its system or rate schedule. Besides, its website is linked to more than 1,000 sites, and some GDS vendors take initiative in offering the partnership.

Variation and Value Creation through Online Market by IT

Providing the real time reservation system, "Hanatour.com" is developed by Hanatour company. And also the Hanatour operates the solution company, "tour total.com" which company provides the entire tourism related system. Now both the system and the market are growing gradually which will benefit to not only the entire e-business tourism industry but also the value creation of our customer. Hantour already recognized the importance and the value of IT. Because of the speciality of tourism industry, all of the airline, hotel, and rental services must be linked to each other in reservation. 3 years ago, Hanatour have already linked the connection between Hanatour and foreign company to strengthen the network system.

All of the airlines are using the web service oriented reservation system. "Galileo", "Sabre", "ABACUS", "Topas" are examples. Tourism companies pay the commission to use the airline reservation system to log on the CRS (Computerized Reservation System). Hanatour has already prepared internet homepage to follow the world system 3 years ago. Now "tour-total.com" offers not only the tourism information but also the accounting system of tourism company.

With great support from the management, they invested in network infrastructure 10 years ago and prepared their own ERP system as well as the real time reservation. This preparation was shocked to the industry. In 2005 late July, Hanatour increased the member of IT planning department from 46 employees to 60. And last year they have invested IT 1,000,000,000 won.

They aimed themselves to be top 10 world tourism company and the world best company in 2020. To realize their vision, Hana realized that the most important thing was the new ideas of system. To avoid the massive competitive situation of off-line market, company realizes that the market need variation of business. One of all, online market helped to create new market as well as to use existing management, product planning by new online data base system.

Although this new digital value chain need a lot of cost however the efficiency grows much higher and that means more value creation. Reduction of employee use reservation and the time saving of customer will create invisible benefit to both customer and the company. Online market has changed the company to all day, all year company to meet the customer. In conclusion, digital market has changed the reduction of cost and more of value chain through network system.

Partnership and the Value Creation through an Affiliation and Outsourcing

With increased demand of internet and the growth of the online market, the exclusive market has reduced between the tourism companies. Hanatour reduced the management structure as well as restructuring, out-source and an affiliation to follow the world trend.

Not only to connect between the foreign companies, Hanatour joined cooperative marketing affiliation with Korea.com, Lotte.com and Samsung mall to diversify the market. Especially, Hana tour joined with "Amtrek, Track America and Alamo Rentcar to give best service to FIT. Hanatour is the wholesale company. It plans the tour product to retail tourism company, shopping channel. Sometimes, the progression is more important than cost reduction. So Hanatour developed the foreign network tour conductor and regional tour conductor to strengthen the market power. And also they have connected with a local subsidiary which now Hanahas captured 60% of domestic wholesale tourism companies. And it was the Hana tour that has stocked their market first.

Furthermore, Hana tour joined the tracking and the hinterland exploration oriented company as well as pilgrimage tourism company "Koryo" to meet various customers' need. This will give company flexibility and maximize the customer satisfaction to enhance the tour product by professional our-source companies.

Hana tour has aim their goal to grow their business up to JTB of Japan in 2010. Hana tour practices variation of market and more competitive advantage through the internet management, knowledge management. This will generally create more brand power of Hana tour in one-line, financial, broadcasting market.

Value Satisfaction through Human Resource Management

Sales, tourism human resource and after service is the key to the value chain of the tourism industry. To have competitive advantage, human resource management is recognized its importance to the industry. Service is the meaning of customer satisfaction. It is obvious to satisfy both inner and outer customer to gain competitive advantage. Especially, controlling and motivating the inner customer, the employee, is the source of customer satisfaction.

The CEO of Hana tour, San Hwan Park, put his heart to knowledge relationship between the employee. Monthly, he opens the public seminar to share the ideas to improve the company. He also prizes the employee who gives magnificent idea. If the idea is realistic, they spontaneously open his or her idea to knowledge share system. This system gives all employee up-to-date information whenever the employee need it. This knowledge service gives organization work efficiency and cost reduction which generates new energy to company that will improve customer satisfaction.

First, information mind is needed. Planning the new product and meeting the customer is part of the information practice. The employee that survived in information society will be the factor of successful company. Second, new ideas are needed. If you are not satisfied with your own idea, use others. The champion of the market is the company who has the brilliant idea.

Thirdly, globalization is needed. The world is growing smaller than ever. We have to strengthen our power to adapt in the global market. Finally, build your own power. To succeed, it is obvious to learn, experience and think more.

This motivation notices not only increase the employee's service mind but will improve skill and energy to serve customer better. And this will be the driving force of company's value.

Tourexpress

Unlike Hanatour, Tourexpress began as an online travel agency. It invited investment from outside sources and developed the system for online retail travel intermediaries from the outset.

Sales volume from the year 2003 was about $4 million and is expected to reach $5 million this year. Tourexpress made strategic partnerships with ten domestic companies such as Daum.com, Auction, KB Card, Joins.com, E-post, Dongyang Magic, etc. Tourexpress supplies the system to such companies via ASP.

Sponsored by $300,000 in venture capital in 1999, it began its business and opened its system in 2000 with a financial support of $300,000 from daum.com, the largest current shareholder, and now has five times as much capital as it did in 2000. Currently, it invests 15% of sales to system development, and its sales volume derived from e-commerce accounts for 95% of total sales. Last year, Tiger Tech, a U.S. venture capital firm, invested $400,000 in Tourexpress, and additional $200,000 was invested by daum.com. Daum.com is the largest portal, having as many members as any other site. Tourexpress is the only travel service provider on daum.com. At the core of Tourexpress lies Hemosu, which is the name of the son of a god in a traditional legend. Hemosu is linked to the CRS of airlines, hotels, or rent-a-car agencies that have a rate database in its system so that customers, via Hemosoo, can access suppliers they want. Hemosu is connected to foreign airlines, GDS, and suppliers from 60 countries, allowing a flexible search.

Once a custom makes a reservation after checking for availability and rates, the result is transmitted to the customer's mobile phone and e-mail and is stored in "My Page" on the Web, enabling the customer to reference it at any time. Recently, it has developed a wizard to do custom travel consulting to individual travellers, although it is restricted to Europe.

What Tourexpress offers to SMTEs is: A business model for online travel agencies with respect to investment and the method of partnership; a possibility of success of online retail travel agencies without branches or agencies.

Conclusion and Implications

The market space, which involves doing business in the virtual world, has resulted in changed processes used in trading and supply chains. Although it was initially predicted that the Internet would result in mass disintermediation, it can truly complement companies' traditional activities. This medium therefore facilitates mass re-intermediation, whereby current intermediaries can take advantage of the virtual value chain. Intermediaries in the tourism industry value chain merely need to leverage their strengths and knowledge about customers, supplier offerings and the travel market. According to WTTC (2003), tour companies should work to achieve the following tasks to have new global value chains in the tourism industry. Suppliers and intermediaries must independently and jointly execute a number of broad transformational programs.

Experience Delivery Transformation

Suppliers must better capture and exchange customer insight between sales and operational touch-points to deliver an enhanced experience. Suppliers should deliver planning and booking information to operational systems to enhance service execution and create additional revenue opportunities. Suppliers need to capture customer data during service execution to improve offerings and generate increased demand. By doing this, suppliers will benefit from increased customer insight capture and improved service delivery.

Online Systems Transformation

Suppliers must manage and distribute content like inventory and build an eCRM foundation to create more customer-centric and profitable booking conversations online. Transformation centres around two key areas – improving and controlling the content across channels and synchronizing and controlling marketing interactions with customers across channels. By doing this, suppliers will benefit from better, more consistent product representation and lower customer acquisition costs.

Off-line Systems Transformation

Suppliers must establish seamless inventory, improve reservations functionality and increase self-service to make off-line channels more customer-centric and profitable. The foundation of all supplier related customer-centric systems improvements, particularly for off-line channels like the call centre, is the replacement and integration of the CRS and location-based systems (i.e., PMS, counter system). With an improved view of inventory, suppliers can layer in capabilities to streamline the booking process and leverage customer insight. A final area of improvement is the increased use of self-service technologies to handle routine customer interactions. By doing this, suppliers will benefit from lower costs to sell and serve while increasing revenue generating opportunities.

Revenue Management Transformation

Suppliers must "close the loop" between revenue management and marketing operations to support the increased profitability goals of the customer-centric infrastructure and the complexities of marketing to increasingly tailored customer segments. Central to this transformation is the ability to forecast soft demand periods, understand and identify target customers to generate demand, and make the necessary changes to price and inventory availability in reservation systems at a customer level to create one-to-one revenue management. The net result for suppliers is increased revenues and higher yields.

Distribution Management Transformation

Suppliers must reposition distribution as an enterprise-level strategic function. Transformation of this magnitude requires organizational changes, new governance mechanisms for decision-making, and tools to capture and analyze the profitability of customer interactions across channels. Beyond increased profitability, this approach to distribution will result in optimal investment decisions and increased compliance in partnership agreements.

8

Shopping Tourism in Germany

Introduction

Shopping has become for many people a manner of passing leisure time and this does never happen in the vicinity of their places of residence. In many one-day-trips, holidays or business trips, shopping has become nowadays an important issue. On every seventh occasion, shopping has become a decisive reason for a trip; this "hard core" of shopping tourists represents 70% of all tourists' expenses in retail commerce. Despite the economic importance of trips to different towns generally and particularly of the shopping tourism, the latter was neither in the past nor at present the main concern of retail commerce in Germany, neither of the tourist service.

Shopping tourism is considered by experts in the field of retail commerce and tourism to be a development segment, which Germany can take a greater advantage of. On international level there a examples of highly successful strategic marketing policies and reasonable cooperation structures not only on the level of individual enterprises or communes but also on regional or national level. The initial situation in shopping tourism and thus especially in the international tourism, i.e. Germany's attractiveness as commercial objective for foreign tourists, registers gaps and unused potential. Therefore, the Federal Ministry of Economy and Labour attributed to the working community consisting of ECON-Consult, EuroInstitute for Commerce and the University Chair for External Traffic Geography of the Trier University the research of the present situation in the field of shopping tourism as well as the draft of some recommendations related to the exploitation of the potential on this market in the future.

The study mainly consists of the following priorities:

- Presentation of the development trends of shopping tourism in international comparison.
- The analysis of the development potential and assessment of the success factors of different forms of shopping tourism in German towns and regions.
- The comparative analysis of the case studies: especially under the aspect of the interaction and use of synergies between commerce and tourism.
- Research on the impact upon the development of the turnover in commerce and tourism as well as upon the subordinate and dominating fields of the economy.
- Evaluation of the framework conditions compared to other countries.
- The impact of the EU extension on cross-border shopping tourism. The present document is a synthesis of the most important results of the study „Shopping Tourism in international comparison– incentives in the development of tourism and retail commerce in Germany".

Behaviour of Shopping Tourists Towards Expenses and the Economic Importance

According to the results of a survey among 2.000 passers-by in 10 different specific shopping tourists' destinations performed in the framework of this study, a shopping tourist spends approximately 152 € for the trip. The daily average expenses for shopping reach approximately 67 €. The other "touristic" expenses (transportation, hotel, restaurant, etc.) reach an average of 85 €. There is a distinction within the study between several categories of shopping tourists:

- Shopping tourists in a restricted sense: the trip is made because of the planned shopping. This category is divided into internal and foreign one day tourists and internal and foreign tourists requesting accommodation.
- Shopping tourists in a wider sense: shopping isn't the main objective of the trip. This category is divided into internal and foreign one day tourists and internal and foreign tourists requesting accommodation. Generally, shopping tourists spend for three categories of merchandise, which make three quarters of the shopping:

- Clothes, with a share of 44 % of the total amount of shopping (daily average per person 29 €).
- Shoes/leather products with a share of 16 % (daily average per person 11 €).
- Food products with a share of 14 % (daily average per person 9 €). Share of shopping tourism to the overall turnover in retail commerce in Germany (no gas stations, no chemist's stores and repairing workshops) reaches in 2004 approximately 3.4%, i.e. approximately 12.5 Bill. €.

The important question is if and at which level was generated a surplus in expenses in retail commerce by the German shopping tourists, therefore it is not only about a transfer of turnover among different locations. Distinction should be made between the impact generated by the German tourists and the one generated by foreign tourists.

An analysis of the sensitivity presents following results for alternative suppositions according to which German shopping tourists spent cu 10 %, 15 %, 30 % respectively 50 % more than usual:

- Supplementary expenses of 10 %: German shopping tourists would generate a supplementary effect of 0.9 Bill. € a year. In this case, shopping tourists would generate a 2.8 times higher effect (2.5 Bill. €).
- Supplementary expenses of 15 %: The turnover generated by German shopping tourists would reach with a balance of 1.3 Bill. € approximately half of those generated by foreign tourists.
- Supplementary expenses of 30 %: The impact of German and foreign tourists is pretty much balanced in this case.
- Supplementary expenses of 50 %: German shopping tourism is based in this case with 6.7 bil. € on the regional transfer but with 3.3 Bill. € on the supplementarity effect. The real supplementary volume of German tourists would be approximately with one third over the one of the foreign tourists.

The calculation shows that for very optimistic premises, meaning at a high level, a positive balance is reached in the touristic shopping activities of the German tourists, foreign tourists being nevertheless an essential target group. For the year 2004 one comes to a gross sum of the contribution of foreign tourists to the gross annual turnover of the German retail commerce of about 2.5 Bill. €, approximately 0.7 %. Shopping tourism is also interested in other economic branches like for instance hotels and restaurants, transport but also services. The transportation of the one-day-tourists becomes more and more important than the transportation of tourists who also require accommodation.

The expenses of one-day-shopping tourists as well as of those requiring accommodation reached 2004 12.5 Bill. € to which one could add 30 Bill. € expenses for restaurants, accommodation, transportation, etc. This means that the overall economic importance is almost three times higher than the commercial expenses.

Types of Destinations for Shopping Tourism

The study contains a further analysis of the destinations for shopping tourism in Germany and their weak as well as their strong points compared to other destinations from abroad. International examples and good practices were discussed, analyzed and compared to the results of the surveys among tourists. The crystallization of the framework conditions and of the success factors of shopping tourism was therefore possible in the end by means of a simultaneous observation of the structure of offer and demand in the field of shopping tourism.

Germany offers mainly three types of shopping tourism destinations, i.e. characteristics of shopping tourism:

- Cities: German cities, bigger or smaller towns with a historic downtown are the classic destinations for the German shopping tourism.

Big towns in Germany are not visited mainly for shopping. These towns are attractive because of many other reasons, not less important, such as culture, international fame, all sorts of events, attractive landscape. The Leipzig/Dresden place is an excellent example for the fact that without an adequate strategy, i.e. marketing measures, no considerable results can be obtained. The premise lies in the existence of excellent offers of other types, of excellent structures. Dresden takes advantage especially of the cultural legacy. There would be therefore no sense in "selling" this region as a merely shopping tourism destination. Shopping is in this constellation rather a successful side effect. Still it can be noticed that all tourists' expenses in retail commerce increased the moment shopping possibilities were intensely communicated. It is further to be noticed that this region is the only one in Eastern Germany registering considerable turnover in the field of shopping tourism. Big German towns do not "sell" under the headlines of shopping tourism. Positive exceptions are – among others – Berlin, Munich and Oberhausen. It is to be noticed that positive potentials of synergies are not fully used, as far as urban marketing bets on centres with touristic attraction but doesn't refer to wide shopping opportunities. The cooperation between commerce, restaurants, touristic organizations, etc. is missing, in most cases commerce is not looking for a proper cooperation.

- Rural area with great potential in the field of shopping tourism: regions with a touristic tradition for decades understand to exploit its regional products like an endogen potential. Towns and regions "on the market" show their need for catching up only since the reunification.

The rural area has more opportunities to participate in the potential of the shopping tourism:

The respective region has a greater endogen offer regarding shopping, the offer being normally sustained by an attractive infrastructure (such as an attractive landscape, hotels and restaurants, leisure time opportunities, cultural events, etc.). In such cases, shopping tourism is an auxiliary product of touristic objectives regarded as main concern. These could nevertheless be considerably extended towards coordinates like attractiveness and potential turnover in commerce.

On the other hand, shopping opportunities can be created by setting up adequate facilities. In these cases, the main target is to attract customers for shopping in remote regions. Infrastructure is under these circumstances the necessary framework for the success of the shopping destinations.

The usual location of FOC (of designers and factories) is the rural area. These are set up so that customers can reach them rapidly and easily from crowded spaces. FOCs are sooner an exception in Germany due to the restrictive approval procedure. At present there are less than a handful of such centres.

These are no doubt a magnet for customers and in Germany they are as good as not existing. From the point of view of the shopping tourism they are successful models but no hopes related to supplementary effects of these centres for the neighboured towns were fulfilled.

- Commercial centres: Commercial centres have existed under different forms in Germany since the 50ies, modern planning–

also in Eastern Germany – refer more and more to relaxation while shopping.

Shopping Malls: No commercial centre has the dimensions of the examples offered by the North-American malls, although based on its functional structure the Centre Oberhausen can be regarded as an example in its essence as a mall.

Urban Entertainment Centres/Urban Entertainment Destinations: as big urban projects following the example of urban entertainment destinations, the Potsdam Place in Berlin or the New Centre in Oberhausen can be understood as such centres in Germany.

Shopping Malls and Urban Entertainment Centres establish – next to the experiences gathered by shopping – an increased priority on entertainment as a commercial centre. Regarded from the perspective of the shopping tourism, these offer a more interesting tourist destination than a commercial centre, whose function is rather related to acquisition of goods.

In these forms of distribution there normally lies a certain professional marketing as shopping tourism destination. Owners take care, among others, of a common presence and also take into account the costs for events and other measures of attracting customers. Cooperation opportunities with urban marketing/urban tourism are simpler, as far as the owners' interests can be combined and retail merchants, restaurant owners and service providers don't have to be brought "under the same roof" – as in downtowns.

Commercial centres are widely spread in Germany. Normally these aren't specific shopping tourists' objectives but could anyway serve as an addition of the existing offer in shopping tourism. Extremely interesting for Germany are the cross-border-shoppings.

- Brand Lands/Flagship Stores: Different brand lands such as the Stollwerck chocolate museum in Cologne, the Volkswagen glassworkshop in Dresden and many other enterprises/ companies aim by self-representation in the headquarters at setting anchor for the respective brand and these centres also have a certain touristic attractiveness. Flagship stores are tied to the brands of contribute to the attractiveness of the respective location, like the Sony centre in Potsdam Place or the flagship store of the clockmakers Glashütte Original in Frankfurt on Maine.

- Factory Outlet Centres: FOCs of Zweibrücken and Wertheim are the two pure outlet centres in Germany, built after the American model. The distribution of the two FOCs is taking place in other locations, far more remote and there they generate big figures in the turnover in tourism such as Metzingen, where, among others, the outlet centre for Boss – clothing has been set up.

The approval procedure of the German FOCs is extremely restrictive. As a consequence, especially owners/foreign investors, crossed the German border, next to it and there they exploit the purchase power at a certain level. A vivid example is the FOC in Roermond, Netherlands, where more then 56 % of the customers come from Germany. This trend is also consolidated by the fact that stores abroad are open on Sundays as well.

- Cross-border shopping: Cross-border shopping in order to purchase goods is taking place in Germany outside the sphere of organizing spare time (for instance shopping for ordinary food products by Danish people in Germany) as well as during the spare time (for instance occasional shopping for clothes, leather articles of Polish people in Germany).

Cross-border shopping is interesting from an economic overall perspective especially due to the fact that this can contribute to the flow of purchasing power. This type of shopping involves anyway a certain kind of competition that can lead to an unwanted flow of purchase power.

A new development is remarked, consisting of the fact that – as mentioned in the case of FOCs – due to the very restrictive approval procedures in Germany for these outlet centres, Germany's neighbours enter the territory with more offers of the kind. Taking into account the fact that Germany, as a comparatively "cheap" country regarding trips and shopping, is surprised by the fact that cross-border shopping looks more an more like a one-way-street to abroad. This is also the case of commercial regions in the border area as well as of the Low-Cost-Carrier for which 80% of the potential is considered to be "exiting".

Framework Conditions and Success Factors of Shopping Tourism

The research crystallized six main groups of success factors:

1st Success Factor: General Framework Conditions

The conditions stability and internal security are mostly fulfilled in Germany, big towns being considered to be more secure than similar towns abroad (Europe).

Essential for the opportunity of developing the retail commerce locations is also the legal framework which should be taken into account in the approval of large land destined to retail commerce. In synthesis, legal provisions issued by the federal authorities as well as those on land and regional level lead first of all to the security of structures and also to maintaining the attractiveness of the traditionally compact commercial centres. Second, especially in dense polycentric areas a high discrepancy is noticed concerning the planning targets – on the one hand – and the unexploited potential, respectively not allowed elsewhere– on the other hand.

According to the experts' assessment one cannot start from the premise that this restrictive attitude is to relax in the following years in a remarkable manner, the frame of space order and territorial planning will continue to hinder the development of new offers. These conditions are considerably better in Europe, which means more liberal, as the examples of the commercial centres show in Roermond, Maasmechelen, Pandorf and Bicester. A disadvantage regarding Germany's location in shopping tourism mostly consists of the interdiction of commercial activities on Sundays. During the week (including Saturdays) – and this is a proved fact in the comparisons performed abroad – Germany is competitive.

Short period tourism in permanent development focusing mainly on weekends cannot be exploited from the point of view of shopping tourism at entire parameters in Germany. This is why experts consider the widely debated proposal regarding the transfer of responsibility connected the provisions referring to opening hours – including on Sundays and holidays – to the lands of the federation as being positive. These can issue much better regulations structured on the regional particularity than the still rigid corset of the still valid law regarding the opening hours of stores could ever do. Especially in the border area there is a great need of flexible opening hours on Sundays because otherwise purchasing power will continue to be redirected over border.

2nd Success Factor: Type and Area of the Offer

Basic premise for the exploitation above the local level of some location of a shopping destination is a commercial area focused on a very clear type of product category. We are talking about international brand offer as well. Besides touristic shopping destination in restricted sense, therefore those places which essentially advertise for shopping offers, one shouldn't lose sight especially small and medium sized towns in such picturesque regions or in regions with important cultural offers, where tourists' shopping is mainly regarded as "side effect" in local commerce.

This is where it is often noticed that local retail commerce – for instance in climacteric resorts – doesn't even exploit the scope still offered by the law regarding opening hours. Tourists' guides for people focused on shopping are also rather an exception. As far as the type and attractiveness of the offer is concerned, German destinations – except some forms like outlet centres – are competitive on international level.

3rd Success Factor: Price

The price level is one of the decisive strong points for the international shopping tourism after Germany. Anyway, this is true only in a restricted sense for clothing, shoes, which are the most important merchandise categories shopping tourists are looking for. Considering that home countries of the customers and destination countries have no common currency (meaning fixed exchange rates), the price level isn't stable, fact which is perceived by the tourists as a risk factor and could generate repercussions.

Germany has – at least what the €-space is concerned and the former Eastern block (highly valuable merchandise, for instance electronic products)– clear advantages at present regarding the price level.

4th Success Factor: Position

A basic premise for the potential turnover in shopping tourism is the geographic position towards important traffic axes or tourists' destinations. Especially for groups of foreign tourists (mostly Americans, Chinese and Japanese), the attitude towards shopping is decisively depending on the European routes. The closure of the shopping destinations in Germany and of the downtowns is to be appreciated as being above the average, compared to the situation on international level. The (free) network of highways, airports, high speed trains and even fuel price, all these are advantages related to position.

5th Success Factor: Infrastructure

An essential success factor in shopping tourism is the "historic or cultural power" of a town, therefore the attractiveness of the image of the town and its construction substance. Towns with outraging constructions and – the ideal situation – old intact quarters of towns or in isolated cases even architectural attraction points revealing the development in this direction of entire quarters offer the adequate "backstage" for the offers in retail commerce, which will certainly be approached by the visitors of those towns.

If other countries use their infrastructure in a better manner than Germany – this is still an open question. Important is the urban/ regional distribution strategy. The analysis reveals that Germany has both destinations, which are sold in a very intelligent way but also destinations, which don't show their strong points of show them only with low amplitude in order to generate shopping tourism.

6th Success Factor: Fame and Marketing

In almost all cases the necessary marketing level can be systematically ensure, provided enterprises in retail commerce, restaurants and service provider cooperate in an adequate organizational structure. Traditional advertising or interests communities have meanwhile been replaces in most situations by urban and city-marketing-organizations, which have a wider basis of members and therefore a bigger budget. Anyway, commerce is (still) very little involved in such cooperation structures. At first, successful examples by means of long term strategies are to be noticed, together with a touristic model, which understands a lot of promoting shopping as main motive next to culture, business or private reasons and reveals them accordingly. A successful position – especially of smaller locations and rural regions – has as premise individualized characteristics which can be created for instance by known products or specific tourists' attraction points.

Finally, a consequent level of services is of an even greater importance for the success of shopping tourism than for the local shopping centres destined to the local or regional customers. This implies first of all the use of the legal opening hours at a wide scale, especially also on Sundays and holidays, as far as this is allowed by local agreements or exceptions to the regulation maybe for locations where foreign tourists are very frequent. Next is the need of specialized personnel with foreign language knowledge and high consulting competence. The acceptance of credit cards, relevant currency are examples for success factors related to services. Integrated measures are necessary in commerce, culture, restaurants and facilities for spending leisure time, consolidated by professional common management and marketing. A successful destination policy needs a compulsory implementation of future oriented centre related concepts for the development of locations both for spending leisure time and for retail commerce in agreement with the neighbour communes. A key position has commerce which is to be involved in the decision making process and needs enough space in order to configure things, so that downtowns are revitalized by means of shopping events and attractiveness for tourists is increased.

Development Potential of Shopping Tourism

The overall framework conditions for commerce in Germany are considered to be rather unfavourable at present and maybe for one or two years to come. We start from the premise that foreign tourists will have a positive impact on the existing potential on the short and medium range of time. Obviously positive are especially the signs of the foreign accommodation facilities. This is to be appreciated as a boom that is expected to increase the turnover in commerce also in the future. USA and Asia are very interesting for the shopping tourism as source markets, as far as the package sightseeing tour offers are mainly coming from these places.

Member towns of the community "Magic Cities" profit most from the foreign trips. The share of foreign tourists and accommodation requests is also above average in the case of other towns, for instance in the border area (Freiburg) or towns with high touristic attractiveness combined with proper relationships between countries (for instance Heidelberg, Wiesbaden/US-Army).

The big market share of the West-European states in the incoming after Germany represents probably a stability factor because the number of visitors depends less on the stable exchange rate or security risks generated by diseases, terrorist attacks or wars. The relative proximity in space and the EU integration determine increasing expectations related to a rather increasing than decreasing number of visitors.

Chances for the extension of the shopping tourism lie especially in the dynamic economic development in Poland and Czech Republic. The dynamic increase of the GIP in Poland is at the same time a signal for the rising purchase power. We are talking about the use of chances of the participation in the expenses over shopping tourism. The German fashion brands have a similar positive image in Eastern Europe as cars, which is to be appreciated as Germany's advantage concerning location compared to other West-European countries.

The Asian market is very interesting for the shopping tourism. After a restriction of the touristic activity which lasted for decades, especially Chinese people register a great need of catching up. Especially because an even greater number of countries are interested and are striving for the purchase power from Asia, it is very important to adopt a position in due time. This group is expected to increase the number of accommodation nights from about 3.7 mil. to about 5 Mil.

Germany could increase in 2003 its market share in all holiday trips of German people with about 2% to about 60 %. Urban internal tourism represents a segment expected to extend in future, based on the strong trend towards short holiday trips. The exchange of urban tourists between individual German big towns and their resident regions will consolidate based on the rapid train connections and reasonable prices in the area of "Low-Cost-Carrier".

In the age group over 55 (so-called "Best Ager") an extension of all traditional source markets in Germany is expected to come. The "Best Ager" as target group of all people aged over 55 represent an important development segment in international trips for urban and event tourism and at the same time for shopping tourism. The aim is to attract older visitors coming from abroad to (shopping) touristic trips to Germany and simultaneously to confirm Germany as an interesting destination for German tourists.

Regarding the high development potential of this target group in the source markets in Great Britain, France and Italy, German big towns and relevant German towns from the point of view of tourism and culture, especially the "Historic Highlights of Germany" will take advantage especially under the circumstances of the extension of aeronautic connections through "Low-Cost Carrier". This is a source of important chances for shopping tourism. The high development rates of the Low-Cost Carrier (LCC) especially at times of weak circumstances represent a supplementary market segment with high development potential in the German urban tourism.

More efforts are needed in order to promote the incoming tourism through LCC. Present estimations of an average 80 % outgoing to 20 % incoming mean a flow of purchase power in the field of retail commerce for each town, i.e. region.

The focus expected for the coming years of the LCC on the Eastern European markets offers good chances for the shopping tourism in Germany. Premise is nevertheless targeted marketing measures in the European source regions as well as in regions which have registered a flow of purchase power based on the dominant outgoing share in the balance. The extension of LCC will come at hand especially to the German big towns and relevant touristic towns.

The World Championship in Football Germany 2006 is an excellent chance for the German tourism. Based on the number of stadiums and the broadcasted games, next to the final-towns, especially the land North Rhine-Westphalia (Nordrhein-Westfalen) and the Ruhr Region will profit from this event.

After an assessment of the described sources and not at last after the discussions with different experts in retail commerce and tourism, one can start from the premise that German hasn't exploited its potentials not even with the level reached so far.

Taking into account the increasing number of arrivals and accommodation requests, especially from the regions Asia and Eastern Europe, one can expect an increased turnover in shopping tourism. More than that, it can be assumed that the emphasis on shopping tourism as trip target, respectively content o the trip, has an impact on the average expenses in retail commerce. The following is an assessment of the dimensions of this development segment called shopping tourism in a long term prognosis for the retail commerce. This prognosis, i.e. estimation of the expected developments is made for a lower and a higher alternative. The lower alternative is rather pessimistic, while the higher more optimistic.

As an average of all target groups in shopping tourism, one can assume that the result lies somewhere in the middle of the two alternatives. This would mean that between 2004 and 2010 the turnover in retail commerce generated by shopping tourism increased from 12.5 Bill. € p.a. with 20 % to about 15 Bill. €. The lower alternative has a result of about 15 %, that is 1.9 Bill. €, the higher of 25 %, that is 3 Bill. €.

The important turnovers in retail commerce generated by foreign tourists have an important share in the increase rate, especially under the circumstances of an increased number of visitors. We assume that the supplementary turnover in retail commerce generated by this group (in between the two alternatives) will increase by the end of the decade with almost 40 %, i.e. from about 2.5 Bill. To approximately 3.5 Bill. €.

Recommended Actions

Shopping tourism requires overall, integrative approaches in order to use the midterm development chances of the respective markets (especially in retail commerce). Regarding the overall cooperation, especially with the participation of commerce, the main goal is to integrate shopping as a component of tourism in Germany. It is about defining shopping tourism as a touristic distribution object. The emphasis of the importance of cooperation and overall marketing strategies and the creation of the needed basis for a cooperative action of the partners is the main premise for the exploitation of the existing potential for each involved party.

The action fields for the distribution of shopping tourism lie in the branches of internal and external marketing, which depend on each other and simultaneously influence each other. In the field of external marketing (abroad as well as in Germany) of shopping tourism, the German Tourism Agency offers structures and much experience. The interest is focused on efforts in the internal marketing, the distribution of the idea among the involved parties and participant institutions.

Action Field 1: Enterprises in Retail Commerce

Interesting touristic offer packages ("Packages") connected to shopping offer the opportunity of generating an added value to a simple sight – seeing tour. Shopping becomes a part of the experience itself. The creativity of retail commerce enterprises is very much needed for these „Packages". It is about the supplementary incentive they can offer to their customers – besides looking at the merchandise.

A special promotion opportunity also lies in the customer cards of the supermarkets and retail commerce enterprises. In addition to this, supermarkets and retail commerce enterprises increasingly settling down in European countries can approach their customers by mailing, from Poland and the Czech Republic and advertise for the German offer.

For a provision depending on the turnover offered to the organizer or a special partner for instance of a foreign travel group, the opportunity is created for the retail commerce enterprise to influence directly the shopping activities of foreign tourists. In many German retail commerce stores credit cards are not accepted, based on the high provision. Nevertheless exactly foreign tourists, especially those coming from the USA are used to paying for everything with their credit cards, so that the low acceptance is often not understood and generates a negative impact on the shopping availability. It's even worse when other card or system providers are asked for, than those widely spread in Germany (for instance American Express). Service standards, which the international visitors know from other countries, should be accepted in Germany as well in the retail commerce and therefore lead to an improvement of the convenience, which is the decisive factor for the shopping experience. Especially the lacking foreign language knowledge when relating to foreign shopping tourists and not enough information about the merchandise, for instance related to the size of the pants, to custom regulations, compatibility of technical details should be improved. German retail commerce can cope in the international competition with its opening hours. Anyway, at present it doesn't even exploit its existing scope. Cooperation of the local commerce is asked for also in this area, stores will keep their doors open for as long as neighboured stores are accessible, because not very many customers will visit downtowns. Development potential lies especially in the opening hours on Sundays.

Action Field 2: Communes

The task of the communes is to take care of the framework conditions in order to allow cooperation in the field of shopping tourism between the involved parties. Nevertheless, they are confronted with the difficulty of coordinating partners with often different perspectives.

The moderation of a common work in shopping tourism should be the responsibility of a superior institution, something like the mayor. Especially in the field of city-marketing initiatives, cooperation with the responsible actors in tourism is extremely reasonable in order to agree upon marketing strategies and to coordinate them.

Cities should transform into destinations presenting target groups oriented offers at a high quality level by the integration of its organizational structures. Cooperation between tourist-information, city-management, city marketing, cultural institutions, etc. is the essential premise for an efficient distribution of the concept of shopping tourism. The criticism towards the increasing finalization of German downtowns comes too short: essential is the consistent and profiled overall impression of a shopping destination. The objective of a local economic promotion should be the exploitation of a series of specific local offers, where quantity (shopping area, turnover) is less important, where it actually comes down to the unique nature and the sympathy aroused.

The issue oriented cooperation becomes very important in connection with the different reasons of the tourists. In order to reduce losses, to exploit synergies and to enter international tourism as a recognized brand, issue oriented cooperation is necessary, due to the limited financial means. In the development of individual locations, legal provisions in the approval of retail commerce on wide areas are regarded rather restrictively. Very often even with the active support of the good old retail commerce. The new locations of the shopping experiences like for instance Urban Entertainment Centre or Factory Outlets offer considerable potentials to shopping tourism but these are approached by the communes in rather exceptional situations, not to speak about isolated cases, rarely approved. Experts consider flexibility as being highly recommended in this area.

Action field 3: The Regional Level

Next to the relevant touristic highlights of a region, attractive, supplementary offers in the field of culture, leisure time, gastronomy, retail commerce are absolutely necessary in order to exercise influence on the quality and duration of a trip.

Recommendation is to set up the working group "tourism-oriented retail commerce" on regional level, focusing upon cultural, economic and specific products in the region. It is especially the case of the Eastern lands of the federation, like Saxony with the Erzgebirge, where the traditional trade, respectively art is highly praised in Germany as well as abroad, while the conscience about these facts is to be increased, due to the relatively new distribution activities.

Action Field 4: Chambers and Associations in Commerce and Tourism

Taking into account demographic developments of the German people, the trend of short travels and the development potential in city-tours, retail commerce associations should explain to their members the parameters of the incomes which can be generated by tourists and the potential increase. Both German and foreign tourists should lie in the centre of preoccupations. Retail commerce associations together with the top organizations in tourism should communicate measures and cooperation opportunities to their members at the decentralized level: Next to retail commerce, other partners should be identified and contacted in the field of cross-marketing. These could be producers or industrial enterprises.

For many non-EU-markets there are shopping-guides of the company „Global Refund, Tax free shopping", in the native language, elaborated in cooperation with the German Tourist Agency. Nevertheless it is reasonable to elaborate a flyer regarding German shopping tourists' destinations, which is not too much dedicated to tax-free-products, but especially focused on comparisons of prices and quality in the European context, on specific retail commerce structures in Germany, on individual characteristics of each city in the field of shopping tourism, etc. Certain manufactured products and regional food or delicatessen should also be presented as well as new shopping forms in the field of Factory-/Designer-Outlets, Brand Lands or Urban Entertainment destinations.

Action Field 5: Federal and Land Level

Shopping experience is of greater importance for Germans as means of spending leisure time than going to the cinema or going swimming. While cinemas, swimming pools, parks or museums are obviously usually open on Sundays and tourists register at those times a considerable consumption, shopping is limited to working days and Saturdays.

Especially in touristic centres and big towns Sunday shopping could generate a greater consumption, as far as about 2/3 of the short trips lead to towns and the touristic goals are related to the shopping issue.

In order to avoid losses in the region, which could appear only when individual destinations are open on Sundays, the alternative were to offer a certain number of stores open on specific Sundays, for instance 20 Sundays, across the land. Flexibility is asked at a wide scale in border regions if purchase power isn't to be redirected across the border. It is only a matter of time before Poland and the Czech Republic are setting up FOC at the border. The federation promotes economic development, setting up of enterprises, investments in private economy, the department for foreign fairs, consulting measures and further more with considerable financial means. These measures should be checked upon the positive impact on the extension of shopping tourism.

Tax-Free-System should be easier to be used. It's been far too complicated until now, considering the forms one had to fill out.

Generally the tasks of the federations lie in the promotions of shopping tourism in the process of moderation. It can contribute by gathering retail commerce and tourism organizations to the same discussion table and by approaching the necessary coordinated procedure. The role of the lands is not enough appreciated, as far as it is much easier for those to approach regional actors and to assist their work by coordinating it. Lands could also support targeted projects in the framework of their economic promotion programs, like the federation. Funding opportunities lie within the context of the GA and EFRD–promotion.

Action Field 6: EU-extension Towards East

Common task of economy, policy and administration is to ensure the location Germany, the own purchase power in Germany and to attract, eventually, the purchase power coming from the neighboured countries towards Germany.

The EU-extension towards East is related to the curiosity-effect and offers especially for the communes in Eastern Germany the chance of attracting potential customers from Germany of Czech Republic. Special shields in native languages related to shopping opportunities, special shopping guides should be made available in traffic knots relevant for shopping activities, such as airports or railway stations.

In order to attract purchase power flows on it, commerce should reveal its strong points and its efficiency. Speaking about product policy, product quality has to be revealed. Regarding the range policy, not only wide ranges but also deep ranges should be emphasized, so that the customer can really find the article he or she has been looking for.

Regarding the price policy, it is all about a favourable relation between price and performance, especially when purchase power in the residence area lies below average. Discounts are asked for especially in the border area. The issue communication and advertising policy is very important. One of the main tasks of the Chambers of Commerce and Industry is the know-how-transfer in form of seminars.

9

LS Retail Suite of Solutions for the Retail

Current Scenario-Retail and Hospitality

Over the past ten years, organized retail has grown to have a 3% market share of the Indian economy. Today, the overall retail market is estimated to be approximately USD 300 billion. Over the last three years, this sector has witnessed an exorbitant growth due to the establishment of numerous international quality formats to suit the Indian purchase behaviour, the improvement in retail processes, the development of retail specific properties and the emergence of both, domestic and international organizations.

Organized retailers are the contemporary formats by which shoppers have the edge of a world class shopping experience. Fine examples of these formats are Pantaloon, Shoppers Stop and Trent. Organized retail may broadly be classified into the following formats-

- Malls. The largest form of organized retailing today. Malls are located mainly in metro cities, in proximity to urban outskirts, this format ranges from approximately 60,000 sq ft to 7,00,000 sq ft and above. They lend an ideal shopping experience with an amalgamation of product, service and entertainment, all under a common roof. E.g. DLF City Centre and Metropolitan Malls in Gurgaon.
- Hypermarkets. This format comprises of a multiple division layout, and usually has an" industrial-look" interior. Hypermarkets generally provide daily necessities and grocery like items. Pricing is competitive and value for money. E.g. Big bazaar; Giant.

- MBO's. Multi Brand outlets, also known as Category Killers, offer several brands across a single product category. These usually do well in busy market places and Metros. e.g. Royal Sporting House.
- Super Markets. Large self service outlets, catering to varied shopper needs are termed as Super markets. These are located in or near residential high streets. Super Markets can further be classified in to mini supermarkets typically 1,000 sq ft to 2,000 sq ft and large supermarkets ranging from a size of 3,500 sq ft to 5,000 sq ft. Eg. Food World.
- Discount Stores. As the name suggests, discount stores or factory outlets, offer discounts on the MRP through selling in bulk reaching economies of scale or excess stock left over at the season. The product category can range from a variety of perishable/non perishable goods.
- Convenience Stores. This format refers to smaller self service stores which do well in bustling locations.
- Departmental Store. Large stores, catering to a variety of consumer needs. Further classified into localized departments such as clothing, toys, home, groceries, etc. Eg. Shopper Stop.
- Exclusive Store. Ranging from a size of 500 sq ft to 5,000 sq ft. & above, this format is owned/managed by the Company or through its franchise. These can offer single brand as well as multiple bands. e.g. Home Store.
- Speciality Store. These formats focus on a specific product category, Medium sized layout in strategic location. Speciality stores provide a large variety base for the consumers to choose from. Eg. Bata.

In similar light, the hospitality industry, despite being an important component of the economy, has contributed only 2% of the GDP in 2003-04. According to recent estimates of the WTTC Indian tourism, demand will grow at 8.8% over the next ten years from 2005-15, which would place India as the second most rapidly growing tourism market in the world. This will result in a total growth of 7.1% in travel and tourism GDP and an increase of 0.9% in travel and tourism employment. With this estimated growth, the size of the hotel industry continues to represent an appalling figure for India's size and growth prospects.

As the consumer demand increases and the retailers gear up to meet this increase, technology is fast evolving to support this growth. The hardware and software tools that have now become almost essential for retailing and hospitality can be divided into 3 broad categories-

- Customer interfacing system
- Operation support system
- Strategic Decision Support System.

Inevitability of IT in Retail & Hospitality

The Information Technology Industry's contribution to the Indian GDP has increased from approximately 1.4% in 1998-99 to more than 4% in 2004-05. The domestic market for software has grown to USD 6 Billion in the FY '06 from USD 4.8 billion in the previous fiscal year. The Indian ERP market is expected to see CAGR of 25.2% over the next five years. The market was USD 83 million in 2004 and is projected to be over USD 250 million by 2009.

With the global players all set to come in, the existing retail companies in India need to update themselves with the latest technology in order to have a competitive edge over the non recognized retail sector. Today, technology is imperative to increase customer satisfaction and make shopping a global experience.

For example, given a situation where a retailer wants to increase its loyalty customer base, an organization with relevant IT systems in place, has a ready customer data base which is updated at every purchase. This is an immediate reference of recipients, to print and send mailers or promotional catalogues too. A retailer can also align its respective merchandise and plan promotions accordingly. Gone are the days when one had to rely solely on direct customer interaction and manual methods of promotion. This also facilitates large format stores to operate with utmost efficiency and accuracy.

In the hospitality sector, the ability to deliver outstanding service to pleasure guests is the key to staying competitive. It is beyond traditional applications of logistics and supply chain management, technology will play a fundamental role in the future growth of this industry.

Retailers all across the country believe that shrinkage due to inventory recording, handling and administrative errors costs retailer's millions.

In an intensely competitive, cost-conscious industry, decisions about IT and telecommunications infrastructure can make a vast difference. Choosing the right solution provided by the right supplier can result in improved productivity and major cost savings through key advantages such as more accurate supply chain forecasting and better inventory management.

Retailers need to understand that technology is not a sunk cost but rather an investment to reduce heavy long term costs, a long term investment for long term growth and maintaining a competitive advantage.

Filling the Gap

Currently, there is an immense operational and technological gap between the domestic and international giants which can only be reduced with the application of Information Technology.

LS Retail has expertise and insight working with some of the world's largest retailers to provide the needed infrastructure and business solutions that extend well beyond pure connectivity. To ensure cost-effectiveness, it is essential to evaluate business demands and requirements so that maximum value is received from retailers' existing technology infrastructure. Retailers need to optimize IT and telecommunications at the store level to ensure that information assets are leveraged for maximum advantage. Data gathering for inventory management at the cash register is the tip of the iceberg. Back-office and supplier integration demands a secure, reliable network infrastructure.

The Indian retail market – which is expected to reach USD 637 billion in 2015, will change rapidly in the coming years. The advent of Information Technology in retailing will change consumer expectations and behaviour, while International retail stores entering the Indian market are making an already competitive landscape even tougher.

A fine example is store management alerted to out-of-place items. An in-store system could use RFID to monitor actual versus intended product location on the floor or in the stockroom. By using RFID-encoded shelf edge labels with embedded shelf readers, a grid could be set up for verifying planogram compliance for standard shelving and promotional displays, with a corresponding alert for misplaced items sent to store personnel. Big payoffs could be realized for frequently moved and misplaced items, such as apparel, grocery's and books.

Technology that is fast, scalable, adaptable, user friendly, proven, localized and customizable will not only propel Indian retailers to optimal growth, but also retain customers through the ability to make timely and accurate decisions.

LS Retail Suite

Companies today want to increase productivity and performance while addressing the full range of information requirements throughout their operation. LS Retail Suite provides a comprehensive business intelligence functionality that allows companies to use any data asset, transform it into useful information, and deliver it in a practical format.

Landsteinar Strengur is one of the principal companies developing retail and hospitality solutions in the international arena. Their retail solutions have been sold to over 130 countries, translated into 30 languages. It is used by approximately 6,700 stores worldwide, including IKEA, Adidas, NAAFI, Debenhams, Pizza Hut and Booths Supermarket.

LS Retail

LS Retail is an end-to-end retail solution that covers everything from POS to back office and head office. The setup can range from a single store with one POS to a complex, multi-store environment that integrates with your overall business operation.

For example, knowing the unpredictability of Indian weather, if a Retailer wants to roll out a Monsoon promotion in the state of Maharashtra within the next hour for all its 50 stores, it is able to initiate this promptly from one minute to the next for all stores. Secondly, for goods that are not selling as per plan, a promotion is made possible at the click of one button with LS Retail.

In brief, it offers the following functionality in Retail-

- It improves Data Integrity,
- Offers comprehensive Business Intelligence,
- Empowers retailers,
- Effectively streamlines inventory control,
- Eliminates paperwork,
- Increases store efficiency,
- Reduces shrinkage,
- POS for Multi-tier Retail,
- Gives an instant business overview,
- Peak versatility,

- Complete integration,
- Schedule operations,
- Mobile technology integration for que-busting.

LS Hospitality

Globally, dining customers do not prefer to wait for long after ordering their meal. Similarly, the restaurateurs also encourage a quicker turn around time in order to generate greater business. Thus a solution which enables wireless order taking, and direct communication to the kitchen, eliminates errors and time. It creates a finer dining experience, and an increased efficiency of the restaurant. In this regard, LS Hospitality is the ideal solution.

LS Hospitality is an integrated, multilingual POS and back-office solution for hospitality organizations worldwide. Designed for managing dine-in, take-out, delivery business and pubs/bars, LS Hospitality provides management and employees with necessary tools to keep the customers satisfied, thereby ensuring repeat business. With increased flexibility, speed of service and improved access to vital information, LS Hospitality streamlines operations and reduces cost.

LS Hospitality solution integrates restaurant activities like dine-in, take-out, delivery and pubs/bars, split bills, table reservations etc.

In brief, it offers the following functionality in Hospitality-

- Dynamic restaurant management,
- Table reservations,
- POS/Dine-in Interface,
- Fast cashier switching for Pubs/Bars,
- Wireless at the table,
- Call centre functionality,
- Deliveries,
- Kitchen monitor,
- Recipe (controlling ingredients & resources),
- Extensive reporting,
- Advanced statistics.

LS Retail Suite of Solutions

With LS Retail Suite of solutions, localized to the Indian Industry, one can reduce the total cost of ownership and prepares one for changes in both, business and customer behaviour. It undoubtedly increases efficiency and allows complete business transparency.

With LS Retail, it is easier to make up-to-the minute decisions alleviating mistakes.

LS recognizes current consumer trends and reduces the total cost of inventory. It is therefore imperative to any organization in Retail and/or Hospitality.

The Use of Narratives in Landscape Design

A Changing Context: Asking for Narratives and Imagination

Both in highly urbanized regions and in peripheral regions, leisure and tourism are considered as important economic supports of future rural economies. In peripheral regions where processes of abandonment take place, local economies have often become very dependent on leisure and tourism. In regions where the dominant position of agriculture is under pressure due to urbanization, high land prices and increasing environmental restrictions, processes of diversification can be observed. In order to profit from growing leisure and tourism economies, rural areas are being "packed, commoditized and presented for consumption; the more authentic the better". Competition is strong in a globalizing market and traditional supplies of sun, sea and pleasure or a simple, tranquil stroll in the countryside no longer do. Consumers have become very demanding. They expect high quality supply and unique, memorable experiences. 'Spare time' has become the 'ultimate experience time'. In their competition for customers or visitors, leisure industries have introduced more spectacular supply.

Theme parks with ever higher and faster roller coasters or shopping malls with a constantly growing and diversifying supply are examples of the tendencies to intensify, enlarge, multiply or accelerate experiences. The counterpart of this trend is noticeable as well: new meanings can be derived from environments which represent modesty, deceleration or ultimate quietness. These processes accelerated the past decades and nowadays, leisure is more diverse and dynamic than ever before. Unique selling points and an elaborate and diverse supply are essential for regions to promote and distinguish themselves. The key to success could lie in approaches which integrate activities, place, facilities and services, emphasize regional or local identity and rouse peoples' imagination; that is, to appeal to people's fantasy, to stimulate amazement, wonder and curiosity. Distinct local and regional narratives can mobilize and unite stakeholders, and connect existing spatial qualities with future economic opportunities.

Leisure, Tourism and Design Tradition

In order to create landscapes which meet leisure and tourism needs and wishes, landscape designers are called in. The involvement of landscape designers concerned with leisure and tourism has a long history. After all, they have been modifying landscapes for leisure purposes for centuries, with 'pleasure' being an essential motive in garden architecture. Landscape design involves functional as well as perceptive and imaginative aspects of space. It is this particular combination that is essential to making contemporary landscapes more attractive.

Initially, landscape designers' activities were restricted to private gardens, manors and estates, but from the second half of the 19th century they became involved in public urban space, in periurban areas and in rural landscapes as well. In the twentieth century a specific design tradition concerned with leisure and tourism in rural areas was developed in the Netherlands. Dutch landscape designers have been involved in re-designing existing landscapes and in creating entirely new landscapes since the 1920s. Leisure has been one of the aspects to take into account, not only in traditional tourist landscapes but also in those that are seen primarily as productive landscapes. These practices have produced a range of design concepts, tools, styles and images which can be elaborated on.

My reconstruction of a design tradition, based on an analysis of landscape designs from the 1920s to the present, shows how it relates to contemporary questions of landscape adjustments for leisure and tourist purposes. It turns out that landscape designers used knowledge and theories about functional use, behaviour and perception in their designs. Surveys of leisure use and behaviour were carried out since the 1930s. The results were standardized into norms for policy, planning and design. Insights from environmental psychology were easily integrated in landscape design practices as they resembled some basic principles of landscape design. Diversity, coherence and orientation for example were familiar concepts for landscape designers.

While aspects of use, behaviour and perception were addressed in landscape design, imaginative aspects received less attention. On the one hand this is due to the dominancy of a rationalist engineering culture which landscape designers were confronted with in rural areas. On the other hand, the landscape design tradition in rural areas itself was predominated by a functionalist approach. Landscape designers developed design approaches and aesthetic preferences based on the well-functioning of the landscape as a system and held on to the Modernist motto 'Form follows Function". Landscape designers' experience of beauty was primarily related to the recognition of a logical and functional arrangement of land use. Landscapes were meant to refer only to themselves. One of their leading concepts was the 'legible landscape'.

The 'Legible' Landscape

In the early 1960s, Kevin Lynch introduced the concept of 'place legibility'; "with which parts can be recognized and can be organized into a coherent pattern" (1960: 3) or, in other words, the ease with which people can understand the layout of a place. Transposed to a landscape situation, legibility was interpreted as the understanding of how the landscape worked from its manifestation based on coherence between climate, soil, water and human occupation; or "understanding relationships between process and material, form and space". Apart from these so-called vertical relations, legibility also comprehended the horizontal relations; the ability to discern the relation between spaces. Landscape designers based their designs on the 'hidden system' of the landscape; the coherent logic of landscape patterns. The spatial organization of plantings for example was utilized to emphasize and clarify the main landscape structure. Hendriks and Stobbelaar (2003) defined this as the first layer of legibility and called it 'superficial' legibility; the ease to understand and memorize a situation.

In the 1970s, the concept of the legible landscape was elaborated with the concept of landscape identity. Landscape identity, which also had been one of the components of Lynch's legibility, resembled one of the basic concepts in landscape design; the 'sense of place' or 'genius loci'. A landscape with signs that related to former days would enable orientation in time in addition to orientation in space. For this reason, landscape designers tried to secure historic objects in land consolidation projects. "The chronology of land reclamation can be read from the pattern of dikes. [...] It is important to preserve the dikes as intact as possible and to emphasize the pattern with plantings". At the same time, several landscape designers thought new elements should be recognizable as well. New additions to the landscape should look as such and not provide the illusion of something gradually grown. "New patterns must be related to historical patterns; not by imitation but by showing both old and new beside each other, each with its own form and nature". By the mid-1980s, the legible landscape was re-defined as a landscape that offered orientation in time and space, recognizability and identity. The extent to which a landscape features coherences that enable orientation in space and time, is called 'geographical legibility', the second layer of legibility. The central question in 'geographic' legibility is: "Where am I?" It gives people the opportunity to experience themselves in relation to their environment.

With the new demands for special experiences, imaginative aspects have become very important nowadays. Contemporary landscape designers search for innovative means to rouse peoples' imagination. An interesting challenge for designers is to explore the concept of the legible landscape beyond superficial and geographical legibility. If a landscape contains signs which refer to people's individual biography or to collective history, the third layer of legibility, 'existential' legibility, comes up. Narratives play an important role in existential legibility. Narratives can provide orientation in time and space and add to personal identity and place identity. Especially when people 'script' their personal landscape narratives, existential legibility enters into the formation of personal identities and people's attachment and appropriation to the landscape. Whiston Spirn described this interpretation and understanding of landscape as follows: "The language of landscape is loud with dialogues, with story lines that connect a place with its dwellers" (1998: 17). "Humans interpret landscape signs and elaborate upon them, reading meanings in to tell stories.

Landscape Design Based on Narratives

A recent debate with landscape architects suggested that the content of the concept of the legible landscape has shifted towards 'existential' legibility. Probably, present-day popularity of history and heritage made designers pay more attention to temporal aspects of landscape. An legible landscape should contain visible references to its cultural history. A landscape without those references would lack identity and the opportunity for orientation in time They were also conscious of the existence of personal representations – individual narratives referring to personal events and memories-in addition to an 'expert canon' representing collective history. There was more than just one landscape narrative and they existed beside one another. Landscape designers indicated that landscapes are being read in many different ways, depending on the knowledge and bond of a person with the area. They asked themselves whether landscape designers should add other narratives and make them explicitly visible and recognizable or not. Wasn't concentrating on orientation in space sufficient as a design problem? No; they posed, certainly not from a leisure and tourist point of view. The recreational and tourist value and appreciation of a landscape will increase when different layers of meaning are open to interpretation, especially historical layers. After all, a clear local or regional identity and the presence of landscape elements that appeal to people's imagination are distinctive factors for leisure and tourist attractiveness. An attractive landscape should contain visible references to its cultural history; without those references, it would lack identity and the opportunity for orientation in time. The landscape designers thought that the design problem was not *if* other narratives should be incorporated, but *how*. If a landscape represents different narratives for a variety of people and every person can have his or her own narratives and emotions, then how should narratives be represented in landscape design? Should the narrative be explained obviously and one-dimensional or should it narrate itself, open to multiple representations?

Some recent examples of Dutch landscape design illustrate the use of historic narratives in landscapes which are being adjusted for leisure and tourist purposes. The first example illustrates how landscape designers, in cooperation with archaeologists and historians, chose narratives which rather focused on the history of *people* than on the history of *landscape*. An interdisciplinary workshop was organized to provide concrete ideas, conditions and suggestions for the area of Haarzuilens, an agricultural landscape which will be transformed into a future leisure landscape for citizens. The workshop focused on cultural heritage as the basis of the area's future identity. The results consisted of diverse design proposals for separate sites and routes. One team developed a network of paths based on linear landscape elements dating from different historical periods. The history of the landscape turned out to be an inspiring source of narratives for those who know how to find them. Each period gave cause to a characteristic appearance. Feudal times for example were represented by an unpaved track parallel to an avenue. The avenue referred to the lord of the manor, the track referred to the inferior position of the peasants. Today, people have the freedom to choose their path. In the past, they wouldn't have had that choice. Present time was represented by the entrance road of the castle which was transformed into a 'fun avenue' with contemporary follies. What used to be the playground of the baron, turned into the playground of citizens.

In the second example, landscape designers were asked to explore how remnants of 16th and 17th century defence lines in the Dutch-Belgian borderland could be exploited to diversify the tourist product of the coastal area (H+N+S 2003). Landscape designers, historians and leisure experts commonly agreed that the defence lines should not be turned into a ready-made attraction, fully renovated and equipped with information panels. They preferred to make special, unique places in the landscape over a predictable museum-like formula. People should be taken more seriously and challenged to use their creativity. The design team and experts observed that many people were interested in history in a broad context but that only a few artefacts were left. They suggested to broaden the historic narrative and to distinguish the landscape as a whole as 'lieu de memoire'. Where historic forms had perished, new meanings could be evoked with land-art-like operations instead of minute restoration. All experts thought it was necessary to create spatial coherence in order to make sure that relicts of lines and forts would be preserved in their landscape context. Sole cultural-historical value wouldn't be forceful enough against agro-economic forces however. Other programs were necessary to guarantee sustainable spatial coherence.

The designers chose to make use of ecological and water management objectives to develop a regional landscape framework, a 'landscape backbone' of watercourses, marshlands and extensively managed meadowlands. It would connect the different defence lines and integrate them into the landscape. A continuous trail would connect the various parts, running along the Defence Line landscape, following the defence dykes and sometimes crossing the agricultural landscape in between. Strolls from the towns and a Defence Line Museum at a strategically situated in the region completed the program. Thus, the designers managed to contribute to a new tourist product and at the same time created opportunities for residents to gain access to their everyday landscape and appropriate to it.

The strolls were worked out in detail, without paving to strengthen the contrast with local roads. "Accessibility of the countryside is of major importance, but so is the staging of the passage. I want to enable a landscape experience along the route in a certain way; unpretending though designed with love and care, and fitting in an everyday environment instead of over-designed". The forts and redoubts were designed as special, exciting places, dramatized by remodelling the surface level and adding upwards elements. On first sight they would merge into the landscape, waiting to be discovered by visitors. Then, if come across, they would suddenly reveal their special character.

The third example of a Landscape Development Plan for the river landscape Gelderse Poort near the city of Nijmegen shows how the landscape designer based his design for the development of recreational networks on existential legibility. He used fictional storylines to restore peoples' involvement and develop local attachment and support. When the project started, the designers were confronted with residents and land users who felt that the landscape was no longer theirs.

For ages, the landscape had been created by its inhabitants. This sense of belonging with the landscape has been lost due to lack of time, more intensive agricultural management and nature and landscape elements being managed by authorities. Villagers missed their local stroll as paths and tracks had disappeared over the years. In their eyes, their landscape had degenerated into a meaningless landscape owned and managed by a handful of farmers and outsiders. "A path, a bench or special sites invite people to make use of the landscape; narratives will grow naturally. The landscape has become inaccessible and has lost its meanings. An inaccessible landscape is also a meaningless landscape". The landscape designer was convinced that accessible space was essential for people's well-being. "It is important for people to stray in the landscape and in their minds. People want to be out now and then, simply go for a walk or a bicycle trip. It is a simple though essential and universal need".

The designers knew that a simple spatial design would not do and tried to restore the relation between inhabitants and their landscape through a participatory design process. At first, spatial interventions were not localized and the future image was not designed in detail. Design models were based on storylines that referred to the actual or fictitious past and present of the area. Storylines referred to ecological potentials, local use or history: the Vista Romana (the reconstruction of scenic views referring to the Romans who settled on the hills due to their strategic position over the river basin), stroll dikes (trails connecting dike remnants into a new recreational network, aligned with reed) and the cherry blossom circle (a chain of blossom lanes referring to former orchards on a bowl-formed slope creating a small-scale landscape on the gradient from the wooded hills to the river basin). The stroll dykes for example never existed as a network. The landscape designer thought of a possible solution of water storage fields surrounded by embankments which could be used as footpaths. One or two existing old trails were enough to suggest that his idea was inspired by historical relicts. "It doesn't matter whether a story is real or not, as long as we can make it alive".

Proposals for new landscape elements were developed in cooperation with farmers and other land owners. These landscape elements combine ecological and recreation networks and will be primarily realized on private grounds. Detailed landscape plans were made at individual farm level and mutually linked up into a coherent regional network. A recently established Landscape Fund will provide tenants or owners the financial means for management and maintenance. The exact terrain modelling, locations of solitary trees and surprising vistas will be determined on site.

To Conclude

Landscape narratives in de voorbeelden izjn neit ready made klip en klaar. Ze bieden uritme voor iegen interpretatie.

The examples show that landscape designers of the present generation have freed themselves from modernist dogmas and relate more directly to the previous, long-lasting tradition of garden architecture. Inspired by concepts like the experience society, they search for design concepts and tools which rouse peoples' imagination. Narratives are represented in such a way that they are open to multiple interpretations. At the same time, narratives create coherence in the supply of routes, attractions, facilities and setting. By using narratives, landscape designers are able to design attractive leisure and tourist environments and to provide a framework for integrated local or regional development as well. They are not just an instrument to commoditize landscapes and to give cause for leisure and tourist experiences. They also stimulate people's attachment and appropriation to the landscape.

Environmental Issues in Leisure and Tourism Choices

On the whole, participants did not think about the environment when making leisure and tourism choices. There were five main reasons.

(1) Leisure and tourism were not seen as environmental behaviours. These behaviours were mainly concerned with fulfilling participants' own needs or their family's needs.

(2) The environmental impacts of leisure and tourism were generally not well understood. Participants focused on the tangible impacts, such as litter and pollution. They also mentioned several misconceptions, for instance.

- Small everyday actions to help the environment such as reusing carrier bags have a greater impact than making changes to leisure/tourism.
- Holiday activities have a greater impact than travel.
- Long haul flights are only marginally worse than short haul.

(3) Some participants were not concerned about the impacts, particularly the less tangible ones such as global warming.

(4) Some participants saw no point in changing their leisure or tourism behaviour unless other people or other countries reduced their environmental impacts too.

(5) Participants objected to making changes for the sake of the environment, feeling that.

- It impinged on their right to do whatever they wanted with their leisure or tourism. This entitlement to holidays and a lesser extent day trips was very strongly expressed and was felt to justify lack of attention to environmental impacts.
- It was something peculiar that only serious environmentalists would do.
- It would simply make their day trip or holiday less enjoyable. Participants were more willing to change their everyday behaviour than leisure or tourism behaviour. They believed changing everyday behaviours was more effective for addressing environmental issues and a smaller sacrifice.

Leisure Behaviour Goals

Participants were fairly open to taking more of their leisure closer to home and would welcome more or better facilities locally. However, in some cases going further away added to the enjoyment of a day out. The main practical barriers to local leisure were lack of facilities and, to a lesser extent, limited knowledge.

While some participants were committed car drivers, others were willing or even keen to use public transport for their leisure. A number of obstacles would need to be addressed to encourage greater use of public transport, particularly high cost and inconvenient services. Participants realised that it was possible to buy low cost tickets if they booked in advance or travelled at certain times but this often did not suit them.

There were many and varied examples of combining several activities into a single trip. However, there was no clear view about whether combining could be encouraged. It could also prove counterproductive by encouraging reliance on cars, which make combining easier.

Popular leisure activities included those that Defra would like to encourage, such as walks in the countryside and picnics in the park, as well as those that may have a higher environmental impact. Participants seemed to feel that they should not have to change their choice of leisure activities for the sake of the environment but they were more open to doing the same activities with greater consideration.

Tourism Behaviour Goals

While some participants were resistant, there was considerable openness to taking more UK holidays, particularly short breaks rather main holidays. The main appeal of domestic holidays was their ease. However, overseas holidays offered sunshine and experiences that could not be found in the UK, among other attractions. Travelling by plane was something that participants took for granted and were willing to endure even if afraid. The recent advent of cheap flights had made overseas travel more affordable and participants were reluctant to give up the opportunities it offered. Nevertheless, there was some willingness to travel by train instead where practical, provided fares come down.

There was strong opposition to the idea of taking fewer longer holidays partly because of practical constraints and partly because several breaks give something to look forward to. However, special holidays or ones that require a long journey would justify consolidating several holidays into one. As with leisure, there was evidence that participants would be willing to continue with their current range of activities but with greater consideration for the environment.

Requests for Industry and Government

Participants generally saw a greater role for government than industry in reducing the environmental impact of leisure and tourism, although they also came up with a wide range of suggestions for industry. There were several reasons including the following.

- Participants did not understand the dividing line between government and industry responsibility.
- They thought that industry would resist taking expensive action due to vested interests.
- They assumed that 'greening' had already taken place which perhaps implies space for choice editing.

However, there was a dichotomy between calls for government to take action and concern about interference.

Participants wanted to know that their pro-environmental choices were part of a wider movement. They requested that public figures, mainly politicians, should lead the way and cut down on their flying in other words that government should exemplify.

There were repeated calls for more information and numerous suggestions about what it should be like, although participants also emphasised that policies/initiatives other than information provision sent out strong messages.

- Some participants asked to be told how their actions would help while others preferred to be told what would happen if they did not take action. However, the latter *"shock tactics"* approach could backfire.
- There were several suggestions about where information could be presented, including some innovative ones such as targeting it through stickers on petrol pumps.
- Participants stressed that information should be presented in a way that was meaningful. They strongly preferred environmental impacts presented in terms of an everyday action ('light bulb hours') to more scientific language (tonnes of CO2).

There was universal support for making train travel more affordable, ideally through simple user-friendly approaches. There was a mixed response to raising the cost of flying through taxes. Participants generally saw it could have an effect but objected to it mainly on the basis of fairness. The idea of a carbon tax also received a mixed response but was discussed less widely, suggesting it was less well known. Participants requested improved facilities. They focused on public transport and leisure facilities. Some requests were basic, such as making buses safer, while others were unrealistically high, such as diverting coaches via villages.

Conclusion

The many requests for action indicate that there is scope for government and industry to encourage sustainable leisure and tourism. However, persuading consumers to consider the environment in this context presents substantial challenges particularly given the limited understanding about the scale of environmental impacts; a belief that there is no point in acting alone; and a strong sense of entitlement and attachment. It may be possible to increase the appeal and feasibility of pro-environmental choices so that they are seen as double wins. However, attachment to flying, driving, overseas holidays and activities such as shopping and theme parks should not be underestimated. Interventions that limit or restrict choice (e.g. limiting or taxing air travel) may therefore be necessary to bring about fast and wide scale behaviour change. Although such interventions may meet with a mixed reception, some consumers already expect them.

The action points below build on the focus group findings. To ensure their effectiveness, further research is needed into the details of their implementation.

Action Points

Focus Effort on 'Open Doors'

With respect to leisure, encourage greater use of nearby facilities and less use of cars. With respect to tourism, encourage more UK holidays and less use of planes and cars.

Encourage and Enable Consumers to make Choices for Environmental Reasons

Provide information to enable consumers to make more informed choices. Make it quantitative, meaningful, tangible, and consistent with other government and industry initiatives. Encourage government and industry action, beyond the provision of information.

Ensure that consumers feel part of a wider movement towards pro-environmental leisure and tourism among their peers. Encourage MPs and other public figures to lead by example and take initiatives for action. Promote motivators and overcome barriers unrelated to the environment Encourage leisure closer to home by:

- providing more leisure facilities and improving existing ones, particularly in areas with new development
- informing local residents about the facilities that are available.

Encourage UK holidays by:

- marketing them as easy and ideal for short breaks.
- challenging preconceptions by marketing domestic destinations as opportunities for adventure and experiencing other cultures.
- finding ways to bring down both the actual and the perceived cost.

Discourage use of cars and planes for leisure and tourism by:

- taking steps to reduce the cost of train travel by adopting a more user-friendly reservation and pricing strategy or making advance booking normative, like booking a flight.
- taking all practical steps to make train and coach travel appealing.
- using financial incentives to encourage consumers to try train and coach travel in order to overcome negative perceptions or experiences.
- giving serious consideration to taxing or limiting air travel.

Moving Forward

Many of the above action points require the involvement of government departments and agencies besides Defra. For instance, Defra needs to link into DCLG regarding the provision of more leisure facilities in areas with new development. It is also crucial to involve the leisure and tourism industries in taking forward the above action points.

Methodology

This chapter describes, and where relevant explains the rationale for, the following aspects of the methodology.

- Focus groups,
- Selection and recruitment of participants,
- Procedure and material,
- Data analysis and reporting.

Focus Groups

The approach taken in this project was qualitative, rather than quantitative. In qualitative research participants are encouraged to give a full description of their activities, experiences, and views, and to explain the reasons underpinning them, rather than answering preset closed questions.

Qualitative research is valuable for several reasons. Firstly, it retains the participant's point of view in its original expression. Secondly, it obtains detailed responses so that understanding is gained of the factors that affect activities, experiences and views. Thirdly, it allows unexpected issues to emerge because activities, experiences and views are discussed in an open ended way. Fourthly, it allows complex interrelationships and the context of activities, experiences and views to be explored. It is therefore ideally suited to exploratory research such as this project.

In qualitative research it is not meaningful to report the number of participants expressing particular views or describing particular experiences. This is because of the small size of the sample and the purposive way in which it is selected. Also in focus groups not every participant is asked to comment on every issue. Therefore only a very broad indication of prevalence is possible in terms of overall recurrence of issues and the factors underpinning them.

Great care needs to be taken when generalising from qualitative research. The methodological annex highlights features of the research design that may limit the inferences that can be drawn. For validation, we would refer readers to the findings from the leisure and tourism literature review and the other projects in Defra's 'public understanding of sustainability' research programme. These are broadly consistent with the findings from this project.

Focus groups are useful when discussing issues that participants may not have given much thought to before, such as sustainable leisure and tourism. Comments from one participant can prompt others to have ideas that would not have occurred to them outside the group context. Focus groups may also be useful when information that is new to participants is presented.

Selection and Recruitment of Participants

14 focus groups were carried out, six on leisure and eight on tourism, with 108 participants in total. The location and composition

of the groups were planned to ensure that a wide range of views and experiences would be heard. Participants who had not taken a day trip/ holiday recently, had not flown recently for environmental reasons, or had no interest in the environment (Defra's 'disinterested segment' as defined in Annex A) were not recruited. There were in fact many participants in the sample with very little interest in the environment (but they were classified as 'long term restricted' or 'basic contributors' according to Defra's as defined in Annex A). It was felt that communication and behaviour change strategies would be more effectively focused elsewhere in the immediate future: the needs of these other parties will be clarified in ongoing Defra research. Participants were recruited by a professional recruiter working to a quota set by the research team.

The groups were held in the north, south east and south west of England; rural, urban and suburban areas (leisure groups); and areas differing in the size and proximity of airports (tourism groups). There were separate groups for high and low income households, using housing tenure as a rough proxy for income. All groups included men and women, a range of ages (except one group composed of 16 to 21 year olds), participants with different levels of activity and views about environmental issues (except one group composed entirely of 'green activists' as defined in Annex A), different day trip or holiday frequencies, and different recent holiday destinations (tourism groups). Although still within the recruitment target, overall in the leisure focus groups there were considerably more women than men and almost half of participants had made 11 or more outings in the last year.

Procedure and Material

In the focus groups, participants were asked about the following issues:

- day trips/holidays they had taken recently and would like or dislike to take,
- perceived impacts of leisure/tourism, particularly environmental impacts,
- willingness to change leisure/tourism in line with Defra's behaviour goals,
- responsibility for reducing the environmental impacts of leisure/ tourism,

- requests for government and industry,
- level of activity and concern in relation to environmental issues in general.

The moderators directed the discussion so it broadly followed the order of issues shown above. Participants were encouraged to talk freely around the issues, rather than being asked a series of preset closed questions.

A set of photographs showing various destinations and activities were presented to the participants. In the tourism focus groups the photos were of the following: Australia wine tasting, Caribbean cruise, Cornwall beach holiday, Edinburgh city break, Euro Disney, France skiing, Greece beach holiday, Nepal trekking, New York city break, Paris city break, Scotland golf, and Thailand beach holiday. In the leisure focus groups, the photos were of the following: bird watching, Blackpool, country house, farmers market, football match, Glastonbury, Lord Mayors Parade, museum/art gallery, picnic in park, shopping centre, walking in countryside.

Participants were asked to sort them into groups, first by desirability and later by environmental impact, and then to explain their thinking. The card sort helped to stimulate discussion about environmental impacts.

To see if information changed participants' views, they were told about the impact of travel to different destinations by different modes of transport towards the end of the focus groups. The information was presented in terms of tonnes of CO_2 emitted from the journey and in terms of light bulb weeks i.e. how long a 100W light bulb would have to be left on to emit the same amount of CO_2 as the journey.

Data Analysis and Reporting

2.14 The focus groups were digitally recorded and transcribed verbatim. Information from the transcripts was systematically sorted and recorded in thematic matrices. The matrices were examined to identify key issues; find explanations for particular views; note where differences or consensus existed among participants; and suggest how differences may relate to the characteristics of participants.

Environmental Issues in Leisure and Tourism Choices

On the whole, participants did not think about the environment when making leisure and tourism choices. There were five main reasons.

(1) Leisure and tourism were not seen as environmental behaviours. These behaviours were mainly concerned with fulfilling participants' own needs or their family's needs.

(2) Participants focused on the tangible environmental impacts of leisure and tourism, such as litter and pollution. Other environmental impacts were not widely mentioned and were generally not well understood. Participants mentioned several misconceptions, for instance.

- Small everyday actions to help the environment such as reusing carrier bags have a greater impact than making changes to leisure/tourism,
- Holiday activities have a greater impact than travel,
- Long haul flights are only marginally worse than short haul,

(3) Some participants were not concerned about the impacts, particularly the less tangible ones such as global warming.

(4) Some participants saw no point in changing their leisure or tourism behaviour unless other people or other countries reduced their environmental impacts too.

(5) Participants objected to making changes for the sake of the environment, feeling that.

- It impinged on their right to do whatever they wanted with their leisure or tourism. This entitlement to holidays and a lesser extent day trips was very strongly expressed and was thought to justify lack of attention to environmental impacts.
- It was something peculiar that only serious environmentalists would do.
- It would simply make their day trip or holiday less enjoyable.

Participants were more willing to change their everyday behaviour than leisure or tourism behaviour. They believed changing everyday behaviours was more effective for addressing environmental issues and a smaller sacrifice.

Introduction

In the focus groups participants discussed the impacts of leisure and tourism and sorted photographs of leisure and tourism destinations and activities according to their environmental impact. They described what they did in their day to day lives to help the environment and how concerned they were generally about environmental issues. They talked about their willingness to change their leisure and tourism behaviour for the sake of the environment and explained their feelings about this issue.

Taking the Environment into Account

There was widespread agreement among participants that they did not think about the environment when making leisure and tourism choices. For instance, the occasional participant had opted for rail instead of air travel to their holiday destination, had decided to take more UK holidays, or had made a point of contributing to the local economy while on holiday. This chapter sets out the reasons why such choices were far from mainstream.

It is important to note that members of the public who had not flown recently for environmental reasons were not included in the focus groups. By definition, this group of consumers do pay attention to the environment when making tourism choices.

Viewing Leisure and Tourism as Environmental Behaviours

On the whole, the environmental impacts of leisure and tourism simply did not cross participants' minds. Participants generally did not frame these behaviours as environmental behaviours, alongside recycling and turning off lights and electrical equipment. However, participants recognised a few environmental behaviours from everyday life, such as re-using carrier bags and cutting down on car use, that crossed over into leisure and tourism.

Instead participants saw leisure and tourism as mainly concerned with fulfilling their own needs or their family's needs. The wider impacts were simply not relevant. Not only did participants disregard the environmental impacts, but they also paid little heed to the economic and social impacts. Even participants who thought the consequences could be seriously detrimental (*"like a tsunami"*, *"dire"*), gave little attention to them.

"You don't think about that when you're getting ready to go out. It's about what fun you're going to have. that's the main factor." (Woman, under 30, basic contributor, Leeds, leisure focus group)

"You just take it for granted. You want to see this or you want to go there. You don't really think about the country. the economy. the environment at all. You just get on the plane. buy what you want to buy. take the kids wherever. You don't

really think about what it is actually doing." (Woman, 30-60, green activist, Watford, tourism focus group)

Participants did, however, think of the impacts when it was possible they could affect their leisure or tourism experience. For instance, a woman said she would not want to go somewhere that was full of coach parties:

"You're not bothered that the coaches are polluting the air [but] you're bothered about the loads of people that are going to do your head in while you're there." (Woman, under 30, basic contributor, Manchester, tourism focus group). When made to think about the impacts of leisure and tourism in the focus groups, some participants commented that they would never travel anywhere if they ordinarily thought about them (*"if you did you wouldn't go on holiday – you wouldn't leave your house"*). In fact, even after discussing the issues these participants were prepared to make only limited changes to their behaviour for the sake of the environment. However, their comments seem to demonstrate the discomfort felt when facing the consequences of their leisure and tourism decisions (*"It might take some pleasure out of it, put a damper on it maybe."*).

Understanding of Sustainable Leisure and Tourism

Participants were asked to describe the impacts of leisure and tourism and to compare the size of impacts from different sources. The photographs used in the card sort provided examples to stimulate discussion. The discussion therefore focused on these examples (for instance Euro Disney and Blackpool) but also covered related activities (such as other theme parks).

There was a great deal of uncertainty among participants when discussing these issues. Even the knowledgeable participants, who knew what some of the impacts were, had trouble when it came to assessing their relative impact.

Towards the end of the focus group, participants were given information about the relative size of environmental impacts associated with different leisure and tourism behaviours. The purpose of this was to see whether participants would change their behaviour in the light of changes to their understanding.

What are the perceived environmental impacts of leisure and tourism?

While the environmental impacts of leisure and tourism were not at the front of participants' minds, with prompting they were able to suggest a number of issues. Some environmentally aware participants thought of impacts more readily and suggested a wider range. Overall, social and economic impacts tended to come to mind before environmental impacts

The core environmental impacts of leisure that were mentioned repeatedly were litter, congestion and air pollution. Other environmental impacts were not as widely mentioned. These included the negative impacts on:

- noise pollution e.g. from traffic and crowds at football matches,
- waste associated with packaging and plastic bags from shopping,
- water resources e.g. visitors adding extra strain during times of water shortage,
- biodiversity e.g. walkers digging up bluebells,
- landscape e.g. erosion from too many walkers or from mountain bikes,
- energy/fossil fuel supplies e.g. due to the amount of energy used to light up in shopping centres,
- global warming e.g. theme parks contributing to the problem.

For tourism, mention was made of a similar range of issues. Participants focused particularly on litter and air pollution. They also discussed the negative impacts on:

- traffic,
- water pollution and water resources e.g. with new building increasing the risk of floods and tourists adding to the problem of water shortages in Australia,
- biodiversity e.g. coral reefs being damaged in Egypt, deforestation in Nepal, and airport expansion destroying habitats in the UK,
- landscape e.g. loss of farmland to make space for hotels and leisure facilities, and coastal areas becoming built up and unattractive,
- energy/fossil fuel supplies for instance with energy being *"wasted"* for instance to run resorts and theme parks,
- global warming.

There was some disagreement whether littering had increased or decreased recently. Participants who believed it had decreased put this down to a number of factors ranging from more bins to stronger social norms on the issue. It was also suggested that less litter resulted in a virtuous cycle.

How are leisure and tourism perceived to impact on global warming?

The focus groups were peppered with the language of environmental issues, particularly references to *"global warming"* and *"emissions"*. Understanding of the concepts varied a great deal across the sample but on the whole they were poorly or superficially understood.

Participants knew what global warming was. Some participants understood that it was affected by, for instance, using electricity to light up theme parks or fuel to drive there. However, other participants had little understanding of the mechanism linking global warming to leisure, tourism and human activity in general. They sometimes muddled it up with other environmental issues that they had heard of. For instance, when asked to say what she meant by global warming, a young woman in Brighton explained: *"Well I don't really know. Just the effects of our everyday lives in terms of pollution. How everything we do [like] recycling affects the planet. Obviously that's why we've got blistering hot days and tomorrow it could be snowing for all we know. It just affects the ozone layer and all that sort of thing."* (Woman, 16-21, basic contributor, Brighton, tourism focus group)

Participants generally did not understand the role of carbon dioxide. When they talked of emissions or even carbon emissions, they generally meant dirty exhaust fumes (*"toxic fumes"*, *"If a train is electric then it won't give out any emissions, surely?"*). This confusion seemed to be due, at least partly, to thinking that carbon emissions were the same as emissions tested in MOTs (*"we have to be tested for emissions on our taxis"*).

However, there were participants with a clear understanding of global warming. For instance:

"The greenhouse gas is carbon dioxide which is a product of any fuel that is burnt and that causes the greenhouse effect. All fuel that we use, aeroplanes, cars, trains, you use up energy and you burn the fuel and you produce greenhouse gases." (Man, 30-60, consumer with conscience, Watford, tourism focus group)

How do the perceived impacts of leisure/tourism and everyday activities compare?

There was an widely held belief that small everyday environmental actions had a greater impact than changing leisure or tourism behaviour, mainly because they were done more often (*"a little difference everyday from everyone, will make a huge difference"*). This view was even held by more knowledgeable participants (in consumer with conscience and green activist environmental segments). For instance, a frequent flyer who made the most of living close to Bournemouth airport believed that reusing carrier bags, changing to low energy light bulbs, and insulating his home were more important for the environment than changing his holiday behaviour. Although this consumer with conscience had a sophisticated understanding of environmental issues he had little feel for the relative impacts of everyday and tourism behaviour.

Some participants concluded that there was no need to make environmentally aware leisure and tourism choices if they carried out other environmental actions instead. They felt that by recycling, for instance, they earned the right to fly (*"at least I [recycled] those two bottles so I won't feel as bad when I get on the plane"*). There were, however, participants who expressed doubts or realised they would have to do a great deal to outweigh the effect of their holidays.

How do the perceived impacts of travel and activity compare?

In the tourism focus groups, there were mixed views about which component of holidays, travel or activity, was more important in determining environmental impact. When asked to rate a number of holidays according to their environmental impact, no one approach was dominant. One set of participants considered both travel and activity. Another set focused on travel, for instance sorting holidays by whether they can be reached without flying. The final set focused on activity. For instance, one participant suggested that the city breaks in Edinburgh, Paris and New York were more problematic than the beach holidays in Cornwall, Greece or Thailand.

Even participants with an in-depth knowledge of environmental issues (in green activist, currently constrained and consumer with conscience segments) made this mistake. For instance, a green activist with a longstanding interest in environmental issues was able to reel off a lengthy list of potential impacts from tourism. However, when sorting holidays by environmental impact, he did not think about travel at all and only sorted on the basis of activity. This demonstrates a disconnect between understanding the relative size of the environmental impacts from holiday travel and activity.

Participants were very aware of the air pollution, congestion and parking problems associated with driving to leisure activities. The environmental impact of the activities themselves, such as the electricity used for the Blackpool illuminations, was also seen as important. However, no attempt was made in the leisure focus groups to find out which component, travel or activity, participants believed had the greater impact.

How do the perceived impacts of different travel methods compare?

When asked to order travel methods according to their environmental impact, participants tended to think that trains were low impact. However, there were mixed views about the relative impacts of planes, cars, buses and boats. A number of factors influenced participants' thinking.

Cars were viewed negatively because, unlike the other modes of transport, each could only carry a few people. However, it was pointed out that trains and buses were often fairly empty (*"I get five in my car and there's many times you.*

Planes were generally thought to be fuel intensive. This was partly because of their size and partly because they would need a lot of fuel *"to get off the ground and to actually get in the air."* However, it was suggested that once in the air they did not use much fuel. On the plus side planes produced pollution at some distance (*"aeroplanes are right up there [so] by the time it gets down to us it's pretty diluted"*). This was generally of less concern than street-level pollution from cars and buses, although not always (*"[planes] put ozone in the atmosphere at the wrong level"*). Therefore proximity to pollution was important: the more distant, the less the concern.

Boats Like planes, boats were said to use a lot of fuel because they were large. There was concern about the pollution they created at sea, with participants generally believing that cruise ships emptying waste into the water.

Buses There were complaints about bus fumes. Some participants believed that diesel was very polluting or that controls on pollution from buses were lax compared to controls on cars.

Trains In contrast, trains were seen as less polluting than the other forms of transport because they relied on electricity and did not emit visible pollution (*"If a train goes down the track you don't really see anything coming out of it so you just assume there is nothing wrong with it."*). However, participants with a more sophisticated understanding of environmental issues pointed out that there was pollution associated with producing electricity:

"If it's an electric train, doesn't it depend on how the electricity is produced? If it's coal-fired electricity, it's very damaging. If it's nuclear, zero carbon content." (Man, 30 to 60, consumer with conscience, Bournemouth, tourism focus group)

There was growing awareness that planes have a large impact on the environment. Participants mentioned that they had a high media profile recently (*"the media are speaking about planes, planes, planes"*) and explained that they had therefore only just become aware of the issue.

However, even some participants who realised that planes were problematic were surprised by just how large the impacts of flying were. When given information about carbon emissions associated with flying to Paris and Australia, they described them as *"shocking"* and *"frightening"*.

Conversely some participants responded with surprise to the comparisons between cars and planes, expecting that the impacts from planes would be much greater. They found it strange that flying could emit less CO_2 than the same journey with one person in a car. Similarly, some participants expressed surprise to find that travelling by train could emit more CO_2 than the same journey in a full car.

How do the perceived impacts of travelling to different destinations compare?

When rating holidays by environmental impact, there was some recognition that travelling to long haul destinations had a greater impact than staying closer to home. Some participants explained that this was because going abroad generally involved flying while others explained that the further they travelled, the greater the impact.

However, there was a misconception that long haul flights were not that much worse than short haul ones. For instance, a motor mechanic believed that flying to Thailand, rather than Paris, would use more fuel but not that much more because most was used in take off and landing (*"When a plane's up cruising up in the air, it doesn't actually burn too much fuel."*) Again this reinforces that participants do not have an understanding of the relative size of environmental impacts associated with different behaviours.

How do the perceived impacts of different activities compare?

When discussing the environmental impacts of different activities, participants focused mainly on energy use, litter and pollution. These were the common threads running through discussions about both tourism and leisure. Activities in busy settings involving crowds were seen as worse on all three fronts.

In the leisure activity card sort, there was general agreement that walking in the countryside, having a picnic in the park, and other outdoor activities such as bird watching, had a low environmental impact. Participants explained that these activities were quiet and natural (*"you don't plug anything in"*), were not usually done in crowds and did not need to involve cars or any transport.

In contrast, there was general agreement that visiting shopping centres and theme parks had a high environmental impact. Participants said that these activities were artificial, used a great deal of electricity, and involved large numbers of people and cars, with the associated litter, congestion and fumes. Shopping also generated plastic bags that would be at best reused or at worst thrown away while football and Glastonbury created noise pollution as well as the other impacts resulting from crowds.

Participants acknowledged that the impact of activities depended on how considerately they were carried out. For instance, if litter was left after a picnic or if large numbers of people walked in one area these activities would be high impact; if plastic bags from shopping were recycled this activity would be lower impact.

Some participants looked at the issue from unusual angles. For instance, it was suggested that:

- Going to watch football is not all that different from being at home (*"maybe have a hamburger, hot-dog and a drink, which you'd be doing anyway"*).
- Leisure activities in places built for that purpose, such as museums, galleries and country houses, would have a lower impact because the infrastructure is there to make sure that there is minimal damage.

In the card sort of tourist activities, participants fairly consistently picked Euro Disney, city breaks, and cruises as high impact. For the first two, they talked about the amount of electricity used, the pollution produced, and the rubbish left by crowds of people. When thinking about the cruise, they worried particularly about sewage and other waste going into the ocean.

As with leisure, consideration was given to whether places were created specially for tourism. On the one hand it was argued that if something had to be built, such as resorts or ski slopes, this caused a negative impact on wildlife and the wider environment. On the other hand, it was said that less damage was caused by visiting places that were geared up for tourism, than those that were not. In a similar vein, it was suggested that one more person going to a city or to Euro Disney would not make much difference. The negative impacts of golf courses were rarely commented on, perhaps because they were the ones that participants were less aware of i.e. on biodiversity and water. Going trekking or sitting on a beach tended to be seen as harmless activities. However, echoing comments in the leisure focus groups, these activities could have a greater impact if done by large numbers of people or if done thoughtlessly, with litter left behind.

Concern About Environmental Impacts

Global Warming

There was a difference of opinion about whether global warming was a cause for concern. Participants fell into three sets.

- The first set was concerned. They were already seeing changes that they thought were due to global warming. However, they tended to fear for their children or grandchildren, rather than worrying for themselves:
  "They say by 2020 or something it's just going to be horrendously hot. My kids are only 4 and 2. It's definitely going to have an impact on them." (Woman, 30 to 60, currently constrained, Chipping Sodbury, leisure focus group).
- The second set was not concerned. They argued that any global warming happening at the moment would not have a significant impact in their lifetime; was part of a natural cycle (*"we've had severe weather like this before, it's nothing new"*, *"there were times when we've had vines over England growing in open areas"*); or would result in changes for the better (*"me being selfish, I like the nice warm weather"*).
- The last set simply felt confused. They explained that they had received mixed messages (*"we're bombarded with so much information and a lot of it is conflicting"*) and did not feel sufficiently expert to know what to believe.

The three sets were not completely clear cut and there were participants who fell in between, such as a woman who believed that global warming was partly natural but that human activity was accelerating it; and another who thought it was happening but was not as bad as people were being told. Level of concern did not seem to be related to any particular personal characteristics. While older participants were concerned for future generations, there seemed to be no greater sense of urgency among young people themselves. For instance, a 21 year old explained *"it's not really your responsibility because you'll never be here to witness it."*

Some participants mentioned the effect of global warming on tourism, pointing out that there would be less snow at ski resorts and that some holiday destinations might become uncomfortably hot in the future. It was suggested that if consumers understood that their tourism behaviour now could lead to fewer holiday opportunities in the future, they would be more concerned. This seems highly plausible, given that participants paid more attention to the impacts of leisure and tourism when it affected their experience.

Other Impacts

Participants who were not concerned about global warming were sometimes concerned about other environmental impacts of leisure and tourism, particularly more tangible ones. For instance, a man in Leeds doubted whether global warming was a problem but worried about the air pollution produced by traffic.

Value of Making Sustainable Leisure and Tourism Choices

Some participants felt it was not worth their while to try to reduce the environmental impacts of their leisure or tourism. This seemed to be a greater issue for tourism than leisure. Two reasons were given. The main reason was that participants felt strongly there was no point in individuals taking action if other people or other countries continued to behave inconsiderately. These views were expressed across a range of environmental segments, mainly by participants with some interest in environmental issues (wastage focused, consumer with conscience, currently constrained) but not by green activists.

"[If] there's other people going to Australia, it just makes you think why am I holding myself back?" (Man, under 30, currently constrained, Bournemouth, tourism focus group).

"What I can do is just a drop in the ocean. If the Chinese are opening the equivalent of one coal-fired power station every week, what chance have I got?" (Man, 30-60, consumer with conscience, Manchester, tourism focus group). It was also said that it was simply too late to take action because damage to the environment had gone too far to be reversed, although this was an unusual view:

"You probably won't be able to ski in the French Alps in 25 years time because there probably won't be any snow there... I would say the way we are living now you should do as much as you can while you still can." (Man, under 30, consumer with conscience, Manchester, tourism focus group). In several focus groups, there was heated debate about whether individuals should take action, even if others did not. Some participants believed in principle that it was important to *"do their bit"* irrespective although they were more willing to follow this principle for everyday environmental behaviours than for leisure and tourism, as discussed below.

Acceptability of Making Sustainable Leisure and Tourism Choices

Participants had three objections to changing their leisure or tourism behaviour for the sake of the environment.

Firstly, it was argued that people should be able to do whatever they want with their leisure and tourism, without having to consider the environment. There was a very strong sense of entitlement to holidays and to a lesser extent days out. They were seen as a necessity (*"it keeps me sane"*) or something earned through hard work (*"a holiday is something you live for, work towards", "I've worked hard for 40 years and I want to play hard and I don't want any restrictions"*). Participants therefore felt that their lack of attention to environmental impacts was justified. Even a young woman who recognised that pollution was a problem explained:

> *"[It] might sound really selfish [but] I work the rest of the year so I have to go away and it's costing me money so I'm going to have a good time. I'm not going to think 'I'm not going to go there because of pollution or because of this or because of that'... I'm just going away and that's it." (Woman, under 30, basic contributor, Manchester, tourism focus group).*

Secondly, pro-environmental leisure and tourism choices were sometimes seen as less appealing or even a sacrifice (*"they can't expect everybody to give up everything"*). The motivations underlying leisure and tourism choices were personal benefits while helping the environment was not seen to have immediate personal benefits, besides guilt alleviation, hence the sense of sacrifice. Participants were much more willing to make changes to their everyday lives which would not feel like a *"massive sacrifice"* or *"too much hardship"* and in fact might not *"do a thing to alter your way of life at all"*.

However, making sustainable choices was generally not felt to be a sacrifice by those who adopted these behaviours. On the whole, participants gave positive reasons for their choices, for instance enjoying holidays in England. Those who made these choices with the environment in mind tended to see them as double wins. Finally, for some participants, making leisure or tourism choices with the environment in mind was not seen as something people like them would do. Some participants viewed it as peculiar. For instance, an older man was happy to recycle and turn off lights and appliances but did not do much else for the environment. He called people who would go so far as to change their leisure for the sake of the environment *"sad"* and explained that this was not something *"the ordinary man in the street"* would worry about. Other participants saw it as worthy. They said that not considering the environment made them feel *"guilty"* or *"selfish"* but it was still not normative for them to do so, as the quote below illustrates. However, some participants really felt that they should be taking the issues seriously in their leisure/tourism choices.

"You should be more aware, you should be more conscious of it... We don't think enough about the environment, definitely not, but we all want to do what everyone else is doing, visiting all these places." (Woman, 30 to 60, wastage focused, Bournemouth, tourism focus group).

Everyday Compared to Leisure and Tourism Behaviours

As discussed, participants generally believed that everyday actions to help the environment, such as reusing carrier bags, were less of a sacrifice and more effective than changes to their leisure or tourism behaviour. They gave several further reasons for preferring everyday pro-environmental actions:

- They knew they were supposed to recycle, turn off lights etc. at home. This reinforces the point made earlier that leisure and tourism are not yet framed as environmental behaviours.
- They were paying for energy used at home and therefore had an incentive to not waste it. This was not the case on holiday.

- They felt more in control when carrying out pro-environmental activities at home. For instance, recycling bins in public places could be knocked over or left uncollected so their effort would be wasted.
- Everyday pro-environmental actions would become a habit and people would then do them everywhere, including on holiday. Some participants did indeed carry their everyday pro-environmental actions into their holidays or leisure, in particular waste reduction and recycling. However, other participants admitted to being careful with energy at home but not on holiday as they were not paying for it.

Social Construction of the Tourist Experience

Although the atmosphere of a tourist destination as part of the travel experience strongly influences visitors' satisfaction with their trip, their behaviour during their stay and their willingness to return, it is a relatively under-researched topic in tourism studies, and the atmospheric characteristics of places rarely provide the basis for destination marketing (a notable exception is the "Australia– a different light" marketing campaign which, however, has been subject of serious criticism on behalf of local tourism professionals).

The notion of the tourist milieu is defined as "the objective manifestation of the experience components of the tourism space, i.e. the result of the gradual process in which individual visitors' psychological perceptions become part of collective knowledge". Consequently, the tourist milieu is based on a consensus of perceptions, i.e. on an almost homogeneous factual reflection of visitors' impressions and sentiments, and, in this respect, it shows significant similarities with stereotypes.

The Characteristics of the Tourist Milieu

Although the tourist milieu is shaped by a specific interpretation of perceptions and, as such, its existence depends on tourist demand, the emergence of the milieu itself is based on the supply-side components of a destination. Within the system of tourism, the tourist milieu comprises of elements of the place product (i.e. it belongs to the supply side of the system), but its evolution is also strongly influenced by certain tangible and intangible components of the tourism system's wider environment.

While the tourist milieu may become an attraction by itself, generally only returning visitors and experienced travellers may be incited to choose a particular destination by the area's milieu elements. On the one hand, the development of the subjective milieu requires direct personal experiences on behalf of the perceiver, and on the other hand, first-time visitors to a destination are usually attracted by the area's landmark sights and major events. It must be noted however that it is not necessary for the traveller to return to the very same destination: it is one of the key assumptions of the milieu concept that various destinations may represent the same milieu due to shared characteristics, thus favourable experiences gained in one destination may lead to demand generation in other places characterized by the same tourist milieu. Due to its complexity, the tourist milieu of a particular destination is hard to define and even harder to communicate; consequently, in most marketing messages it is only represented as the background to a few selected sites. However, the authors believe that an area's milieu plays an equally – if not more – important role in affecting travellers' satisfaction and willingness to return as the major tourist sights; visiting key attractions only occupies a certain amount of time during a trip, while the destination's milieu surrounds the visitors throughout their whole stay.

While being a component of the tourism system's supply side, the tourist milieu also incorporates certain elements of the social, economic, political, technological and natural environments of the system. Although any of these environmental components may prove to be decisive in creating the tourist milieu, it is the social environment and its physical representation, the cultural landscape that have the most intensive role in shaping the milieu. A further assumption of the milieu concept is that the milieu of the same area is perceived differently by tourists with different cultural background; i.e. different aspects are perceived and different details are noticed. The closer the tourist's sociocultural background and the milieu of their place of origin to the destination's milieu, the more meticulous observations are made, while in the case of greater cultural distance, the visitor is more likely to discern the significantly different, thus more easily distinguishable components of the visited destination's milieu.

The de-differentiation of the tourist experience suggested by e.g. Lash and Urry (1994) and Uriely (2005) also highlights the importance of the tourist milieu. While the development of mass media as well as the potential development of virtual reality may replace travel as a means to 'see the world', and for many tourists, visiting the Louvre may soon be substituted by looking at the museum's collection on television or on the internet, the complex audiovisual and sensual stimuli of the milieu cannot be reproduced yet by artificial or virtual reality. Even the probably most publicised, most professional and – in commercial terms – most successful attempt to recreate a place's milieu, the construction of The Venetian in Las Vegas failed to replace the real Venice, and this failure can mainly be attributed to the artificial, sterile milieu of the casino and hotel complex. The details are carefully replicated, the scale and the exterior of the buildings are thoroughly designed and executed, but the sense of history, the smells and sounds of the real Venice are missing. (Which is not to say that The Venetian project fell completely short: it created a new place product that exists parallel to the real Venice and it does have a distinctive milieu – dissimilar to historic Italian cities, but sharing distinct characteristics with other new, artificial, purpose-built attractions.). However, the question of the tourists' experiences arises again in this example: those who have first-hand experience of historic Italian cities may perceive The Venetian as a commercialised replica without the 'right' atmosphere. Those, on the other hand, who have only seen the real Venice on photos and films, may enjoy the combination of visual authenticity and shopping mall-cleanliness in the case of The Venetian, and a subsequent visit to the real Venice may even prove to be a disappointing experience, due to the difference between expectations and reality. The sociocultural characteristics of the local community are embedded in a given destination's milieu; therefore, its typical features will be reflected in tourists' experiences. Obviously, the perception of the milieu also strongly depends on the guest's personality. Similarly to the individual nature of travel behaviour, spatial experiences are also influenced by the socioeconomic and sociocultural characteristics of the visitor.

The extent to which tourists engage in communication with the local population, their familiarity with the place, the intensity of their participation in the activities offered by the destination, and their sociocultural attitudes all influence their experience of the social components of the tourist milieu. The diverse milieu interpretations of tourists of different cultural backgrounds will in turn influence the milieu itself: consequently, highlighting target market-specific milieu elements in marketing communication may alter in the long term the actual tourist milieu of the destination.

The Structure and Components of the Tourist Milieu

The tourist milieu may be understood as a meta-level of the destination as a tourist product: "it contains the abstract components of tangible reality, and while each milieu element may be perceived individually during the routine consumption of the site, it is the elusive totality of all the elements that is able to create a feeling of attraction in visitors". The kaleidoscopic structure of the tourist milieu – it comprises of the destination's physical environment and heritage values, the tangible and intangible elements of the tourism supply as well as the site's human characteristics such as behaviour of locals and fellow travellers, expressions of religion or the tourist-host relationship. One of the main assumptions of this study is that the tourist milieu is generally not limited to a single destination: due to comparable geographic location or cultural background, larger regions frequently embody similar milieu elements. Consequently, while certain settlements may provide an absolutely unique milieu, resemblances are often experienced within regions including several countries. The findings of an empirical survey of the social construction of the Mediterranean tourist milieu in Hungary justified the existence of a shared tourist milieu in the study area, although visitors' associations with the region included both well-known tourist attractions and typical milieu elements such as colours, ambiance, landscape, and the visual and behavioural components of local life.

The analysis of the survey results also suggested that the personal construction of a destination's milieu does not depend on visitors' deeper cultural and historical awareness – as opposed to the sense of place of a destination which requires a certain level of familiarity with the history of the area. However, the perception of the tourist milieu necessitates the existence of certain physical components including both natural and man-made landscape elements, since it is based on actual observation and participation of the destination environment.

According to the survey results, the most distinctive components of the Mediterranean tourist milieu with the highest level of social consensus proved to be the weather conditions, the flows of tourists, the bustling crowds, the multitude of restaurants and cafes, the sight of historic buildings and that of people sitting on terraces. The results of a factor analysis indicated that the Mediterranean milieu was essentially organised along five dimensions which influenced respondents' perceptions to a different extent: visitors' experiences were most affected by everyday life in public areas, by the built historic heritage and by the natural features of the destinations, while the physical reflection of material welfare and the neglected environment proved to be less influential in shaping their milieu concept. The role of the tourist milieu in the social construction of the tourist experience The tourist experience is a combination of perceptions, emotions, reactions, moods, level of satisfaction and memories created by visiting a certain destination. It is a complex phenomenon – various people embark on journeys for different reasons and return with different experiences. These dissimilarities are significantly influenced by the travellers' motivations to visit a certain place, their previous expectations, their sociocultural background, their psychological needs, and by the destination's perceived characteristics.

It shall also be noted that the tourist experience is affected by a multitude of external and internal factors before, during and after the actual visit. Visitors' advance expectations of their travel experience are mainly influenced by their subjective image of the destination, non-commercial and objective information that they collect before the trip, and the promotional efforts of the tourism sector. The on-site visitor experience is mainly affected by the tangible elements and the service delivery elements of the tourist product (particularly visitor attractions, accommodation, F&B services and transportation), the milieu of the destination, and the social interactions between the visitor and the representatives of the tourism industry, local inhabitants and fellow travellers. Experiences are situated in specific space and time that are socially and culturally interpreted. Depending on the sociocultural distance between the visitors' and the destination's culture, their previous travel experiences, motivations and interest, different people will pay attention to different details of the tourist product and the destination milieu, even if they participate in the same activities and seem to have the same experience. Thus the basic characteristics of the human attention significantly influence the individual perceptions of the tourist milieu, and the attention structure framework of understanding tourist experiences suggested by Ooi (2005) may prove to be a useful theoretical approach for the further analysis of the milieu's social construction. Following the trip, the actual experience will be gradually modified by the selective memory of the traveller, and it generally becomes an incomplete narrative based on and limited by photographs and memorable stories. The milieu of a destination plays an important role in the post-trip recollection process of the tourist experience. Although it is a relatively difficult concept to convey to those who have never visited the destination or at least a similar area, emotions are generally easier to remember than facts, and sharing the same milieu experience creates a sense of familiarity among travellers, so it contributes to the efficient communication of the travel experience.

Due to the intangible nature of the tourist product, the image of a destination plays a particularly important role in influencing tourists' choices and their satisfaction, since they are motivated to act by perceptions rather than reality. The significance of the destination image – a relatively well-represented notion in tourism – in affecting the tourist experience, demands further analysis of the similarities and differences of the concepts of destination image and tourist milieu. The destination image is a mental construct of ideas and conceptions held individually or collectively; it is comprised of cognitive, affective and conative components. Although both the image and the milieu of a destination are dependent on visitors' subjective perceptions, image formation is possible on the basis of preconceptions, while the milieu corresponds to the interiorization of personal impressions and first-hand experiences. Potential tourists frequently create mental images of destinations in spite of their limited pre-visit knowledge. In contrast, the tourist milieu develops as a result of the visitor's sensual experiences of the destination's attributes, so it is predominantly based on actual observation and participation rather than on advance expectations produced by marketing communication and the general media. (It should be noted that although certain forms of communication, particularly films and novels, may also contribute to the prospective tourist's milieu perception, personal involvement and experiences are essential for the development of the milieu concept.)

Obviously, the perceived milieu of an area does not always conform to its image; travellers' images are generally modified after visiting a particular destination, and significant differences exist between first time and repeat visitors' image perceptions. It is the assumption of this study that the perceptible milieu elements – particularly those that are difficult or impossible to communicate by traditional promotional methods such as temperature, smells, sounds, general ambiance – play a significant role in the transformation of the visitors' preliminary images.

As we could see earlier in this paper, the tourist milieu is defined as the objective projection of the subjectively experienced tourist space. Consequently, the tourist milieu of a destination is based on an informative consensus that reflects the visitors' emotions and impressions.

The tourist milieu – represented in the kaleidoscopic model – is a complex sphere where the tourist experience takes place and which, at the same time, has an influence on the traveller's personality. This sphere – the phenomenal environment – includes both tangible and intangible components: objects and persons on the one hand, and sociocultural phenomena on the other. The phenomenal environment filtered through the sociocultural set of values of the individuals becomes the behavioural environment which forms the basis of the milieu. Individual values and factors include the visitor's personality, education, previous knowledge of the destination, image, and the traveller's attitudes and stereotypes, among others. Obviously, this is not a one-way process: while experiencing the behaviour environment as a network of interrelations, humans react individually or behave in a controlled way, which again influences the phenomenal environment. Sharing individual perceptions and attitudes through various commercial and non-commercial communication channels, e.g. personal discussions, photographs, films, literature or other mass media forms, contributes to the development of a certain level of social consensus concerning the tourist milieu of a destination. The projection of the generally accepted milieu concept affects, in turn, the expectations of future travellers, and, due to the fact that visitors tend to reaffirm their perceptions and stereotypes when consuming a place product, it has a major impact on their satisfaction and experiences.

10

Retail Service Dynamics in a Rural Tourism

Introduction

Travel and tourism are well integrated into the consumption patterns of many people in the USA. Forecasts from the World Tourism Organization (2003) indicate tourism will continue to grow significantly into the foreseeable future. In the USA, tourism is one of the nation's largest employers, generating 7.3 million direct travel-related jobs (TIA, 2006). It is also the third largest retailing industry segment, with average spending of 1.7 million dollars a day by domestic and international travellers in the USA (TIA, 2006). Furthermore, tourists devote approximately one-third of their total expenditures to shopping. Thus, it is important to more fully understand the products, services, and overall shopping experiences preferred by tourism customers.

Within the past two decades, the effects of downsizing in manufacturing and agriculture have had lasting economic impacts on many rural communities. As a result, some rural areas have sought non-traditional paths toward sustainable economic activities. Tourism has emerged as a popular rural development strategy, due to associated entrepreneurship opportunities and its ability to bring in dollars, generate jobs, and support retail growth. Rural tourism can also aid transitioning rural communities by providing more diverse economic/development options.

Rationale and Significance

The demand for touristic utilization of rural areas has increased in recent years due to the inherent qualities that many rural settings possess. These qualities include: personalized attention and genuine interaction with the customer, enthusiasm for sharing local culture/ heritage, and overall authenticity of character. Such attributes may represent value added features that resonate well with an increasingly urban-based population. Retailers in rural tourism communities may thrive from the effectiveness and uniqueness of services they provide, yet many have not developed a strategic approach that fosters sustainability. If successfully implemented, service offerings may have significant impact on rural retailer competitiveness due to the visible nature of service interactions and the positive word of mouth created by satisfied customers.

Rural tourism retailers are ideally suited to offer customized service, as their small size can allow them to quickly change and adapt to meet local and tourist customers' expectations and capitalize on the experiences, attractions, and natural amenities present in the community. However, providing customized service that leads to ongoing relationships with local and tourist customers is not an easy task. Perry et al. (1986) state that understanding and exploiting the benefits of rural tourism communities while trying to maintain a traditional lifestyle is often difficult. To be sustainable over time, rural tourism retailers must be able to balance service efforts to meet the needs and expectations of diverse customer segments.

The current study acknowledges not only the important economic contributions of rural tourism, but also the critical role of service delivery and customer service segmentation that can enhance the success of rural tourism retailing. We specifically address local resident and tourism customers' expectations for retail service, their perceived post-service satisfaction (i.e. perceptions), and their projected shopping outcome behaviours based on perceived service quality. Implications and recommendations are discussed regarding service strategies that may enhance customer loyalty and rural community business sustainability.

Despite growth in rural tourism, a gap exists in the literature regarding the challenges and opportunities of operating a service/retail-related tourism business within rural markets. Many rural communities are in need of economic activities that are complementary to the changing nature of agriculture. Rural tourism retailing can provide opportunities for distinctive customer offerings and attractions such as interactive food and farm activities, authentic products created by local artisans, vineyards complete with wine tasting rooms, and events that build on local or regional natural amenities.

Additionally, a void in the tourism literature also exists in regard to rural tourism communities that service a dual market; where retailers must cater to both local customers and tourists. Moreover, in small rural tourism communities (such as that in the present study), it is rare to have separate retailers catering primarily to tourists and those focusing just on local customers. They must do both to survive. Therefore, more research is needed to understand the unique aspects of retail service quality in rural tourism settings and strategies to promote successful service delivery to both local customers and tourists.

The present paper provides foundational insight into the little understood process of retail service relationships and service quality in the rural tourism context. Findings will provide theoretical understanding of rural tourism service dynamics with implications for academics and practitioners.

Purpose

The overarching goal of this study was to examine and profile service quality expectations and perceptions for three focal groups in a rural tourism market setting in an established rural tourism community in Iowa: local customers, tourist customers, and retailers. This in depth case study focused on retail customer service as a value added component and potential success strategy for rural tourism retailers. We examined the meaning and importance of service quality as it related to each of the three market segments. Finally, we assessed the impact of perceived retail service quality for local customers and tourist customers on two dimensions of shopping behaviour: customer purchase intentions and retailer loyalty.

In this study local customers were defined as individuals who reside in the focal rural tourism community year-round as validated by residency, voter registration, and mailing address. A tourist customer is an individual who resides in this rural community for up to a week to three or more months at a time. They may own property in the area, or have rented the same property for consecutive years. Tourists are away from home on non-routine travel such as vacation or visiting family and friends. A retailer is any business that offers a product, service, or experience to customers. Examples of retailers within this rural tourism community included apparel and souvenir shops, restaurants, marinas, parasailing, golf courses, night clubs, collectibles and gift shops, pharmacies, etc.

In the Iowa context, tourism thrives not only because of the authenticity of the beautiful rural setting and the service/retailer offerings, but also because of the demand for outdoor recreational activities (i.e. biking, boating, fishing, golfing, swimming, skiing, camping, etc.) that the area provides to both locals and tourists. This unique backdrop makes it an ideal context to examine the specific expectations that are held for retail service by local and tourist customers, how their satisfaction or dissatisfaction with the service experience translates to purchase behaviour, and the potential impact of met retail service expectations on rural community business sustainability. The current study fills a void in the literature by providing a community based view of retailer service quality from the perspective of local and tourist customers. The following research questions were used to frame the study:

(1) Do local customers and tourist customers have differential views of service quality (i.e. expectations and perceptions) in rural tourism settings?

(2) Do service quality perceptions influence patronage behaviour and retailer loyalty?

Tourism-based retailers customarily supply goods and services that make tourists' visit to the area more enjoyable and memorable. However, for many rural tourism retailers, catering only to the tourist customer does not ensure business survival during the off-season. Therefore, many rural tourism retailers are increasingly seeking ways to enhance their service quality and build greater store loyalty by implementing customer relationship programs. Within the service sector (i.e. retail environment), research has suggested a number of important benefits for firms in regard to building relationships with customers. For example, Beatty et al. (1996) found that salespeople provided extra value to their customers by learning about their particular needs and catering to those needs. This "relationship customization" practice enable retailers to deliver unique customer service and value to customers, making their service delivery resistant to imitation and providing a baseline of true differentiation in an increasingly competitive retail marketplace. Research also indicates that fostering a close salesperson-customer relationship may help retailers position themselves to build satisfaction and loyalty around relational benefits rather than undifferentiated service strategies.

Relational retailing is a significant means by which to build and enhance customer loyalty.

However, in the context of small rural markets, retailer service is often provided informally, lacks a specific strategic focus, and is essentially a taken for granted relational process. If this is so, rural tourism retailers may be missing a key opportunity to attract and keep both loyal local customers and repeat visit tourists. This may be a particularly salient concept for small rural retailers given that researchers have found important crossover effects between loyalty to the salesperson and loyalty to the store. This finding may suggest important linkages between customer perceptions of rural tourism retailers and the community overall. Iacobucci and Ostrom (1996) further suggested that important differences exist between person-to-person and person-to-firm or organization relationships and that interpersonal loyalty is highly important to the formation of loyal customer relationships.

In rural tourism communities, retail service may have particularly important implications because different types of relationships may be expected and desirable for local customers and tourist customers. For example, tourist customers may be more focused on service quality and relationships at the firm or community level, whereas local customers may seek to form relationships of a more personal nature. Treatment received by small local stores are often viewed as extensions of the owner and perhaps even extended to the overall local business sector. It is important for retailers to keenly discern the unique nature of customer needs and refine their ability to differentiate and customize their service efforts. Thus, our research perspective for this paper suggests that the local and tourist customers' perceived satisfaction with service interactions and relationships may have significant and different impacts on individual patronage behaviour, store loyalty, and the sustainability of community retail businesses in the rural tourism setting.

Conceptual Background

Importance of Retailing in Rural Tourism Communities

The retail sector plays a critical role in the US marketplace, generating sales of $3.7 trillion in 2005 and accounting for 17 percent of total employment. Relative to metropolitan areas, retailers are even more important to small rural communities where they account for about 24 percent of the number of business establishments including stores, restaurants, and tourist destinations. Locally owned businesses are key drivers of local and regional economies, employing over 25 percent of the private sector. These businesses must implement marketing and service strategies within tight resource constraints; lack specialized marketing/management expertise; experience difficulty in purchasing this expertise; and operate under less aggressive objectives than large firms. The very small size of some firms means that they need to carefully and creatively leverage their capabilities and resources in order to survive in the highly competitive retail market. Businesses operating in tourism communities also have distinct competitive challenges in contrast to other rural settings. Retailers in rural tourism communities must overcome obstacles of remoteness and seasonality, while acknowledging the diverse needs of two distinct market segments: local customers and tourist customers. In order to sustain economic growth, rural retailers must provide a balance of products, services, and experiences that simultaneously caters to both groups. Finding the precise mix of retail services that are imperative to customers (local and tourist) and retailers is a formidable task. In Dalal et al.'s (1994) study regarding the loss of retail trade in small towns, they found convenience, location issues (parking, hours, nearness to other services), degree of hometown morale/support, and the attitudes of local merchants and retail clerks to be major reasons for customer out-shopping. Rural retailers must simultaneously address these issues to remain financially viable.

Bartlett and Peterson (1992) suggest that successful small businesses focus on and create unique niches for products, services, and experiences in the market. Similar recommendations have been made by researchers regarding small tourism based businesses. Little is known, however, about factors that drive the success of retail business ventures in rural tourism communities or the role of customer service quality in this process. Addressing retailing in rural tourism communities is critically important as retailers are not only major employers in the local market, but also places for primary social interactions. Much of the social interaction in retailing and tourism occurs through customer service delivery. This suggests that service relationships and the perceived quality of interactions may play an important role in retail sustainability in tourism areas that may in turn promote the vitality and resiliency of rural communities. Community resilience, the ability of a community to adapt to change, is reflected by a community's social and cultural diversity, economic diversity, social infrastructure, and amenity infrastructure. These aspects of resiliency point to the major role retail service relationships may play in promoting long-term sustainability of rural tourism businesses and communities. Despite the emphasis placed on customer service and relationship management in the literature for larger firms, little attention has been given neither to the importance of service quality for smaller businesses nor those operating in rural communities. This gap is important as the quality of business offerings (including a mix of products, services, and experiences) and the ability to consistently deliver them within the scope of available resources frequently jeopardizes rural business survival. Though limited in size and sometimes isolated, rural businesses offer great potential for economic development and support other ventures such as tourism. They are the cornerstone of local economies and dominate the local civic environment.

Success for small community businesses has social as well as economic impact on communities and geographic regions of the US Mark Drabenstott, Director for the Centre for the Study of Rural America, has identified five challenges that "will be critical in shaping the rural economic outlook: tapping digital technology, encouraging entrepreneurs, leveraging the new agriculture, improving human capital, and sustaining the rural environment. Clearly, rural tourism and related retail operations are essential to meeting these challenges in the years ahead.

Hypothesis Development

This study is framed by the services literature, specifically the expectations-perceptions-satisfaction paradigm and the SERVQUAL scale. Prior research suggests that customers' expectations frequently influence their perceived service quality. We define service expectations as the level of service that customers believe a tourism retailer should offer, whereas service perceptions are the customers' views of actual retail service performance.

Service quality is a combination of overall service expectations and perceptions resulting from a comparison between actual retail service performance and prior expectations for services. Good quality service typically leads to customer satisfaction, which in turn, has a positive impact on a customers' ongoing loyalty and purchase intentions. Our aim is to develop a conceptual framework for understanding retail service quality dynamics in rural tourism communities that has theoretical underpinnings from the service quality literature. We will then test a series of hypotheses based on the service quality literature within the rural tourism context.

Service Quality in Retail Settings

Service quality is conceptualized in this study using dimensions of the SERVQUAL scale. The SERVQUAL scale is the most prominent instrument used to measure customers' opinions of service quality expectations and perceptions regarding actual service received. Originally, the SERVQUAL scale was used in pure service settings, and included ten dimensions (tangibles, reliability, responsiveness, competence, courtesy, credibility, security, access, communication, and understanding the customer). The original SERVQUAL scale was later revised to ensure that there was no overlap of dimensions, and resulted in the five dimensions of responsiveness, assurance, empathy, tangibles, and reliability. Dabholkar et al. (1996) adapted the original SERVQUAL scale to the retail setting, and concluded that retailers could use this adapted scale as a diagnostic tool to improve their service delivery. To date, retail service has not been assessed in rural communities in the USA using the SERVQUAL scale. The present study therefore contributes to the literature by its application of the SERVQUAL scale in a rural tourism context.

Service Quality in Tourism Contexts

Kandampully (2000) emphasized the importance of quality in regard to tourism, stating that quality will be the major driving force of travel and tourism firms as they strive to meet the competitive challenges of the future. Few empirical studies within the realm of tourism have utilized the SERVQUAL approach. O'Neill et al. (2000) studied four tour operators in Australia using the SERVQUAL scale and found the "assurance" dimension to be the most important indicator of service performance. Juwaheer and Ross (2003) measured service quality in the hotel industry using a modified version of SERVQUAL, and found the dimensions of "assurance", "reliability", and "responsiveness" to be the most salient determinants of service quality. Atilgan et al. (2003) evaluated the difference in German and Russian tourists' expectations and perceptions of service quality in tour operations and found that various cultural groups can have differing expectations ,and perceptions of service quality. Additionally, in Jonsson Kvist and Klefsjö, 2006 study of British and Italian tourist customers in Sweden, they found that some of the service quality dimensions differed in importance between the two nationalities. Together, these studies highlight the fact that tourism experiences are unique and complex, and that the needs and expectations of tourism customers can be influenced by a number of factors, including time at which needs are assessed, cultural differences/ norms, and/or past experiences. In sum, customers' assessments of service quality may change according to customer values for service, level and type of service needs, the environment or culture in which the service occurs, and how the service delivery is perceived by the customer.

Although it has been extensively used, the SERVQUAL scale is not without criticism. Keating and Harrington (2002), Buttle (1996), and Teas (1993) questioned the validity of the SERVQUAL instrument; Ekinci et al. (1998) pointed out the difficulties in analyzing the differences between expectations and perceptions; Armstrong et al. (1997) illustrated the influence of cultural background on the measurement of service quality perceptions; Baker and Fesenmaier (1997) found the SERVQUAL approach to be inadequate within their multiple-stakeholder setting that included visitors, employees, and managers of theme parks; and Cronin and Taylor (1992) criticize its basic methodology and conceptualization.

Despite critiques of the SERVQUAL scale, the quality dimensions upon which the instrument is based are frequently employed when discussing and measuring service quality in a variety of service sectors, including tourism. Thus, use of the adapted SERVQUAL's quality dimensions in the present study facilitates comparison with other empirical findings and supports the need to continually modify and adapt the SERVQUAL scale according to context (i.e. retail setting, tourism setting, cultural background).

Retail Service Expectations and Satisfaction

Satisfaction is critical to repeat retail business, but is not the only factor that determines customer loyalty. Customers also need to feel a sense of commitment and involvement from the retailer regarding their purchases, and the products or brands they have selected. Commitment and involvement can only be conveyed to customers through the service interactions and relationship development efforts of retailers. The concept of service augmentation stresses adding value above and beyond what is expected by the customer. It may very well be a primary way for rural retailers to differentiate the products and services they offer compared to those of their competitors. Retailers in rural tourism communities may thrive on the effectiveness and uniqueness of services they provide. Service offerings can add uniqueness to a business, aid in developing a distinct competitive advantage, and increase store presence in rural communities.

In addition to service, price and product mix are other essential tools used to attract local and the tourism customers to the retail setting. Heung and Cheng (2000) found that tourists do not consider price a main determinant in formulation of their overall impressions of a retail shop. Tourism customers do, however, engage in a great deal of leisurely or "nonessential shopping". Retailers need to cater to the needs of tourism customers who are shopping leisurely, and concurrently meet their expected service needs. In order to achieve the objective of customer satisfaction, retailers must first know their target customer and understand how they choose and evaluate retail offerings. This is especially critical for retailers in rural tourism areas, because of the diversity in customer segments. If customers' expectations are exceeded, then their experiences are positively confirmed, leading to the following series of hypotheses regarding service expectations and perceived satisfaction in rural tourism-based markets:

- Customer expectations for pre-service quality will be different for local customers than for tourist customers in rural tourism contexts.
- Customer perceptions for post-service quality will be different for local customers than for tourist customers in rural tourism contexts.
- Expectations for pre-service quality will be greater for customers (local and tourist) than for retailers.
- Perceptions for post-service quality will be greater for customers (local and tourist) than for retailers.
- Tourism-based retailers will perceive service treatment as more important to the tourist customer than the local customer.

Outcomes of Tourism Retail Service Interactions

All customers expect a certain level of retail service. If their needs are not met, they quickly become dissatisfied, and take their business elsewhere. Rural tourism retailers rely upon repeat business to generate profit and meet their business objectives. Customers will likely continue to patronize a particular store when they feel their needs have been met. On the other hand, if a customer is dissatisfied, it may be largely due to a discrepancy between their expected and perceived levels of service.

In a focus group study regarding service quality and tourism, Augustyn and Ho (1998) found that as the tourism industry evolves and becomes more prominent, so do the expectations of tourism customers. Also related to service expectations, Le Boeuf (1987) explored reasons why customers stop shopping at a particular retailer. Of the participants, 68 percent stated that they became disloyal to a store due to retailer indifference toward the customer. These findings provide support for the second series of hypotheses: H2. Retail pre-service quality expectations will predict local customers', tourist customers', and retailers' post-service quality perceptions.

- Local customers' and tourist customers' satisfaction with their overall retail post-service quality perceptions will predict their purchase intentions.
- Local customers' and tourist customers' satisfaction with their overall retail post-service quality perceptions will predict their retailer loyalty.

Research Methods

Case Study Approach

A case study research strategy was employed for this study as it supported the logic of our research design, data collection, and data analysis. Yin (2003) states that a case study is an empirical inquiry that assists in the investigation of a phenomenon within its real-life context. Additionally, according to Kitay and Callus (1998), case studies deal with the complex relationships (i.e. multiple perspectives) within a unit as well as the interactions between the unit and its environment. Hence, using a case study research strategy enabled us to better understand: the complex relationships between local customers, tourist customers and retailers, in this rural tourism community; and the unique nature and richness of this specific tourism community in Iowa that has been an established rural tourism destination for over 100 years (IGLCC, 2003).

Survey Development and Measures

As a basis for instrument development relevant to rural tourism, interviews were first conducted with local Chamber of Commerce representatives in the selected well-established rural tourism community in northern Iowa. This insight, together with existing literature and tested measures for service expectations, service perceptions, and purchase intentions, formed the foundation for instrument development. The instrument contained seven parts:

(1) assessments of the tourism market environment;
(2) motivations to engage in retailing;
(3) enticements to shop;
(4) service quality expectations;
(5) service quality perceptions;
(6) shopping outcome behaviours; and
(7) demographics.

Also, to ensure that we captured accurate classification regarding the two customer groups (local and tourist), each survey included appropriate criterion variables. For example, at the top of local customer's survey, they were asked if they "rented" or "owned" residential property in the area, and how many months out of the year they resided in the community. The tourist customers were asked how long they planned to be in the area (with responses ranging from "1 week or less" to "three or more months". To assure reliable and valid measures, the survey was pre-tested with relevant groups of local rural customers, rural tourism customers, and tourism retailers. The instrument was subsequently refined and modified based upon results of the pretest. For the current study, we were primarily interested in respondents' responses to the following: service quality expectations and perceptions and service satisfaction outcomes (i.e. retailer loyalty and purchase intentions). For the service quality expectations and perceptions, we used a modified version of the SERVQUAL scale.

Respondent Characteristics

A total of 302 usable surveys were received out of the 375 distributed, for an overall response rate of 80.5 percent. Of the 125 participants approached in each respondent group, 100 were local customers (80.0 percent), 94 were tourist customers (75.2 percent) and 108 were retailers (86.4 percent).

For the local residents, 28 percent were between the ages of 18-44, 47 percent were between the ages of 45-64, and 25 percent were

65 or older. A total of 46 percent owned property in this area for 16 or more years. In contrast the tourists were slightly older with about 12 percent between the ages of 18-44, 46 percent and 32 percent were 65 or older. About 70 percent of the tourists owned property in the area; hence, the fact that so many tourists have a second/summer home in this area contributes to the uniqueness of this rural tourism community.

Of retail respondents, 45 percent were owners, 25 percent were managers, and 26 percent were both owner/managers. Overall, 41 percent of these retailers have owned a business in this community for less than five years; however, approximately 30 percent have owned a business in this community for 16 to 21 þ years.

Data Analysis

Data were analyzed with SPSS 14.0. Analysis included descriptive statistics, factor analysis, t-tests, and multiple regression analysis. A multi-step process of factor analysis was used to assess construct validity and dimensionality. Factor analysis, using a principal component method with Varimax rotation, was performed on multiple items of the five SERVQUAL scale dimensions: responsiveness, assurance, empathy, tangibles, and reliability. Parallel sets of 18 items addressing customer and retailer service expectations and resulting service perceptions were used in the analysis.

Factor Analysis

Principal components analysis with varimax rotation was initially conducted on both pre-service expectations (18 items) and post-service perceptions (18 items) for each group of respondents (local customers, tourist customers and retailers) in order to assess the degree of service gap (perceptions minus expectations). However, after finding minimal significant gap-score differences, it was decided to focus solely on post-service perceptions because they are better indicators of resulting service quality experiences and proved to be significant predictors of outcome variables (i.e. retailer loyalty and purchase intentions) during exploratory regression analyses. Results of the principal components analysis and reliabilities obtained are summarize. To assess resulting factor structures, eigenvalues greater than one served as the decision rule for retaining a resulting factor item. Factor loadings less than 0.30 are not generally considered substantial. Thus, only items with loadings of 0.30 or higher, and an eigenvalue of 1 were used to determine salient factors. Reliabilities were also computed for each factor (Cronbach alphas range from 0.82

to 0.98). Items were summed and averaged to create a factor score per dimension. Finally, each factor was matched to common service themes and given a new variable name relevant to the focus of this study.

Principal components analysis results revealed differentiation by respondent group for post-service perceptions. Local customer perceptions loaded on to two dimensions, compared with the original theoretical five dimensions proposed by Parasuraman et al. (1991). Based on the content and themes of these variables, we retained two names from the original SERVQUAL dimensions: (1) responsiveness (a ¼ 0.98, M ¼ 5.58); and (2) tangibles (a ¼ 0.85, M ¼ 7.01).

Total variance explained by local customers' responsiveness and tangibles dimensions was 77.71 percent (responsiveness ¼ 53.07 percent and tangibles ¼ 24.64 percent). The amount of variance captured by these two dimensions is an indication of how important retailers' willingness to efficiently help customers (i.e. responsiveness) and to attend to their store image and physical environment (i.e. tangibles) are to local customers.

Principal components analysis of tourist customers' post-service perceptions loaded onto only one dimension. Based on variable themes from the existing service quality.

literature, we chose to name the one dimension responsiveness (a ¼ 0.98, M ¼ 7.65). Total variance explained by tourist customers' responsiveness dimension was 72.59 percent. This suggests that rural retailers need to adjust their customer relationship management strategies to allow them to simultaneously cater to local and tourist customers. The fact that tourist customers' perceptions loaded into one singular dimension, and the local residents' and retailers' perceptions loaded into two almost identical dimensions, is noteworthy. These findings suggest that each customer segment (local and tourist) has a unique way of interpreting service quality. This observation is further supported by the fact that each group demonstrated differences in the indicators associated with each resulting satisfaction (i.e. post-service perceptions) dimension. These one and two-dimensional constructs were then used to test H2-H2b. Principal components analysis of retailers' post-service perceptions of customer service quality appeared to mirror those of the local customers. A common set of variables loaded highly on the same factors, with the exception of survey questions V3.10 (Quality of merchandise offered) and V3.11 (Overall effort of retailers towards customers). Since all but two factors loaded identically (i.e. V3.10: Quality of merchandise offered and V 3.11: Overall effort of retailers towards customers) between the local customers and the retailers, the dimension names of responsiveness (a ¼ 0.96, M ¼ 7.84) and tangibles (a ¼ 0.82, M ¼ 7.45) were again applicable. Retailers' responsiveness and tangibles dimensions explained 67.99 percent of the total variance (responsiveness ¼ 44.09 percent and tangibles ¼ 23.90 percent). Since these two variables explain about 68 percent of the variance for retailers and about 78 percent of the variance for local customers, this indicates that retailers' and local customers' perceptions of service quality follow a similar pattern. These findings also suggest that these two dimensions are identifiable customer relationship management strategy themes that rural tourism retailers could utilize to better accommodate local customers. In sum, local customers and retailers conceptually differentiated responsiveness (i.e. prompt service, willingness to help customers, etc.) from tangibles (i.e. convenient business hours, visually appealing store, etc.), which tourists did not. While retailers may have limited time to attend to tangibles during the tourism season, these should definitely be attended to in the off-season.

Results of Hypothesis Testing

In H1, customer expectations for pre-service quality in the rural tourism community were hypothesized to be different for local customers than for tourist customers. Support was not found for this hypothesis. In fact, results of an independent t-test indicate that local (M ¼ 7.67) and tourist (M ¼ 7.65) customers' expectations were identical (t ¼ 0.12; p ¼ 0.90), suggesting there is no difference between local customers' pre-service quality expectations and the tourist customers' pre-service quality expectations. H1a posited there would be a difference in post-service quality perceptions by length of residence (local versus tourist). Significant support was found for this hypothesis for local (M ¼ 5.59) and tourist (M ¼ 6.12) customers' post-service quality perceptions (t ¼ 22.67), implying that tourist customers have greater levels of perceived satisfaction (i.e. perceptions) post-purchase than do local customers. In sum, these finding suggest that the two customer groups (local and tourist) have similar expectations going into a retail purchase; however, local customers were much more disappointed after purchasing. This implies that length of time spent in the community (i.e. year round evident vs. temporary visiting tourist) does indeed impact resulting satisfaction with retailer service treatment regarding greater relationship development expectations and perceptions (i.e. post-purchase satisfaction).

Next, H1b and H1c were used to test if there were greater pre-service quality expectations (H1b) and post-service perceptions (H1c) for customers as a whole (local and tourist) than for retailers. Significant differences were found for H1b between customers (M ¼ 7.66) and for retailers (M ¼ 8.24), (t ¼ 5.69), suggesting that customers (local and tourist) have lower expectations going into the shopping experience than retailers anticipate. Support was also found for H1c for customers (M ¼ 5.85) and retailers (M ¼ 7.71), (t ¼ 12.20, p, 0.001), implying that customers perceive a considerable difference between the pre-service quality they expect from rural tourism retailers and the post-service quality they actually receive from these retailers. However, it appears that retailers are unaware of the severity of this pre/post-service quality difference.

For H1d, five questions on the retailer survey were used to evaluate if tourism retailers perceived service treatment as more important for tourist customers than local customers. A one-sample t-test of retailers' perceptions of the service treatment they deliver to local and tourist customers revealed significant results; however, evaluation of mean scores indicate only partial support. Mean scores reveal that retailers feel their business caters more to the local customer than the tourist customer (M ¼ 4.02); however, they believe that tourist customers are likely to spend more money in their store than local customers (M ¼ 3.31). Retailers also feel they deliver similar service treatment to both customer groups (M ¼ 1.71). This suggests that there is a substantial disconnect between the service quality the retailer believes they provide to the two customer groups (local and tourist) and the service quality customers believe they receive. For local customers and retailers, two perceived service quality dimensions (responsiveness and tangibles) that resulted from principle component factor analysis, were used in testing hypotheses H2-H2b. For the tourist customer, one service quality dimension (responsiveness) that resulted from principle component factor analysis was used to test hypotheses H2-H2b. A factor mean score was calculated by summing and averaging responses to items in each dimension. Mean scores were used in hypothesis tests of relationships between service quality perceptions, purchase intentions, and retailer loyalty.

In H2, we posited that customer pre-service expectations predicted customers' and retailers' resulting post-service perceptions. Support was found for each group (local customer: b ¼ 0.31, p, 0.00; tourist: b ¼ 0.21, p, 0.05; retailer: b ¼ 0.60, p, 0.00), indicating that expectations do play a role in predicting resulting service satisfaction for customers in rural tourism communities. To assess the importance of customer service quality dimensions of responsiveness and tangibles, and their affect on customers' service satisfaction, a series of hypotheses was tested related to outcome behaviours: purchase intentions (H2a), and retailer loyalty (H2b) (. Support was not found for the ability of post-service perceptions (service quality dimensions of responsiveness and tangibles) to predict purchase intentions (H2a). Results indicate that purchase intentions were not influenced by local customers responsiveness (b ¼ 20.09, p, 0.37), and local customers tangibles (b ¼ 0.10, p, 0.54), or by tourist responsiveness (b¼ 0.05, p, 0.65). Since previous research suggested that purchase intentions are affected greatly by customers' value perceptions, product quality (what the customer actually gets from the exchange), and price, these results may indicate that retailers in this rural tourism community have not successfully mastered the appropriate mix of price, products and promotion.

Support was found for the ability of post-service perceptions (service quality dimensions of responsiveness and tangibles) to predict local customers' retailer loyalty (H2b): local customer responsiveness (b ¼ 0.28, p, 0.00), and local customer tangibles (b ¼ 0.29, p, 0.00). Conversely, tourist customers resulting post-service perceptions (service quality dimension of responsiveness) was not a significant predictor of retailer loyalty (b ¼ 0.04, p, 0.69). This indicates that the measures for retailer loyalty were more dependable for local customers, and that customers' service quality perceptions (local) do indeed affect their degree of retailer loyalty in tourism markets. However, these results also suggest that for tourist customers, retailer loyalty is quite unpredictable; possibly indicating that rural retailers have not successfully mastered strategies for catering to both local and tourist customers.

It is surprising that even though the local and tourist customers have the same expectations going into the shopping experience and the local customers are more dissatisfied after the shopping experience, that the same local customers also demonstrate greater retailer loyalty. This suggests that local customers choose to support local retailers, regardless of their satisfaction, but is this enough support for long-term sustainability? Ultimately, this finding presents a major opportunity for tourism community retailers to build customer loyalty through improved service offerings and relationship management. For customers, the evaluation of service quality and satisfaction is a result of them comparing the observed service performance with prior expectations of what and how the service is performed. Customers tend to base their overall satisfaction with a retailer on individual perceptions, and those perceptions do indeed influence future patronage behaviour.

Discussion and Implications

This study sheds light on the little understood domain of retail service relationships in rural tourism markets. Our findings suggest that local customers believe they receive substandard service quality treatment in retail service interactions in contrast to tourist customers, and retailers indicate some degree of differentiated treatment between local and tourist customers. While tourism customers may seem to have greater short-term purchase potential, our findings suggest that tourism retailers need to realize who comprises their customer base during the off-season. As highly visible representatives of the community business sector, tourism retailers are well positioned to effectively meld community sentiment and tourism development into their business and service quality efforts. Results of this study further suggest that developing a customized approach to retail customer service and associated relationship management strategies may better meet the needs of the diverse customer base. This will require training by business consultants, intervention, and a rethinking of how these rural tourism retailers go about doing business in a seasonal market. It is apparent that neither a "one size fits all" approach to service nor a distinct bend toward preferential treatment of possible big purchasers meets the expectations of either local or tourist customers in this study. Focusing on service strategies that attend to personalization, customization, genuineness, and the authenticity of the rural setting appear to be major ways for these small firms to improve their service quality and leverage relational capabilities they already posses. Such an approach may simultaneously meet expectations of both local and tourist customers by blending delivery of what Gwinner et al. (1998) call social benefits (relationship based on familiarity and friendship) and special treatment benefits (based on information, efficiency, and economic outcomes such as discounts) into their service strategies. These authors note that customer perceptions and feedback regarding such benefits have been linked to loyalty, satisfaction, and repeat patronage intentions.

These findings lend further support for our recommendation that rural retailers differentiate and customize their service and relationship management strategies to satisfy both local and tourist customers. This dual strategy is also supported by findings of Huang and Stewart (1996) who indicate that tourism development can strain or at least change relationships among community members and systems (business, social, cultural). If local customers feel part of the tourism development process versus alienated by it, the overall effort will be more effective. Local and tourism customers have the choice to patronize local retailers. This patronage choice is a broad translation of their resulting satisfaction regarding service quality expectations and perceptions. Customer patronage and store loyalty are ultimate deciding factors that impact the economic sustainability of rural retailers. Thus, it is critically important for rural retailers to determine what attributes will encourage customers to engage in rural tourism retailing, and to use this knowledge to create customer relationship management strategies that satisfy both local and tourist customers. Feedback retailers receive from customers may provide cues on how to build and/or enhance their customer relationship management strategies and fulfil their goal of being a vital, fully functioning retail sector that has year around sustainability.

Implications for Customer Service in Rural Tourism Markets

Theoretically, the failure of the SERVQUAL dimensions to fit the five-factor structure is supported by previous research, in particular the tendency for the dimensions of responsiveness, empathy and assurance to overlap. In the current study, these three dimensions, along with the reliability dimension loaded onto the same factor for the local customers and retailers (responsiveness), creating the two-factor solution of responsiveness and tangibles. For the local customers, all five of the dimensions loaded onto the same factor (responsiveness), creating a one-factor solution.

Baseline information was yielded by this study regarding important service quality dimensions from the perspective of local customers, tourist customers, and tourism retailers. This insight provides specific guidance for a research agenda regarding service delivery in rural tourism settings. The service quality dimensions of responsiveness and tangibles were identified as core service quality themes by both local customers and tourists, suggesting that they should be foundations of rural tourism retail service strategies. It is noteworthy that the importance assigned to service responsiveness and tangibles varied among the two customer groups, signaling a need for differentiation (i.e. convenient but potentially different business hours year-round) and customization (i.e. selection of merchandise to meet both tourist season and non-tourist seasonal needs) of service approaches for these customer segments. The less busy off-season may offer a time for retailers to focus attention on store appeal and maintenance, special events, and other relation cultivation efforts that demonstrate service tangibles that are important to year-round customers.

Another revealing finding was that both the responsiveness and tangibles dimensions were of much less importance to retailers in their current conceptualization of their retail service offerings than to the local and tourist customers. The responsiveness dimension included items such as: level of service employees provide, attention provided by retailer and employees, readiness to respond to customers' needs, and overall effort of retailers towards customers. The tangibles dimension included items such as: convenient business hours, visually appealing store, modern fixtures and displays, and selection of merchandise. These findings provide explicit strategic guidance for rural tourism retailers and a means of targeting resources and efforts toward areas of greatest importance to their primary customer segments.

Since many retailers frequently offer the same merchandise and typically mimic each other's pricing and promotions, the potential for sameness in retailing is increasingly present. Therefore, for service-intensive retailers, like those operating within tourism communities, the key to differentiation lies within the scope of how they treat their customers (i.e. service delivery or relationship retailing). According to Berry and Gresham: [...] the heart and soul of relationship retailing is personal attention: treating the customer as a client rather than a face in the crowd, individualizing service, tailoring it, adding a touch of grace, making the client feel special. Accordingly, an important implication from this study is that rural tourism retailers need to develop a comprehensive service strategy, particularly one that emphasizes longer-term relationship management with local customers through service and relationship interactions. Being knowledgeable of and attempting to meet service expectations for these core customer groups may be a primary business success strategy that can provide year round sustainability in rural tourism markets. Understanding core customers' expectations for service quality may provide retailers in rural tourism markets with insight and strategic direction needed to improve service offerings, enhance employee training, and target scarce firm resources to areas of greatest need. In communities where businesses have concurrently improved their scope of product and service offerings for local customers concurrently with tourism offerings have found greater success in tourism and economic development efforts. The combined implications of this study will aid rural tourism communities in understanding service expectations for these core customer groups, and how they impact shopping behaviour and retailer success and sustainability in the local market.

Limitations and Recommendations for Future Research

While this is one of the few studies to date that specifically addresses service quality in rural tourism markets, it has several limitations that will provide opportunities for future research. One limitation is that it represents an initial test of the modified SERVQUAL scale (i.e. service quality expectations and perceptions) in a single rural tourism community in Iowa. Therefore, findings may only be generalizable to the unique nature of the tourist population (i.e. second/summer home) in Midwestern regions of the USA. Additionally, this study was exploratory and continued refinement and testing is needed for the SERVQUAL scale and other measures (i.e. purchase intentions and retailer loyalty) used in this study relevant to retailing and tourism shopping contexts. This study also shows that a well-validated measurement instrument for retail service quality within the rural tourism industry is still lacking. Our research suggests the need to develop and test scales with a broader population of customers in diverse rural tourism areas in order to improve the validity and reliability of the SERVQUAL instrument across differing market segments (i.e. local and tourist customers and retailers). Of particular interest is assessing why rural tourism consumers do not appear to differentiate retail service quality in a similar manner to local residents and why both groups do not seem to differentiate service quality in as complex a manner with the five dimensions as identified in previous research.

Since the tourism community in our study has a strong focus on outdoor recreational activities (i.e. boating, fishing, biking, hiking, etc.), future efforts should focus on testing the research model in a broader scope of rural tourism settings, such as those focused on agri-tourism, historic or cultural venues. Replication of the case study approach used in the current study would allow for greater understanding of shopping behaviour for core customer groups and their expectations for products, services, and experiences desired in diverse rural tourism markets. Examination of differences in customer expectations and perceptions of service varying with type and duration of tourism experience would also provide insight to tourism shopping patterns and preferences.

Spatial Planning For Cruise Tourism: Maximising The Benefits

In recent decades there have been major shifts in the pattern of uses within port cities. Specifically, the technological development of port functions (arising from factors such as containerisation and transport technology) has led to a shifting of port uses away from historic dockland areas, with the development of specialised dockyards, container ports and distribution centres in peripheral areas of cities, served by new communications links. The result has been the creation of voids in many historic docks areas, which have compounded wider processes of economic and social decay. In many cities this has been exacerbated by the disconnection between such areas and central business districts, including retail and cultural uses.

The implication of the voids created as a result of the shifting of port functions away from historic docks areas has been the need for regeneration, and indeed such areas have often been seen as opportunities to 're-image' the city, provide new leisure and cultural uses, and restore linkages between the waterfront and the city centre. Hence new and innovative retail, residential, leisure and cultural uses have been created, often applying 'masterplanning' principles in relation for instance to integration of uses, and large-scale 'flagship' developments have frequently acted as a focus of such development partly to ensure the maximum effects of 're-imaging'. Tourism and related uses have often formed an important part of regeneration schemes for port-cities, since they can provide an alternative to employment and income based on port or shipping activities, and can allow such cities (for instance in the Mediterranean region) to make use of advantages arising from location, climate and historic heritage. It is helpful in this respect that tourism as an activity is increasing in importance globally, relative to other economic activity, and cruise tourism – often a significant component of regeneration strategies for port cities – continues to grow faster than most other types of tourism activity.

The Cruise Industry

There has been significant growth in this activity in recent decades, with expansion leading to increased capacity both in terms of ships and cruise passenger terminal facilities. There was significant expansion in the 1960s, as well as in the 1980s and 1990s when standardisation increased the capacity of cruise ships and passenger terminal facilities. The cruise market in the Mediterranean has been a particular focus for growth; this is the result of the diversity of the region, allowing innovative itineraries to be organised in a relatively small area, as well as improvements in security standards and port facilities such as passenger terminals.

More recently, niche operators have exploited the changing image and appeal of cruise tourism, targeting a younger 'mass' consumer base, linked to more flexible travelling routes and seasons, and provision of a broader range of facilities and activities (both on-and off-ship). Hence there were around 1 million British cruise passenger tourists in 2004, and some forecasts suggest there will be 2 million by 2012.

The growth in the global cruise tourism industry has led to increased capacity in terms of ships. Indeed, around £1 billion was invested in new, larger cruise ships by the world largest cruise firms in 2008; this included the new 160,000 tonne 'Independence of the Seas', for the Royal Caribbean International cruise company, which has a capacity of 3,600 passengers and contains facilities such as a climbing wall, an ice risk and a shopping mall. In addition, the P&O cruise operator has developed the 116,000 tonne 'Ventura' which has a capacity of 3,100 passengers. Furthermore, Royal Caribbean International's 'Project Genesis' involves a ship under construction, of 220,000 tonnes, with sixteen decks, able to carry 5,400 passengers, and with an internal park over 300 feet long. This is planned for completion in 2009 and will operate from Fort Lauderdale, Florida. It will be the largest cruise ship in the world.

Clearly, an important implication of this increased capacity in terms of cruise ships is the need for enhanced capacity in terms of cruise passenger terminals, which many cities have sought to develop in order to compete more effectively in the global market for cruise tourism, particularly where cities aspire to become 'home ports' (from where passengers start or end their journeys) since such cities may enjoy economic benefits in terms of tourism-related income.

Benefits

Cruise (and other tourism) activity can offer significant benefits which can contribute to the achievement of regeneration outcomes for port-cities, and this has caused cities to compete to develop terminal facilities so as to exploit such benefits. Specifically, economic benefits can include: increased visitor spending and job creation [including direct and indirect effects]; enhancement of the city's image due in part to the cachet associated with cruise tourism (arising from associations with modernity, leisure and luxury); the attraction of new service industries in the wider port area linked to this change in image; the extension of the tourist or visitor 'season' with the increasing operation of year-round cruise tourism; and additional revenues from passenger terminals where these include other uses such as retail and leisure in additional to the terminals' primary function, leading to a synergetic effect on the regeneration of the wider area.

There are also clear environmental benefits, for instance: the re-use of docks areas as 'brownfield' sites with particular advantages in terms of location, as well as the preservation of historic heritage where this can house new uses; more effective use mixing compared to the city as a whole, which can result from a 'master-planned' approach which prioritises integration of uses, with improved linkages between the waterfront and the city; more sustainable urban densities than many other parts of the city, arising from the possibility of incorporating relatively high residential densities; and an improved overall environment, particularly where resources and planning allow the best use of the visibility of the waterfront area, representing the city as a whole and acting as a gateway (for instance by applying high-quality iconic architecture as a feature and focus of regeneration). These factors reflect in part the potential of activities based on maritime transport to achieve sustainable development outcomes.

In addition, social benefits of cruise tourism may include the potential use of 'planning gain' or community benefits, which are benefits funded by developers and designed to offset the potential negative impacts of the development. Such benefits could include for instance community facilities, environmental improvements and enhanced infrastructure, which could be of benefit to local communities as well as visitors. In addition, developments associated with cruise tourism, such as cruise passenger terminals, may allow greater access to the waterfront (for instance via public walkways) than was previously available, and this too can be enjoyed by local communities as well as visitors. There may also be other facilities that can be enjoyed by local communities within cruise-related developments, such as retail and leisure facilities. In addition, related tourism developments may enable local communities to 'reconnect' with historic port areas, particularly where interpretation techniques are used effectively, without compromising authenticity.

Moreover, the development of cruise terminals may involve 'planning gain' or community benefits which offset negative effects of such developments. This occurred in the case of Palma de Mallorca, where there was provision of a new road system, a new public walkway, and the handing-over to the municipality of the ownership and management of the seafront promenade.

Problems

However, cruise tourism development (and other tourism development) in port-city waterfront areas may also involve costs or problems. For instance, much of the employment created may be seasonal, low-wage and low-skilled. In addition, the income (direct and indirect) derived from visitors may be small, particularly where visitors spend minimal time in the city. Such income is also vulnerable to global shifts in fashion as well as the effects of events in terms of perceived risk. Moreover, the economic impact of visiting cruise ships may be relatively small largely because competition amongst host ports leads to relatively small fees for users, reducing the overall benefit to port-cities. In addition, on a broader level, it may be argued that the increasingly globalised pressures for cruise tourism may lead in the longer term to a homogenisation of the waterfront areas of port-cities, in the context of pressures for place branding which emphasise the need for local distinctiveness. Income from products sold on board ships may also accrue direct to ship owners, minimising benefits for host cities (Figueira de Sousa, 2001). Furthermore, tourism-related regeneration strategies for economic regeneration may create long-term vulnerability to external factors such as visitor numbers.

There may also be environmental costs deriving for instance from the inadequacy of infrastructure such as transport to cope with large numbers of cruise passengers. This may be particularly important for 'home' ports where passengers embark or disembark (sometimes with a throughput of over 10,000 passengers per day with more than one ship disembarking), resulting in congestion, and effects may be felt particularly in sensitive historic urban areas where heritage conservation is a key issue. Such problems may even affect cities where cruise terminals are planned carefully in the context of the wider city. Congestion may be exacerbated by the (albeit decreasing) seasonality of cruise (and other) tourism (particularly in Mediterranean ports, which lack space in comparison to those in northern Europe for instance) although efficient scheduling of cruise traffic can seek to minimise this.

Other issues include environmental pollution arising from noise and reduced air, ground and water quality as well as loss of natural habitats. Air pollution may derive from sulphur-rich exhaust fumes, and water pollution may derive from the waste from cruise ships, comprising for instance waste water, sewage and oil-contaminated water. The United Nations has indicated that passengers on a typical cruise ship account for 3.5 kg of garbage daily, and it argues that since most regulations concerning pollution were developed prior to the development of cruise tourism, there are many loopholes and exemptions within the regulations which result in significant pollution effects, though these may be related to the passage of ships through open seas rather than within port cities. There may also be loss of natural habitats.

In addition, social costs may derive from increased crime and anti-social behaviour in some contexts, as well as a broader decrease in the quality of life for local communities, linked to environmental effects such as congestion. There may also be a degree of marginalisation or even displacement of local communities as a result of the gentrification effects of prestige waterfront development which may result from tourism development.

Examples

Malta presents an interesting case of cruise passenger terminal development since the country has become increasingly dependent on tourism, but it also has an extremely valuable historic heritage, particularly in the Grand Harbour area of Valletta, where the new cruise terminal is sited (the Grand Harbour is also a World Heritage Site). Hence there have been some tensions between the need for tourism development and protection of historic heritage. The area for the cruise passenger terminal in Valletta was identified in the city's strategic spatial plan, and a development brief was prepared for the scheme. Part of the area selected for the scheme was of great value in terms of historic heritage, comprising seventeenth century stores as well as historic bastions, though many of the buildings were in a state of decay, and other parts of the area were vacant and derelict and used for car parking and port-related storage. Partly due to the requirements of the development brief, the scheme includes a new-build cruise passenger terminal, a new retail complex, and a range of leisure and recreation uses with new bars and restaurants on the waterfront.

Elements of good practice include the emphasis on high quality design which is carefully integrated into the site, adaptive re-use (or re-creation) of historic buildings, new landscaped areas and a new walkway along the waterfront. However, there were several problems with respect to the Valletta terminal development. For instance, while there is a range of uses as required in the Development Brief, this does not include residential uses (as set out in the Grand Harbour Local Plan) which form a desirable component within such schemes. In addition, it may be argued that, in terms of regeneration benefits, the uses incorporated within the scheme cater primarily for visitors rather than local people – as indicated for instance by the restaurant and associated uses in the scheme. This reflects wider concerns of waterfront regeneration in port cities. Moreover, in terms of integration with the surrounding area, it may be argued that the scheme does not provide sufficient linkage between the waterfront and the city centre, largely as a consequence of the problem of the change in level from the waterfront to the city centre. In overall terms, the scheme is therefore likely to result in increased congestion affecting a designated Urban Conservation Area and surrounding areas of sensitive heritage quality. Furthermore, the visual impact of the scheme may detract from the unique historical context as reflected by the Structure Plan and this could ultimately erode the area's distinctiveness which is critical for its wider tourism function. Finally, the scheme does not appear to have involved inclusive partnership, perhaps in part because of the priority for national economic regeneration and the possible limitations of the Maltese development planning system in encouraging community benefits.

Other European examples include a new cruise passenger terminal in Amsterdam, which shows innovation in design and highly-developed transport infrastructure to minimise congestion (but with problems in terms of lack of public access to the adjacent waterfront because of heightened security concerns). In addition, the case of a terminal development in Genoa illustrates the use of a detailed masterplan with a resulting high level of integration of uses. Here, the scheme allows year-round operation, combining passenger services with commercial and other tourism-based activities, and helping to link the port and the city.

Critical Analysis

The case of Valletta illustrates the difficulty of balancing the need for cruise tourism and cruise terminal-related development with environmental protection. Clearly, the cruise terminal here has the potential to help exploit growing international demand for cruise tourism, and to promote Malta as a Mediterranean hub for passenger vessels. As a consequence, the Development Brief for the cruise terminal site states that 'Given its strategic geographic location, and the importance of tourism to its economy, Malta*cannot afford to miss* the opportunity to capitalise on this trend'. This is certainly understandable given that around 25% of Malta's economic activity is dependent upon tourism-related activities. Moreover, the terminal was intended to enhance the international image of Malta by providing an important landmark. Nevertheless, it is equally clear that the scheme is problematic in some respects, for instance in terms of its effect on local heritage and amenity.

The case of Valletta and others therefore show the need for spatial planning to manage the potential conflicts between tourism and related development and heritage or amenity interests, and to take account of such conflicts in decision-making for the strategic regeneration of city-port waterfront areas. Such decision-making should involve a wide range of interests including local communities, so that appropriate community benefits are included. It should seek to ensure that development schemes involving tourism-related activities include appropriately-integrated uses, and that schemes are integrated with the wider city, with adequate provision of transport infrastructure. It can also assist in ensuring that the distinctiveness of the area is maintained, which is necessary to ensure its long-term attraction for tourists and visitors.

Moreover, with relevance to the development of cruise passenger terminals – clearly an important physical effect of the expansion of cruise tourism – there would seem to be a need for clearer and more careful regulation of the process of development and expansion of such terminals, taking account of all potential impacts. In fact an analogy may be suggested here in terms of the process of 'containerisation'. Like the expansion of cruise tourism, this led to significant changes in the way that (commercial) ports operated; while there were major associated benefits including wealth creation, there were also significant associated problems including congestion and adverse environmental impacts, which the regulatory infrastructure was often slow to respond to. In such circumstances, areas of heritage value (for instance within historic port cities) are likely to be particularly vulnerable.

One potential means of evaluating the potential effects of cruise passenger terminals – as a key component of cruise tourism promotion – could be by the application of generic criteria to ascertain the potential contribution of such development schemes to broader regeneration outcomes. Such criteria could include for instance: internal functional integration of an appropriate mix of land uses, including re-use of historic buildings where appropriate; integration with the surrounding area, particularly the city centre; regeneration effects on the city as a whole; and inclusive partnership in the development of the scheme. These are based on case studies of waterfront development in practice, and they reflect a degree of consensus that on good practice in waterfront development/regeneration.

For instance, Bruttomesso (2001b) stresses the desirability of a mix of a plurality of functions and activities; Rogers and Power (2000) highlight the need for adaptive re-use of historic buildings; Marshall (2001a) shows the importance of linking the scheme with the surrounding area; Tunbridge and Ashworth (1992) show the need to ensure linkage of leisure and tourism-related uses to others in the area; Van der Knaap and Pinder (1992) suggest the need to ensure linkage with city centre uses; Burwood and Roberts (2002) indicate the importance of broadly-based, inclusive and equitable partnership; and Jauhiainen (1995) highlights the need for community involvement.

In addition, in terms of specific mechanisms in spatial planning, it may be argued that greater certainty within spatial planning might have been helpful; in this context, Home (1997) suggests that Malta's spatial planning system may compromise aims for environmental quality by its use of discretion. It may be suggested that a 'master plan' approach, incorporating a clear and specific vision for the Valletta waterfront, could have assisted in providing a more useful framework for development than that afforded by statutory plans. In the case of

Genoa, for instance, such a master plan provided a design vision for the area incorporating the proposed cruise passenger terminal.

Tourism in Saudi Arabia and its Future Development

International tourism has become a major industry worldwide and travel and tourism activities generated US$3.6 trillion in 2000. The rate of expansion has been impressive and international arrivals increased annually by an average of 4.3% between 1990 and 2000 (WTO, 2003). Developing nations have sought to take advantage of this strong upward trend, prompted by an appreciation of tourism's positive economic consequences which include income and employment creation, foreign exchange earnings and inward investment. Tourism is vigorously pursued as a catalyst to general growth and means of diversification, despite its disadvantages as a vehicle for economic development. It is now responsible for 19% of the developing world's exports and more than 40% of its gross domestic product. According to Mastny (2002), as many as 65% of the 200 million jobs created by tourism every year are to be found in less developed countries.

Tourists are unevenly distributed around the globe, however, and Europe and America continue to dominate the industry as both generators and destinations. The Middle East recorded 24.1 million arrivals in 2002, only 3.4% of the world's total, although this compares with nine million in 1990 and there was an average annual growth rate of 9.7% throughout the 1990s (WTO, 2003). Sharpley (2002: 221) terms it 'one of the least developed tourism regions in the world' where leisure travel is rare and often seen as 'culturally undesirable and economically unnecessary'. For many Middle Eastern societies, Western style tourism is considered to be fundamentally incompatible with the Islamic religion and way of life.

Other barriers in operation are the absence of infrastructure, harsh climate, visa restrictions and a lack of commercial interest amongst tour operators and travel agents of major generating markets. Regional instability and the heightened threat of terrorism worldwide is another critical issue. Nevertheless, there is a rich endowment of tourism resources and the Middle East offers a host of natural attractions such as deserts, mountains, green valleys and the Red Sea with its beaches and world class diving.

There is also a diversity of archaeological, cultural and heritage sites like spectacular tombs and dwellings carved in sandstone. Accessibility is improving and the WTO forecasts that inbound tourists will rise from 12.4 million in 1995 to 35.9 million in 2010, reaching 68.5 million in 2020 when the Middle East's market share will be 4.4% (WTO, 2000).

Saudi Arabia originally devoted little attention to conventional international leisure tourism for a combination of social, political and economic reasons. There were few financial incentives to do so given its wealth accruing from the discovery and exploitation of oil reserves and the fourfold increase in oil prices in the 1970s. The central role of religious tourism must be stressed, however, with over a million travelling annually for the Hajj which requires a massive organizational effort by the authorities. The Hajj is a pilgrimage to Mecca which all Muslims are expected to make, if their circumstances permit, at least once in a lifetime. Umrah also involves a visit to the holy cities, but is not restricted to a specific date and may be undertaken on numerous occasions. Those on the Hajj and Umrah together accounted for 3.6 million of the 6.3 million tourists in 2000 and almost half of tourism expenditure. In comparison, business and conference travel constituted 17% of spending while the proportions for VFR and vacation or leisure tourists were 18% and 2% respectively.

Although support for the tourism industry has been limited, Saudi Arabia was a leading Middle East destination by the beginning of the new millennium when it was drawing 27.1% of regional tourists and 29% of receipts (WTO, 2002). Domestic tourists were also a significant sector with about 14.5 million participants annually. Tourism is now Saudi Arabia's third largest industry after energy and manufacturing, and has recently emerged as the second most important in terms of foreign exchange earnings and job creation. In 2001 tourism contributed US$9.6 billion or 5.6% of GDP and employed 489,000 people. By 2020, revenue from the tourism industry could exceed SR86 billion (US$22.93 billion) and it is anticipated that it will provide 1.5 million additional jobs for Saudis. There will be spin-off benefits in the wider economy and tourism could boost revenue in the communication and housing sectors by between 20% and 25% (ITP, 2003)

Such figures and projections have led to a shift in formal attitudes to tourism at a time when oil revenues are no longer as lucrative as they once were, leading to the exploration of alternatives. There is also concern about unemployment levels amongst the rapidly expanding and young population. At present, only 10.5% of the jobs in Mecca and

Medina are taken up by Saudi nationals and the Secretary General of the Supreme Commission for Tourism (SCT) would like to see this increased to 70% or more. A relatively new phenomenon is that of Saudization which entails reducing the number of expatriate workers and replacing them with Saudi nationals. Senior government officials recently ordered the establishment of a committee to implement such a move across 21 job categories in several stages over the next three years, at the end of which the workforces should consist entirely of Saudis.

Greater official interest has thus been expressed in tourism in recent years with the formation of specific policies and an administrative framework. There had been no formal agency devoted to tourism prior to 1999 when the SCT was established to promote the sector. Another national body, known as the High Tourism Authority (HTA), was set up in early 2002 to further encourage tourism and is chaired by Prince Sultan, Second Deputy Prime Minister and Minister of Defence and Aviation. It is tasked with developing the tourism industry, implementing the recommendations of earlier studies and preserving key archaeological sites and monuments. Seminars and discussion forums on tourism and its future prospects have also been organized, additional evidence of its higher priority.

A long term tourism master plan was prepared by the SCT and is now being implemented, while provincial plans are about to be drawn up. The intention is to attract 8.1 million arrivals in 2010 and 10.9 million by 2020, 3 million of whom will come from outside Arab areas and the countries of the GCC (Gulf Cooperation Council whose members are Bahrain, Kuwait, Oman, Qatar, Saudi Arabia and the United Arab Emirates). The principal target markets will be Saudi residents and expatriates living in the kingdom, followed by Muslims worldwide and then niches of those interested in culture and heritage, ecotourism and pursuits such as diving and trekking. Possibilities of enhancing religious tourism have been acknowledged with initiatives such as 'Umrah Plus' which aims to boost the movement of pilgrims outside the main centres of Mecca and Medina, exploiting a relaxation in visa regulations (AME Info, 2002). There are also opportunities regarding extended short break travel by GCC nationals who do not require visas.

Selling to non-Muslims internationally is more challenging due to matters of cultural sensitivity and security, fears about the latter intensified by the terrorist bombings in Riyadh in 2003 and general regional instability. There are also problems related to mutual suspicions between the Islamic and Western worlds and political uncertainties which are likely to deter many visitors. Although visa restrictions have been eased to some extent, the rules are still inconvenient for foreign tourists who wish to visit certain more remote locations. Nevertheless, and assuming the presence of a degree of political stability, long haul tourists might be attracted by the county's unique culture and landscape and the national flag carrier has already had some success in transporting groups from Europe, America and Japan. A Mintel report describes Saudi Arabia as possessing much unrealised potential and 'outstanding cultural, heritage and natural sites'. It cites the cities of Riyadh, Jeddah and Mecca as examples. Madain Salah is said to surpass the huge rock tombs of Petra and Al-Jouf is home to antiquities linked to the origins of the Nabatean and Assyrian cultures. There are many parks and the Asir National Park covers over a million acres in the Asir region which offers comparatively green countryside, a mild climate and many leisure facilities. Other nature-based amenities are those of the Red Sea and Arabian Gulf coasts and the SCT has identified 10,000 attractions overall. However, it should be noted that many well known landmarks have given way to development projects as part of the drive towards modernization, thereby reducing the country's attractiveness as a tourist centre. Wildlife reserves are also under threat, despite a policy of public exclusion which needs to be revised if ecotourism opportunities are to be maximized. The kingdom already has a satisfactory accommodation stock of 7,068 hotels and 41,000 rooms which is half that of the total volume for the GCC collectively. Most rooms are in Mecca and international chains control over 80% of five star properties. Another 50,000 hotel rooms and 74,000 apartments are planned in order to meet projected demand (ITP, 2003). Communications are also good and there are 22 regional and four international airports, Jeddah and Riyadh being the busiest, as well as an ever-expanding road network and extensive motorway system which will connect most regional centres by 2005.

Saudi Arabia thus exhibits both strengths and weaknesses as a tourist destination, the former indicative of scope for further expansion and a positive future. However, there are many uncertainties ahead and it is therefore valuable to seek the advice of experts regarding their opinions about the future as a foundation for decision making. The Delphi technique was selected as the most appropriate approach to this subject and is summarized below, followed by an account of its application in this particular instance.

Research Methodology: The Delphi Technique and its Application

The Delphi technique is a qualitative forecasting tool which has been widely applied in various disciplines In essence, the method attempts to make constructive and systematic use of informed intuitive judgments through a series of questionnaires which explore the knowledge and experience of a selected group with relevant expertise. The procedure allows a panel of chosen experts to refine their opinions in a series of stages until a consensus is reached. The method is obviously not foolproof and relies on subjective opinions, but these are collected in a carefully planned and orderly program of sequential and impersonal exchanges. Communication can be conducted through various media including personal interview, the telephone, email and traditional mail.

The approach has proved especially popular with many marketing researchers. Bolongaro (1994) for example, argued that the Delphi technique is more dynamic compared to other instruments which produce comparatively static results. It is helpful in picking up the weaker signals in the market, thereby assisting planners to predict changes that might occur in the business environment with greater accuracy. Michman (1987) also preferred the Delphi method and Lunsford and Fussell (1993) adopted it to examine export opportunities for Western firms in the emerging economies of certain Eastern and Central European states, leading to recommendations for constructing a business services marketing strategy.

A literature search also reveals the extensive adoption of the Delphi technique in the tourism and hospitality field, often within the context of destination marketing. Kaynak, Bloom and Leibold (1994) projected scenarios for the South African tourism industry until 2010 and Yeong, Kau and Tan (1989) explored the future of Singapore's tourism industry and possible marketing strategies to remain competitive. A more recent study was conducted by Tideswell, Mules and Faulkner (2001) to measure the domestic and international tourism potential of South Australia. Adopting an integrative forecasting model combining quantitative methods and the qualitative Delphi technique, the researchers succeeded in validating predictions for both types of visitor. In view of such studies, the Delphi methodology would seem a sound choice for evaluating the changing nature of Saudi Arabia's tourism and the challenges to be confronted in the future.

Major methodological considerations with regard to the current project were the selection of panelists, questionnaire design, feedback provision and the number of rounds of decision making. Martino (1983) and Dalkey (1969) proposed a minimum requirement of 15 to 20 panelists to achieve reasonable forecasting accuracy, but other researchers maintained that the number could range from only a few to more than 100. There appear to be no hard and fast rules and the optimal panel size depends on the nature and scope of the study as well as the level of knowledge and expertise of those taking part.

Two panels of experts were invited to contribute in this case and the data was analyzed separately in order to enhance the validity of the results. Both panels consisted of key individuals in Saudi Arabia's tourism and hospitality industry and were classified into six groupings of government ministries; foodservice, hotels, airline industries; travel agencies and tourist attractions. Aiming for a final panel size of 15 and assuming a favourable response rate of 50%, a total of 30 correspondents were initially contacted. They were informed about the purpose, scope and the duration of the study and were invited either to participate personally or nominate someone whom they believed most suitable. There were a total of 20 positive responses, with each grouping almost equally represented. All the panelists had experience of the tourism industry as tourism academics, industry professionals or government staff. They had also travelled widely and acquired understanding of local, regional and world economies.

The first questionnaire was designed in accordance with prevailing market conditions in Saudi Arabia as well as in response to the ideas expressed by tourism industry personnel who were consulted. It contained generally worded questions which became more specific in later stages, building on the previous reactions. In phase one, the questionnaire asked respondents to assign probabilities to a list of tourism events or developments and provide reasons for their answers. A summary of the first set of results was prepared and the statistical report was distributed, along with an amended questionnaire. Panelists were requested to revise their estimates if they wished or justify their original opinion and, after this, a summary was produced which showed the emergence of consensus. The experts were then sent a third questionnaire and had to indicate whether they supported the stated propositions. Three rounds of questioning were judged sufficient due to the fact that Saudi Arabia has an evolving market research culture, although more phases could have been added. Twenty-six event statements or scenarios were finally developed related to future trends in the tourism industry, the global environment, technological progress, regional collaboration and Saudi Arabia as a Middle Eastern tourism hub and a training centre. Perceptions were appraised of the probability of the occurrence of each event or scenario from zero to 100%. The popularity of Saudi Arabia as a result of tourism development and the year of probable success of Saudi Arabia as a popular destination were also ranked, the latter on a five point scale from 2005 to never (2005 being 100% probability and never being 0%). In addition to the questionnaire, the panelists were also supplied with secondary information to assist them in forming their estimates. The material included documents such as tourism related publications from the Ministry of Commerce, HTA, Saudi Chamber of Commerce, and articles from magazines and newspapers. The panelists were also encouraged to provide their own comments, documents or information to enrich the whole process. The list of events and final responses of both panels are summarize, with a discussion of the results in the next section. The table columns contain the probability and ranking figures for both the panels, with the former expressed as a percentage. The Mann-Whitney U test was applied after ranking all the probabilities in order from the lowest to the highest. When some probabilities were found to be repeat items, rank values were averaged to untie the data. The value of the Z statistic obtained through the Mann-Whitney U analysis was found to be-0.475 and it was determined that the critical Z value for an area of-0.475 was 1.64, the sample U statistic further standardized (U-mU/?U). The resulting Z score arrived at was -1.758 which was considered insignificant at the 0.05 alpha levels. This meant the sample statistic did not lie within the critical values of the test and it was concluded that the two samples were not the same, but independent of each other.

Event

(1) Saudi Arabia is growing as a major tourist attraction for the entire world.

(2) Tourism destinations of Saudi Arabia are gradually becoming attractive to foreign tourists as a result of regional collaboration.

(3) Ancient castles, museums and other historical places and sand dunes will be accessible to foreign tourists in future.

(4) Visas for Saudi Arabia are relaxed now.

(5) Transportation advances will continue lowering the travel expenses in Saudi Arabia.

(6) Travel and tourism will be non-discretionary expenditure.

(7) Local travel and tourism will continue growing rapidly in Saudi Arabia.

(8) Saudi Airlines will keep on developing rapidly as a major international airline in terms of passenger volume and travel frequency.

(9) Riyadh, Jeddah and Dammam are gaining popularity as shopping paradises in the Middle East region.

(10) Airlines, hotels, foodservices and retail industries in Saudi Arabia will require more specialized and formal education in the area of tourism and hospitality.

(11) Top convention centres now exist in main commercial cities of Saudi Arabia.

(12) Safety, security and political stability in Saudi Arabia are helpful in attracting foreign tourists to visit varied destinations.

(13) The Saudization drive in the country will result in promoting tourism destinations in future.

(14) Adequate training and education programs in tourism and hospitality exist to meet the demand for personnel in Saudi Arabia.

(15) Business travel to the Kingdom of Saudi Arabia is threatened by video-conferencing, Internet, satellites, view phones and similar technologies.

(16) The Saudi Riyal is a stable currency and will continue that way for a long time.

(17) The Saudi Riyal is increasingly becoming an exchangeable currency internationally.

(18) As a result of tourism development, the Kingdom of Saudi Arabia will become a popular destination internationally.

(19) The probability of Saudi Arabia's success as a popular tourism destination will occur after year 2005.

(20) The growing trend of sales over the Internet has an impact on tourism in Saudi Arabia.

(21) Most of the hotels in Saudi Arabia offer room reservations via the Internet.

(22) Saudi Airlines offers speedy service for self reservation through its websites.

(23) The Internet is gaining popularity for creating tourism prospects for Saudi Arabia.

(24) Video conferencing will have a significant impact on large and small businesses in Saudi Arabia.

(25) The website of the Supreme Commission will remain attractive to foreign tourists intending to visit Saudi Arabia.

(26) The advancement of telecommunication and IT networks will enhance tourism prospects of Saudi Arabia.

Discussion and Recommendations

There was not overwhelming support for the ideas that Saudi Arabia is growing in importance as a major destination worldwide with an increasing appeal to foreign tourists, perhaps reflecting a realistic assessment of current conditions. Local travel and tourism was viewed more favourably as likely to continue expanding quickly, encouraged by the relaxation of visa restrictions, and this indicates an appreciation of its mounting economic value. However, it was believed that Saudi Arabia could achieve greater success as a destination after 2005. Such a trend would be assisted by advances in transport and a lowering of costs and the improved accessibility of cultural and natural heritage attractions. Both panels endorsed the revival of traditional activities and members felt that emphasis should be given to devising new tourist attractions, improving recreational facilities and cultivating Saudi Arabia's image as a regional tourism centre. Awareness of shopping facilities and the presence of convention centres were deemed to be significant. Travel and tourism was seen as essential expenditure, further boosting demand, and the Saudi currency to be stable and acceptable internationally. Safety, security and stability were recognized as key determinants of inbound tourism flows. In terms of industry sectors, the national carrier was judged to have favourable prospects regarding its passenger volumes and services and to be already operating an efficient Internet reservation system. While it was generally agreed that training and education programs in tourism and hospitality were adequate, more specialized and formal education would be necessary in the future for the airline, accommodation, catering and retail industries. Information Technology was believed to be widely accepted with a marked trend towards Internet booking. Hotels would offer online reservations and the web pages of official agencies be used as a source of information. Improvements in telecommunications would also enhance the country's prospects, although video conferencing and other technologies could prove a threat to business travel.

With the latest advances in telecommunications, the panelists predicted that much Islamic travel would be booked and arranged through the Internet in future years. It was accepted that the latest developments have made an array of potential products, services, and channels of distribution available that were previously either technically impossible or economically prohibitive. A basic substitution of broadband communication for business travel might impact negatively on the travel industry, but videotext services providing travel and shopping information in other countries could make international visits a more enjoyable experience. An international databank with tourist information would have implications for international tourism advertising and affect traditional distribution channels for products. Nevertheless, both panels also pointed out that there was under-utilization of the Internet in Saudi Arabia due to the quality of service and the literacy rate in the kingdom. In addition, its people do not always have confidence in transactions conducted by computer. Equipment such as video conferencing and satellite communications are only installed in a few large hotels so its availability should not be exaggerated. The comments made suggest areas in which action might be taken in an attempt to capitalize on favourable trends and deal effectively with any anticipated problems. Evidence of long-term growth indicates a need for investment by both the public and private sectors. Government is responsible for providing the necessary infrastructure of communications and services with private funding needed for projects such as hotels, restaurants, shopping malls and recreation centres. Existing tourism products should be refined in response to consumer demand, making use of the latest developments in science and technology. Opinion surveys could be conducted in order to monitor consumer attitudes and experiences, ensuring an appreciation of changing preferences. Efforts should be directed at creating new products that portray traditional ways of life which are likely to appeal especially to tourists from outside the region. The importance of culture and nature as tourism resources means that conservation measures are necessary to protect such sites and prevent their disappearance due to modernization and urbanization.

Intensified marketing is necessary with scope for greater collaboration between the public and private sector. The focus of promotion should be on neighbouring GCC countries initially and then beyond in the longer term. Questions of safety and security, as well as religious and cultural sensitivities, will need to be resolved if leisure tourists from Westernized nations are to be attracted in significant numbers. The service sector is the backbone of tourism, yet there is room for great improvement in standards. While tourism traffic and revenue have grown substantially, the quality of service provided by hotels, restaurants, stores and travel agencies often remains disappointing. It is therefore imperative that initiatives be launched to raise standards and this is linked to the provision of education and training. There is an urgent need for vocational and executive training in the hospitality and tourism areas. Both panels agreed that new colleges to prepare management and technical staff should be opened in principal cities. Major universities could offer hospitality and tourism courses incorporated into their existing business curriculum, or even create new departments to run specialized programs. Leading hotels, restaurants and travel agencies should also encourage their staff to register for professional certification and upgrade their skills and competences.

11

Market Segmentation in Tourism

Goals

This discussion paper has three key goals:

- For tourism operators and planners to better understand Market Segmentation;
- To provide an indication of trends in the market, with special focus on emerging segments; and
- To provide a useful backdrop of information for the Product Club Advisory Board to assist in the development of new or enhanced product lines.

Market Segmentation

Market segmentation can be defined as the process through which people (both tourism providers and consumers) with similar needs, wants and characteristics are grouped together so that a tourism business/ organization can use greater precision in serving and communicating with these groups (marketing). There are associated benefits of segmentation (e.g. identifying partnerships to promote networking and guiding research and development) but the bottom line is that it enables better marketing decisions, and promotes more viable operations. In more general terms, segmentation comes down to ties that connect two or more individuals (or businesses) together; it could be their age, their love of certain music, the magazines they read, or what their son or daughter is doing in school. The possibilities are endless.

Approaching Segmentation

Market segmentation can be approached from two broad directions: supply side (e.g. grouping similar products together) or the demand side (e.g. demographics and behavioural patterns of tourists). The objective is consistent: trying to reach out to potential customers in a more cost effective manner. The levels of segmentation can be broad (e.g. businesses offering an 'outdoor' experience) or narrow (e.g. a segment of the population in a set geographical boundary, who have a certain medical condition, with children, in a particular income bracket).

The approach to segmentation is important however. There is debate about 'Product Push' versus 'Market Pull'. The former is designing a product and packaging it and hoping that there is a market for it, while the latter attempts to find a niche market, identifying the needs and wants of individuals within that market, and designing a product to meet those needs. Generally it is more effective to undertake the market pull approach, but at the same time it is important to understand the strengths of a region's product. This is especially important when it comes to developing partnerships and products that fit with local community and cultural values. A mixed approach-market pull and 'manipulated or value-added' product push-is likely to be valuable when developing new product lines.

The following comments focus on the three main bases for market segmentation: product related, demographic and behavioural. Generally the more defined a market segment, the easier it is to reach out to individuals. Whichever approach is used, the segments (or niche markets) should be at least one of two things-*Focused* or *Targetable*-preferably both.

Focused: the stronger the ties that link people together the better; not just age and income but expectations, passions, habits, affiliations etc. The niche market does not have to be small to be focused, but usually the larger the market the weaker the ties.

Targetable: The easier it is to reach people in a niche market, the better. If they are all receiving the same newsletter or visit the same location on a regular basis, the better. An example of a focused market is 'ringers' (i.e. those who ring birds for counting and monitoring purposes) within the bird-watching segment. This niche is also targetable because it has its own specific newsletters, associations and conferences. An example of a niche market that is not particularly focused but is targetable is the 'David Thompson' segment. (This idea arose at a recent TASK meeting-to have a retreat inviting only those called David Thompson!). It is not focused as the only connection is the name;

individuals are likely to have disparate interests and passions. With today's technology, however, it is a targetable audience. [Suggestion for a key note speaker: David Thompson, past president of Whistler Tourism Association!]

Product Related Segmentation

- Without listing all the subgroups, typical product-related segmentation may be along the lines of the following,
- Adventure Operators/Organizers *(from family adventures and motorcycle tours to* hunting and bird-watching),
- Attractions *(from museums and theme parks to sports clubs and festivals),*
- Transportation and Services *(from train and van tours to restaurants and gas stations).*

Another product-related segmentation strategy is based on seasons, for example grouping Winter or Fall activities. The Product Clubs of the Canadian Tourism Commission (CTC) are diverse, from focusing on Greek or Aboriginal businesses to particular styles of accommodations, such as 'charming inns'. For those with an outdoor theme the product segmentation is often similar to the above, or even broader. One promotes the four choices of:

- Land Travel
- Water
- Winter
- Mixed Activities.

The use of technology, and more specifically websites, can be very beneficial for segmentation and steering potential customers to their particular vacation interests. Websites can quickly lead consumers to the same tourism package/business via different 'routes'. For instance, a cat skiing operator can be reached via 'Adventure Seekers', or 'Winter Activities'. The use of technology should also be utilized in segmenting the market into further subgroups.

For many years there has been a movement from mass production (and marketing) to customized production (e.g. with a computer manufacturer, customers can choose online their preferred specifications and have it 'built to order'). So too, with the tourism product. Given the consumers' limited time (and tendency to book last minute vacations), they may choose a vacation with a variety of outdoor activities, even offered by different operators. The message here is not to offer consumers what the operators *think* they want, but to provide a wide array of choices, ask them what they want and then organize it for them.

Nature-Based Tourism

The Kootenay region as a whole can largely be viewed as a nature-based tourism product given the plethora of national and regional parks, small communities, lake systems, mountain ranges and truly outstanding natural beauty. Cultural and heritage tourism will continue to play a strong role, but the major draw will be the natural surroundings. Segmentation has already occurred with the creation and naming of the new Product Club. *Explorers of the Western Canadian Wilderness Product Club.* Aside from the geographical identifier, there are two key words: *Explorers* and *Wilderness.* These conjure up an image of unspoilt natural beauty and outdoor activities – it is a nature-based tourism product. The nature-based tourism industry has grown so much in recent years that it now contains four broad sub-markets or segments:

Eco-Tourism: Travel for a learning experience about natural environments, using tourism products and services that are sustainable and sensitive to its surroundings. It should be noted that one recent local project 3 identified a regionally useful definition of Ecotourism within the nature-based tourism segment:

"Ecotourism is responsible travel to natural areas which conserves the environment and improves the welfare of local people".

Adventure Travel: *Personal accomplishment though thrills of dominating dangerous* environments.

Wilderness Travel: *Personal recreation through travel in natural environments which are devoid of human interference.*

Car Camping: *Family travel, providing a safe interface between wild and civilized.* All of these descriptions or definitions are open to interpretation. At one end of the spectrum for 'wilderness travel', for example, may be a tourist on a mountain-bike traversing a logging road though a planted forest. Others may believe that wilderness is non-existent in South-East BC because there are few mountain ridges where there is absolutely no visual human intrusion. This is an important aspect with regards to marketing (and product development) as it is important that the region does not attempt to 'sell' something it does not have. It is equally important not to put off potential visitors because they perceive that the area as too wild and rugged. When undertaking product enhancement or development it should be recognised that these four subgroups are at different stages of the typical life cycle. Broadly speaking, wilderness travel is likely nearing the peak of its business life cycle. This is because true wilderness areas are diminishing and only a limited number of tourist activities can take place in wilderness settings before the product can no longer be categorized as wilderness.

Car-camping too, on a global scale, is either approaching the peak of its life cycle or even started the down-ward slide. One component of 'vehicle camping' is still on the rise, however, and that is RV travel. Nearly one in twelve (or seven million) vehicle owning households in the USA own an RV, exhibiting nearly an 8% increase in the last four years. There is expected to be a further 15% increase over the next decade. Baby boomers are fuelling this growth and many have yet to reach the prime purchasing age of RV ownership. The rising cost of gasoline and the continuing weakness of the Canadian dollar might provide opportunities for South Eastern BC to offer alternatives to the 'Alaskan experience'.

Both eco-tourism and adventure travel are likely to have greater growth potential and are still on the upward curve of the life cycle. Eco-tourism was recently identified in a series of local community consultations as "the greatest opportunity for tourism growth in the region". 4 Sustainable tourism should not be confused with eco tourism. The latter is a sub sector of sustainable tourism and is a more narrowly defined segment within nature-based activities. Sustainable principles, on the other hand, can apply to all types of tourism activities.

Examples of Segmentation of Outdoor and Learning Travellers

Outdoor travellers and learning travellers are reviewed in more detail given the nature-based local tourism product and the, as-yet-untapped, potential of learning vacations.

Outdoor Segment

Even though a large part of the local tourism product is based on the outdoor experience and natural beauty, this does not mean that all tourists regularly participate in outdoor activities. The graph below provides a picture of the outdoor segmentation of the US market. As seen, a large component of the segment is categorized as 'outdoor inactives' (36%).

There are many market segments that overlap. The pie chart above provides the segmentation split for outdoors travellers. Another market segment, the 'Learning Traveller' was identified as an emerging market. The learning Traveller may overlap with a number of above segments of the outdoor traveller, some being naturalists, some resort lovers, etc.

Outdoor-Wilderness Segment: There are many different ways that markets can be segmented, and an equally diverse number of descriptors that could be attached to each segment. With respect to outdoor wilderness travellers, the Adventures of the Northern Wilderness Product Club identified three main sub sectors for wilderness travel to the Yukon. Its research consisted of 800 telephone interviews and mail surveys to California, Vancouver, Calgary, Chicago, and Ontario. The identified segments were:

- Earthly Explorers: (*24% of respondents*) *like to keep it simple, lower budgets, into nature and roughing it, prefer to keep to one activity rather than trying them* all;
- Adventure Collectors: (*18% of respondents*) *like to sample lots of different* activities, looking for higher quality, with fun, shorter trips;
- Pampers Consumer Boomers: (*14% of respondents*) *Smaller segment but market expected to rise; looking for high quality, want to relax, but also* experience activities in a non-threatening way.

There was a fourth segment identified (*'No Thrills'*), but this sub-market prefer to stay closer to home for their wilderness trips and are not looking for any risk or adventure. Although this was noted as a weak market for the Yukon given distance and remoteness, it may hold some opportunities for the Kootenay region. In terms of product development and target marketing it would be beneficial for the Kootenay region to focus more on the Adventure Collectors and Pampered Consumer Boomers given their ability to pay, interest in winter, and the relatively more desirable (compared with the Yukon) climate offered in the local region, especially in the shoulder seasons.

Learning Traveller Segment: Learning travellers are often referred to as 'educated travellers' not because the trips they take have educational components but because they themselves have higher overall education levels than the population at large. *Elderhostel Canada* (since 2000 it has been re-named *Routes to Learning Canada – RTC*) has been the single largest provider of learning travel programs in Canada for 20 years. The North American Elderhosteller is on average 68 years old, and 90%

have post secondary education (in a time when post secondary education was less accessible). Nearly 1 in 5 report having 7 or more years of post-secondary education. 7 The segments for learning travellers are:

Explorers are those looking for learning programs that offer opportunities to explore a new part of the world and learn about local area history, customs and cultures;

- *Activity-Oriented* are those seeking outdoor experiences and are interested in the natural environment;
- *Content-Committed are people who look for a specific subject of interest (e.g.* lepidoptery – the study of moths and butterflies);
- *Convenience-Oriented look for programs that are within a six-hour driving radius of* home.

Of the four segments, the last one is the one that would fit least well with the location and tourism product in the Kootenay Region. 'Activity-oriented' individuals and 'explorers', however, mesh perfectly with the strengths of the local tourism product, and the direction of the new product club.

Demand-Based Segmentation

Demographics

Understanding demographics is imperative to product development and segmentation, especially with regard to understanding trends in the market place. Demography (the study of age, sex, education, family status, life cycle etc.) is an excellent tool for product developers and marketers. According to the well respected demographer, David Foot, demographics accounts for "two-thirds of everything", (markets, social problems, demand for services etc.).

The subject therefore plays a key-role in decision-making regarding demand for tourism products.

Age in particular is an important example. The baby-boom generation is of prime importance due to its size (roughly 1/3 of the Canadian population – proportionally the largest of all the industrialized nations) and characteristics. It is well educated with above average income. The front end is also approaching (within 10 years) retirement age and will therefore have the money and the time to travel. The 'echo' generation (children of the boomers) are also creating peak demands on certain products and services. Born between 1980 and 1995, the front end is into their twenties and taking part in independent, adventure travel. They are also much more technologically advanced and have been brought up in a generation with strong concerns for the environment Other sub sectors and age cohorts also need to be understood to more effectively communicate with them.

Lifecycle Segments: A recent and comprehensive travel motivations survey was undertaken for both Canadian and US travellers. The data was used to provide a series of reports and one 9 focused on demographic analysis of the various tourism market segments. The life cycle segments were as follows:

- Youth Market (18-35, no children under 20 living at home);
- Family Market (with children under 20 living at home);
- Mature Market (36-65 – no children); and
- Seniors Market (over 65, no children living at home).

Each one of these is broken down into sub categories, as shown in the pie chart below. The two largest segments are the Family Market and the Mature Market – accounting for over two thirds of the entire travel market. This, again, reflects the boomer bulge in the population. The single largest segment, at nearly one quarter of all travellers, is Mainstream Young Families (children under 12 living at home). A quick overview of the characteristics of the various segment follows:

Youth Market: (20% of the travel market): lower than average incomes, high energy approach to travel (extreme sports), high participation rate in activities, especially likely to seek out personal indulgence travel, use the internet as a research and booking tool.

Family Market: (33% of the travel market): above average education and income, most affluent of the four markets. Tends to be shorter-haul travellers (with children); important domestic market; greater focus on recuperative vacation experiences; less likely than average to take day and overnight tours; less than likely than typical American traveller to visit Canada.

Mature Market: (32% of the travel market): relatively well educated and affluent; slightly more than average likely to seek out exploratory vacation activities; more than likely to have gone on natural sightseeing vacations & visited cultural attractions; above average users of travel packages.

Seniors Market: Smallest of the four markets (15%): lower than average education and income levels; American seniors more likely than the average traveller to visit Canada, and most likely of all the markets to seek out exploratory vacation experiences, much less likely to view vacations as opportunities for relaxation. Above average participation in natural sightseeing (although generally less active in outdoor activities) and above average in cultural and heritage attractions; more likely than average to take guided tours; rely more on printed material and television for travel opportunities and information.

Although currently smallest, special attention should be paid to the seniors market, as its members look for exploratory experiences and prefer value-added components such as guided services. Although currently not a wealthy segment, the baby boomers are approaching retirement with higher income and education levels.

As can be seen, the largest sub-markets are mainstream young families, mainstream mature couples and mainstream youth. All the affluent segments are very important to the tourism sector as they tend to be better educated, well travelled, have the means to travel and are often looking for new experiences. The affluent sub-markets account for over one-quarter of all travellers.

Behavioural Segmentation

People's *'activities, interests* and *opinions* (AIO's) also play a key role in decision-making and travel habits. These behavioural characteristics (also known as psychographics), when used in conjunction with demographics, provide a much stronger marketing tool for tourism businesses and planners. By understanding people's AIO's and their subsequent motivations, certain sub-groups can be targeted more effectively, as well as reflected in new product lines.

Another TAMS report (Emergent Vacation Interests) 10 focussed on emergent themes in tourism and indicated which demographic sub market was likely to drive which emergent theme. A more detailed description of the report's findings (relevant to The Product Club) is outlined in the *Tourism Trends Discussion Paper.* Suffice to say the key emergent themes (in order of anticipated net change) were as follows:

- Intimacy & Romance,
- Experiencing Different Cultures,
- Natural Wonders,
- Fine Cuisine and being pampered,

- Escaping winter weather,
- Adventure and Excitement,
- Experiencing Unspoiled Nature,
- Historic sites,
- Hands on Learning,
- Hobby or sport.

Any product development should try and incorporate one or more of these themes if it is going to meet future markets. Selecting a couple that are most relevant to The Product Club-*experiencing unspoiled nature* and *adventure and excitement,* the predominant sub-market driving both experiences is mainstream mature singles. Other important sub-markets that show great interest in these vacations are the young mainstream and mainstream young family markets.

The affluent family market is also a key driver. According to some travel writers 11, one of "the hottest trends in travel in 2002 was the family vacation", especially for affluent families. This may have arisen, in part, from the events of Sept, promoting a desire not to stray too far from loved-ones. With regard to transportation segmentation there is now even an airline designed exclusively for family travel: FamilyAir based in Los Angeles.

What the Sub-markets will be looking for

As noted, the largest sub-market is the mainstream young family market, accounting for 23% of North American Travellers. This group is looking for a number of outdoor activities, four out of the top five (in terms of anticipated net increases) of which are offered in the region. These are:

- horseback riding (12% expected increase);
- downhill skiing (11%);
- white-water rafting (10%); and
- kayaking or canoeing (10%).

The one not offered regionally (in the top five of emergent activities) is whale watching.

Other notable outdoor experiences that are gaining in popularity within this single largest market segment are snowmobiling on organized trails (8%) and recreational biking (7%). Although smaller than mainstream markets the affluent segments require special attention due to their larger discretionary spending. In each sub-market the level of affluence varied. For example with affluent young couples, two-thirds of the market have household incomes between $40K and $80K with a third having $80K plus. With the affluent mature and senior couples 100% had income in excess of $80K. The table below lists the top three emergent vacation experiences in each of the affluent segments, followed by the emergent vacation experiences in the three largest segments.

There are a number of common threads. Intimacy and romance was top of the list of emergent themes in three of the five affluent markets and top of the list of two of the three largest markets. Natural wonders, different cultures, hands-on learning, being pampered and adventure vacations were all repetitive emergent themes.

The growing demand for exploratory and learning travel was highlighted with a recent travel write-up of a Scottish whiskey school (a 3-day learning experience). One individual was there after being involved in a climbing accident: "as he lay on his back looking at the stars [he] realized that he had always loved the night sky but knew nothing about it. He promised himself that, if he lived, he would never be so negligent with his passions." [Incidentally at least two of the individuals on the course (in their 30's) went because they had received it as a gift].

In the near future, increased numbers will have greater awareness of the fragility of life and there is likely to be an increased push in making memorable vacations. The Vancouver office of the Canadian Institute for the Blind, for example, has one new client walking through its doors every ten minutes. This is expected to double, to one person every five minutes, within the next fifteen years.

Activity-Related Accommodation

Nearly all (19 out of 20) activity-related accommodation types were more likely to be stayed in over the subsequent two years (at 2000) compared with the previous two years. Again this confirms the importance of experiential vacations.

Especially promising increases were expected in the bed and breakfast market. Less common activity-based accommodations (in other words niche markets, stayed-in by less than 10% of travellers) showed great potential relative to their market size. These included health spas, learning experiences, working farms, and wilderness lodges, which all suggest that more exotic forms of vacation are on the increase. Of particular note is the 'staying at a wilderness lodge that you can drive to by car', showing a two-fold (anticipated) increase. This study was conducted prior to September 11, and the increased fear of flying (and cost) may contribute to enlarging this segment still further. The increased interest in activity-related accommodation types amongst American and Canadian travellers.

Conclusions

A number of conclusions can be drawn from the data above, especially with respect to creating or enhancing product lines. These are:

- Market Segmentation is crucial. No business can be everything to everyone and those that can differentiate their markets will be in a much stronger position.
- Segmentation should not based purely on similar product attributes; a 'market pull' approach should be adopted where planners/operators first understand the needs/desires of individual market segments and then design packages/products to meet those needs.
- There is no right or wrong way to segment the products or market but segments, or niche markets, should be both focused and targetable.
- Developing and implementing new product lines is only half the battle; other real work comes in trying to reach the target market-identifying accessible (and focused) markets first and then designing packages and products that will draw tourists in.
- The Product Club should not expend significant effort and dollars on undertaking primary research into market segmentation. Significant analysis of the market place already exists.
- The Product Club should primarily focus on its strength: delivering a nature-based tourism product. Within this, there should be a mix of different activities and experiences offered, from themes promoting intimacy and romance to learning vacations.
- The Product Club should not solely focus on one lifestyle segment, e.g. the needs of current baby-boomers, because

these will be replaced by a much smaller ("bust" population) in the years ahead. A mix is required and planning for future changes is important.

- The lines of segmentation are becoming more blurred as people mix activities.
- Special attention should be paid to emergent themes among segments. These include learning, intimacy and romance, heritage and historical trips, adventure and excitement, experiencing unspoiled nature, being pampered, health and spa retreats, bed and breakfasts related to activities, and lodges that can be driven to, among others.

The Application of Benefit Segmentation in Tourism Promotion

A basic starting point for tourism marketing efforts is a formal or informal marketing plan. In such a plan target market analysis or market segmentation is usually the first step and the most important part. An excellent market segmentation is half success of a marketing strategy. Promotion is particularly important in the tourism marketing strategy. A recurring problem in the tourism promotional area is "at whom should the promotional effort be aimed" and "what should be said to the prospective tourist". Market segmentation may give these questions good answers. Many people have proposed guidelines for dealing with the problem of identifying tourism target markets. They have attempted to position tourism products in the mind of the prospective tourists, or split up the market based on latent or overt psychological desires., price trip purpose, use type, or other characteristics of tourist in geography, socioeconomics and demography. However, some researchers have found with respect to the inability of demographics to explain important differences in travel and vacation behaviour. What is proposed here is a benefit segmentation approach which can combine many different ways of looking at the tourist and the travel market and actually simultaneously reduce marketing and promotional costs while increasing tourist demand. In other words, clever segmentation strategy can improve marketing and promotional efficiency for the tourism marketer. In addition, a tentative procedure will be rendered to help one to conduct a benefit segmentation research.

Tourism Marketing

In 1985 the American Marketing Association defines marketing as the performance of business activities that direct the flow of goods and services from the producer to the consumer or user. However, tourism industry is unlike many other industries in many ways: unseen before selling, intangibility, paying time and money before actually using, direct or indirect reservation in advance, far away from customers, combination of resources from a variety of businesses, cannot be stored, limited supply in the short term, instability of demand, and high elasticity of demand. The objective of marketing is to reflect the present marketing plan assessment, create the right image for the tourism product, and satisfy consumers. The most widely accepted method for this has been the development of marketing programs based on the 4 p's (product, place, price, and promotion). Within tourism generally price and place to visit is very difficult to be manipulated by tourist agencies in the short run. However, the product itself (various attractions in tourism industry) and promotion of that product (mass communications, direct mail, brochures, etc.), are much more controllable. The product itself can be improved to better match market desires but product calibration decisions involve long-term consequences since substantial developments require extensive time for planning and actual implementation.

The tourism industry can be differentiated from many tangible product businesses by the consumers' perception of risk when they buy intangible services. Promotion can reduce consumers' perception of risk. In addition, some features of tourism business, such as seasonal demand, price sensitive, selling without viewing the product, low brand loyalty, severe competition, and high substitution have made promotion play important role in tourism marketing. Promotion decisions involve the determination of copy appeals, media strategy, and production costs, and are easily controlled in the short run. Proper execution of the promotion task requires a thorough understanding of the levels and types of market heterogeneity faced by the tourism marketer. That is, a marketer needs to know his/her markets and their desires. Segmentation research can help with this task of identifying markets and can lead to more effective promotional strategies.

Market Segmentation on Benefits Sought

Generally speaking, market segmentation is based on four assumptions: (1) Tourists can be grouped into different but homogeneous market segments; (2) People in different market segment have different tourism needs and preferences; (3) A specific destination or tourist experience will appeal to some segments of the market more than others; (4) Tourism suppliers can improve their marketing efforts by market segments. Many ways exist to segment a market. The marketing literature is replete with examples of ways to group consumers based on geography, purchase behaviour, socioeconomic and demographic factors, use type, price, and various cognitive measures.

A method that has the highest usage in recreation or tourism is "benefit segmentation". It also uses a behavioral approach to segmentation but is the hardest to identify. This approach groups consumers according to benefits desired from a particular product category. It seeks to identify that part of the market that derives specific benefits from the product/service. The variables that a supplier has that are benefit based include recreational facilities and equipment, length of stay, transportation mode, experience preferences, and benefit expectations. With benefit-based segmentation, a supplier must determine what benefits potential customers are seeking from their tourist experiences. Groups are then formed of people who assign a similar amount of importance to the same product benefits. It is based primarily on cluster analytic method and has enjoyed widespread application. Once this is done, those benefits are presented to this market segment to encourage additional business.

The Procedure of Benefit Segmentation

The general approach of benefit segmentation consists of collecting data from various tourists by using survey instruments designed and applying appropriate statistical procedures to analyze these data. In brief, this approach includes two major phases: segment creation and segment testing.

Phase 1: Segment Creation

The first step is developing a set of attributes (benefits) which exhaustively describes the range of attributes available from and desired in the product. This list of attributes may include redundancies which are either real or perceived as real by the consumer. These benefits, for example, may be like scenery, cost of vacation, social activity, friendliness of people, cleanliness of environment, quality of shopping, quality of sporting opportunities, cultural opportunities, quality of accommodations, quality of entertainment, and so on. In practice it is usually developed from previous studies (content analysis of related literature), from judgment of a jury of experts, from perception testing of the relevant sample in the field (perhaps through focus groups), and pilot study of the instrument. This step is conducted to assure the list of attributes is clarity, concise, relevance, and validation, Engel, et. al.,., furnish a more thorough discussion of product attributes and their measurement.

The next step is eliciting subjects' assessments of the relative importance of each of the various attributes by Likert scale. For instances, "1" is very important and "5" is less important. In this way, an importance vector is created for each individual. Practically speaking, random sampling from a population of tourists is an impossible task. Generally, we can try to obtain a representative sample through randomizing time and location of questionnaire distribution. Cluster analysis.usually factor analysis of the importance vectors, is then employed in identifying groups of individuals in a benefit segment which is the package of benefits that they all are looking for when choosing a product or a service.

Phase II: Segment Testing

Segment testing directly describes the market structure. Each segment is described using several groups of variables such as principal benefits sought, general activities (lifestyle), interests, trip purpose, alternate destination favoured, different media habits and strengths, and opinions in travelling. These also include demographic and socioeconomic variables such as age, income, and size of family. Sometimes the discriminant analysis will be taken to test if demographic or psychographic variables are significant difference across each benefit segment. A summary of the overall profile of each benefit segment will be presented. Ultimately, promotional strategies are proposed for each of the segments which management wishes to reach.

Initially, each segment is described in terms of the unique, differential benefits sought by its members. This analysis is usually enhanced by a comparison of segments on their lifestyle and personality traits. Schewe and Calantone provide an example of this kind of comparison in a travel context. Also, demographic and socioeconomic statistics (SES) comparisons are made between groups to facilitate media purchases that efficiently reach target segments.

Next, purchase behaviour of each segment is evaluated. The assumption is that people tend to choose products which most closely fit their "ideal" in terms of benefits sought. Each group is identified by the benefits it seeks and the attractions (or brands) it prefers. From this point marketing strategy development draws on the manger's understanding of the situation. Key variables have been identified which make a segmenta i.e. market position) unique.

Managerial Implications

Sometimes the benefits that customers seek determine their purchasing behaviour much more precisely than do geographical, demographic, or psychographic factors.. The tourism marketer can develop demographic profiles of those groups identified in the benefit segmentation in order to promote to those segments. This and other valuable information in such research have provided marketer for designing promotional appeals to its consumers and potential consumers, brochures, package tours, direct selling, point-of-purchase materials, or other media, to the product in the study, and training of branch office personnel. When introducing a new product/brand, the manager can develop copy appeals based on benefits of the new product/brand matching the desired benefits of an identified target segment. This can be especially effective where a new product or brand possesses more of a desired benefit, a differential advantage, than an existing product or brand. Alternatively an existing product/brand might be repositioned with new appeals to better appeal to a particular benefit segment. Each of these strategies, as well as others, depends on the strength each existing product has in its position and each segment's demand for the product's benefits.

Also important is the stability of the segments over time. People change, the environment changes, enough promotion to segments will in and of itself change the market. Just people's need for variety causes segmentation schemes to change over time. Thus, all segmentation schemes have time limits on their usefulness. In addition, this kind study provided the impetus for further marketing studies in the travel and tourism industry.

Conclusion

Benefit is one of key factors in tourist's decision process. People pay to buy a service or product because they can gain some kinds of benefits from this' service or product. Therefore, the tourism marketer should understand purchase behaviour based on the-benefits the consumers seek. Choosing target segments and promotional themes are crucial to marketing any product or service. Benefit segmentation provides an excellent technique for effective and efficient marketing. The wealth of information provided by the benefit segmentation technique can be directly translated into marketing and promotional strategy. No technique can eliminate the need for good managerial judgment and knowledgeability concerning products and markets. However, it is hoped that the above discussion of benefit segmentation with research recommendations, furnishes a convincing argument for its usefulness in tourism promotion.

The International, Local and Social Efforts Involved

India expects a tourist inflow of around 10 million in 2010. The country's tourism sector was growing steadily with 3.92 million tourist inflow in 2005 and 4.43 million in 2006, a confidence is being generated that the inflow would touch the eight million mark in 2009.

There is considerable government presence in the travel and tourism industry. Each state has a tourism corporation, which typically runs a chain of hotels/motels and operates package tours, while the central government runs the India Tourism Development Corporation. Divestment of these state-run tourism corporations have either already taken place or are in process.

Incoming foreign tourist arrivals have shown a 6% compounded annual growth rate over the last 10 years. The government has realised the potential and has advanced several incentives to promote infrastructure growth in the tourism sector. Current investments are likely to see hotel room capacity increase by 20% over the next three years, with several international hotel chains entering the hotel industry. With specialised types of tourism becoming a craze throughout the world, India is coming up with Dubai-type shopping tourism facilities at several places besides focusing on health tourism. At least four such destinations would come up soon and another is likely in West Bengal. Aurangabad near Ajanta-Ellora in Maharashtra is one of the leading shopping tourism destinations coming up amongst others like Noida in Uttar Pradesh with world class facilities, Shilpagram near Hyderabad, permanent art and crafts fair at Bhubaneswar.

Tourism in Aurangabad

The incredible India campaign has given a brand new dimension to the marketing of India as a country. Aurangabad and particularly

Ajanta-Ellora have enjoyed a steady stream of local and international visitors from a long time, even before any specific promotion or campaign was done for it. The tourists are classified as " Budget Tourists" and " Star Tourists". They can choose the type of vacation they want to enjoy in this part of the country. It also enables the government and other bodies to subsequently divide their efforts on them The centre organizes exhibitions and trade shows especially in the Aurangabad region. These give an excellent platform for rural and ethnic culture of the region to be displayed before the international tourists. Various handicrafts, local crafts, food etc. are exhibited. Over the past 5 + years, Aurangabad has seen a regular flow of both national and international tourists. Acknowledged as one of the fastest growing tier-II city, Aurangabad offers a range of site seeing, shopping and experiencing opportunities. But amongst all, the most visited and most revered, still remain the beautiful Ajanta Ellora caves. In addition, the city has seen the development of relevant education providing institutes, courses – vocational, developmental etc. to provide world class atmosphere and service to the customers. The contributions of such entities were indeed exemplary.

Mentioning the infrastructure actors, the presence of three five star hotels in a tier–II city speaks a lot. Good quality roads, renovation of squares, bus stands, and railway stations, restoration works have been the focus to give a world class experience to the tourists. Promoting the place as a 'must see' on the list of the international Buddhist traveller has indeed been a national effort, but in line with that the contributions of local authorities can be seen in their adaptation of every heritage signage, symbol and story in their day to day activities.

The JBIC project

An entire project named 'Ajanta – Ellora Conservation and tourism development project' is dedicated to the conservation of Ajanta – Ellora site. MTDC (Maharashtra tourism Development Corporation) an undertaking of Maharashtra state conceived the Ajanta – Ellora Conservation and tourism development project and prepared in 1991 a master plan from Tata Consultancy Services, on the basis of which the Government of India requested the Government of Japan to consider grant of financial assistance for the project. The Government of Japan got the plan assessed from the Overseas Economic Cooperation Fund (OECF) now Japan Bank for International Cooperation (JBIC) and offered loan assistance for the implementation of the master plan as phase –I of the project. The government went into agreement for the loan in 1992. A Joint Venture of Pacific Consultants International (PCI) and Tata Consultancy Services (TCS) were appointed in November as consultants for planning and overseeing the implementation of the works under the loan. The objectives of the project are:

1. To conserve and preserve monuments and natural resources in the Ajanta-Ellora region.
2. To improve infrastructure in order to accommodate the increasing number of tourists to the region and enhance their experience by providing improved facilities and services.

The first phase consisted of building up essential infrastructure facilities. The consultants, then as was stipulated in Terms of Reference drafted a proposal for Phase –II. It was presented by the Ministry of Tourism for consideration of OECF in the Interministrial Meeting in 1998.

Phase –I and Extended Phase –I Expenditure

The project cost was estimated at Yen 4,406 million which is equal to Rs.817.1 million at the exchange of Rs. 1 = Yen 5.39. The support from JBIC was Yen 3,745 (Rs. 498.8 million) which was 85% of the total project cost.

Ajanta-Ellora Conservation and Tourism Development Project

Phase-II

The second phase of the Ajanta-Ellora Conservation and tourism development project with the Japanese Bank of International Cooperation (JBIC) sanctioning a soft loan of Rs. 300 crores became effective from July 31, 2003. The loan clearance was announces after JBIC held a series of talks with the central department of tourism and culture and MTDC in Delhi. The first phase of Ajanta– Ellora heritage circuit up gradation scheme won appreciation not only from Japanese government but also UNESCO. The second phase envisaged taking forward the conservation and a development scheme initiated in the first phase.

The second was targeted to be completed in 5 years time and was meant to generate additional employment in Ajanta-Ellora region. The plans envisaged restoration and repair of entire cave circuit of

Maharashtra i.e. between Mumbai and Aurangabad. The work carried out at these places includes structural reinforcement, chemical conservation of the paintings and artifacts, preservation of percolation within the caves, upgrading the environment, training conservation staff and improving visitor management system.

A Brief Account of the Work Being Done

Monument Conservation

It included the conservation and repair of he cave belt. Project packages of ASI (chemical branch) for chemical conservation of monuments., survey and maintenance/operation of equipments and purchase of equipments for conservation laboratory at Aurangabad and detailed documentation of heritage monuments.

The package included:

1. Protection of rock mass,
2. Prevention of water seepage in the caves,
3. Slope stability of caves and adjoining hills,
4. conservation, preservation and protection of sensitive paintings,
5. Surface water management,
6. Landscaping the adjoining region,
7. Visitor management,
8. Restoration of essential/structural elements and investigate/ exploration of surroundings.

Aurangabad Airport (Executing Agency – Airport Authority of India)

The major work included to facilitate domestic and international flights to land in Aurangabad and the airport facilities to be upgraded. The development was aimed to significantly boost the international tourist traffic. The package included:

1. Construction of new passenger terminal building and ancillary support facilities.
2. construction of new apron 500 x 400 and construction of taxi track.

Afforestation (Executing Agency – Forest Department, Maharashtra) The central idea was to enhance the greenery adjoining the classic plains surrounding the caves. This was aimed to improve vegetation cover which will prevent soil erosion subsequently reduce pollution vicinity of the caves.

The package included:

1. Major afforestation activity in adjoining areas of the caves.
2. Information and maintenance, erection of fire tower, fire line cutting every year, fire fighting equipments, display card on trees.
3. Tourist facilities, camping and accommodation facilities, establishment of nature trails and watch towers.

Road (Executing Agency – Public Works Department, Maharashtra State)

A number of roads were selected for repair and up gradation. All the roads lead to tourist destinations and it was considered that these improvements will lead to reduction in time and commuting costs. Also the towns and villages in the vicinity of these roads will also benefit.

Water Supply (Executing Agency – Maharashtra Jeevan Pradhikaran)

Water supply and sanitation was the main focus. The aim was to provide essential facilities to tourists visiting the caves.

Tourism and Marketing and Visitor Management System (MTDC) Development of Ajanta Tourist Complex: which included construction of visitor information centre, arrival area, interpretation centre, site museum, virtual reality hall, cave replicas, restaurants, plazas and service areas.

Development of Ellora Tourist Complex: which included construction of visitor centre, arrival area, interpretation centre, site museum, virtual reality hall, restaurants, plazas, and service areas.

Public Awareness Activities

For promotion of Maharashtra and Buddhist circuits along with Ajanta-Ellora region using press, print, audio visual and electronic media.

Human Resource Development

Training of staff for maintenance and operation of tourism destinations, visitor management systems, and tourism planning and environment conservation was the main focus.

Computerization of tourist information: A new system to be set up for computerization of tourist information.

Conservation of State Archeological Monuments

A number of sites, monuments and gates in the Aurangabad city and its vicinity were chosen for repair and conservation and also beatification so that it would act as an additional tourist attraction in line with the caves.

Development of Lonar crater: Lonar is the lake formed by an meteorite. Hence the focus was to promote it as a "must see" site. Roads, fencing, restoration, clearing of prosopsis plants, creation of visitor information centres etc. were undertaken. Additional sub projects at the vicinity of the caves: These included restoration and maintenance of various cave belts and regions. Development of access roads, signage, power and water infrastructure at these tourist places were on the list.

Micro Credit for Low Income Tourist Service Providers

This is the first of its kind in tourism sector in India and aimed at organizing and training service providers at tourist sites who are otherwise considered as nuisance by tourists and planners alike but are essential part of Indian tourism scenario. Along with the development of infrastructure in Aurangabad there is a need to cater to small necessities of tourists which are met by mushrooming hawkers whose service to tourists leave much to desire.

The micro financing sub projects aimed at organizing, training, and financing this low income segment. Women entrepreneurs will be given preference and suitable NGOs ha been identified to training, disburse and monitor the micro credit funding credit and recovery. The beneficiaries include of the scheme small restaurant owners, tea shops, kiosks, guides, photographers, hawkers, fruit vendors and taxi operators. This would make them more presentable as well as increase their entrepreneurial skills and abilities. The loan amount of the will be chanelised through rural banks.

Marketing the Shopping District

Aurangabad has an exclusive set up of mini markets and lanes dedicated to selling ancient craft. The areas near Panchakki, Ajanta – Ellora, Paithan, Daulatabad and the Aurangabad city have their own shops, which sell exclusive speciality items. Aurangabad has seen the thriving of many retail, government owned privately held outlets that offer a variety of regional handicrafts, clothes, jewellery, food etc.

This has immensely contributed to local employment generation. The marketing of Ajanta as a shopping destination is also a driving factor that made customers come to buy region specific products like Himroo shawls, jewellery etc. A best example is 'Paithani Saree' which is handmade and known to have originated at Paithan which is a 30 minutes drive from Aurangabad. On the way to Ajanta-Ellora there are number of government owned and also privately owned shops which sell Paithani sarees, Kurtas, Scarves handkerchiefs etc. All of these have a contributing effect on the marketing of India.

The shopping markets that have evolved in the form of mini shopping districts around the place/site made the shopping experience more relevant to the heritage promotion of Ajanta and Ellora. Even the five star hotels that are running successfully here have exclusive galleries dedicated to the handicrafts made in this region. Here the international traveller gets a glance at the Indian culture. This is a good place for shopping for the tourist who does not want to be bothered by local vendors and sellers.

Rural Tourism-" Atithi Devo Bhava!"

This is the central idea behind all the tourism activities done by the government. The tourists are given the taste of the Indian hospitality and treated as 'God' just the way it is written is scriptures and taught to every Indian.

The authorities have very strategically promoted the theme of 'Rural Tourism'. The focus is on promoting rural culture and enabling employment generation. Tourism is considered to be the major revenue generator in these regions. Typically the allied and dependant areas like restaurants, tourist guides, handicraft shops have been considered to be the focus areas for revamping and enhancement. An active platform is given to boost the generation of income in rural households. Tourists can now stay at the very homes of rural citizens.

The government has started the ' Bed and Breakfast scheme' where they can stay at a local household and get an exclusive experience of the ethnic and rural flavour of India. The housewives get a chance to earn as they provide Indian food and shelter to these travellers. While staying with these local families these tourists get a chance to enjoy the day to day life of an Indian village. As this region is extensively dependant on tourism, here the government is also helping them out to get a more professional way to carry on their business.

Along with the handicrafts that are widely sold, special promotion is given to the Indian wear like sarees, kurtas etc. Also women are given a chance to set up their units where they can put mehndi on the hands of the tourists. An entire package of rural site seeing, staying with a local family and enjoying Indian flavours, traditions and handicrafts is being successfully sold to the tourists. India is internationally known to be a diverse yet very vibrant and colourful country. Marketing it as an 'rural experience' that is a must have for every tourist has many varied dimensions to it. The basic beneficiary is rural India and also the international tourist in many ways. On one hand it gives a good platform for rural India to showcase its culture and also earn from it. And for tourist, it is a very different and exclusive experience. The incredible India campaign has given a real boost to the inflow of international tourists. The global and local authorities are striving hard to maintain the eco friendly zone which they have recently declared around the caves.

Ajanta-Ellora Festival

A large crowd is pulled annually by the Ajanta Ellora festival, formerly known as Ellora festival, which sees a lot of national, state, local and international involvement. It is one of the best ways to study the marketing mix involved in promoting the site as a tourist attraction. Local students from institutes like hotel institutes, tourism courses etc. are invited to join the organizers and delegated various tasks to be a part of this mega event. It has been one of the drivers of tourism has been the Ajanta –Ellora festival that was started as a cultural event by the authorities. Many well known Indian artistes perform on this occasion. Of all the 4 P's the most used, necessary and exemplary were the heritage place itself, people involved, products/services offered and the simplified processes in making Ajanta to top the traveller's list.

12

Shopping Tourism in South India

Tamil Nadu Shopping Travel Tours

Chennai

Chennai is well connected to little getaways from the city. These small towns, away from the rushing city life, give a closer insight into the Tamil and ancient Dravidian culture. Be it Mallapuram, Pulicat, Cholamandalam artists' village, Kovalam, or Kancheepuram, each has its own way of inviting people to Tamil culture Chennai Shopping Travel Tours. Chennai is known for its cotton & silk sarees, handloom works, Tamil handicrafts, gold jewellery, and other traditional Tamil stuff. It is home to some of the most swakiest retail outlets in the country. Poompohar emporium, Cottage emporium, Victoria Technical Institute market, T Nagar market, Nalli's Rasi and Kumaran Silks are some of the best places to shop from Chennai Shopping Travel Tours.

Chennai is a city where the traditional and the modern blend in life everywhere. From traditional vegetarian fair to fast foods, from nine-yard sarees to the latest in fashion, from ancient temple architecture to modern high-rise-with Indo-Saracenic and Victorian as stops along the way-from classical music and dance to discos throbbing to heady beats, Chennai has them all and many more vivid contrasts that are a pleasant surprise. And perhaps the most striking of them all is that here is a modern metropolis with beaches, parks and even sanctuaries in the heart of the City Chennai Shopping Travel Tours.

Chennai offers a wealth of nature and a rich historic past to visitors in the ambience of a city with every modern facility. Modern Chennai grew out of a small village when in 1639 a fishing hamlet called Madraspatnam was selected by early English merchants of the East

India Company as a site for the settlement Chennai Shopping Markets India. There are a number of churches in Chennai that are connected with the life and times of St. Thomas Chennai Shopping Travel Tours. There are also several ancient temples around Chennai, and, within the city itself are two magnificent temples-a temple in Triplicane and another in Mylapore.

Shopping Attractions: Chennai offers a wide variety of traditional and trendy merchandise such as carvings on brass, stone, wood and ivory, leather bikinis, bags and shoes Chennai Shopping Markets India. Traditional items from all over Tamil Nadu can be bought from Chennai like Pattamara Mats and the leaf and palmyra-fiber handicrafts from Tirunellveli, Metal works from Tanjavur, bronze and brass castings and traditional jewellery from Kumbakonam, stone carvings from Mamallapuram and Silks from Kanchipuram. The most popular shopping centres are in Rannganatha Street in T. Nagar and Anna Salai Chennai Shopping Markets India.

Prime Attractions: Fort St. George: The British East India Company under the direct supervision of Francis Day and Andrew Cogon built Fort St. George in 1640 AD Chennai Shopping Markets India. The fort houses St. Mary's Church and fort museum. St. Mary's Church is the oldest Anglican Church in India built in 1680 and the tombstones in its courtyard are the oldest British tombstones in India. This ancient prayer house solemnized the marriages of Robert Clive and Governor Elinu-Yale, who later founded the Yale University in the States Chennai Shopping Markets India. Today the fort is used by the state legislative assembly and as the secretarial offices of the Tamil Nadu government Chennai Shopping Markets India.

The flagstaff at Fort St. George is still the tallest in India. South of the Fort is the War Memorial, a graceful monument built in 1939 in memory of the warriors who sacrificed their lives during the First World War. The Island Grounds, the biggest lung space in the city is situated on an island formed by the river Cooum. This ground is the eventful venue of Trade and the Tourist Fairs held periodically which are seasonal attractions. The High Court with the decorative domes and corridors reminiscent of Indo/Saracenic architecture and the adjacent Parry's corner are the important landmarks of Chennai.

Kapaleeshwara Temples, Chennai Holiday Tours

Fort Museum: This museum contains many relics pertaining to the tenure of the East India Company and British India. It has a collection of contemporary paintings as well as the rare exhibits of weapons, uniforms, coins, costumes, medals and some other artifacts dating back to the British period.

Kapaleeswarar Temple: The biggest temple in the city, it is dedicated to Lord Shiva. The temple contains inscriptions dating back to the 13th century AD, and is a fine specimen of the Dravidian style of architecture. The 37-metre gopuram is especially noteworthy for its intricate carvings that depict stories from Hindu mythology.

Sri Parthasarathi Temple: The temple built in the 8th century is dedicated to Lord Krishna. It was built under the patronage of the Pallavas. It houses the idols of the five avataras of Sri Vishnu and has a small temple shrine dedicated to Vishnu's consort, called as Vedavalli Ammai in the native language of the region.

Santhome Cathedral: San Thome at the southern end of Marina derives its name from St Thomas, the apostle of Christ who is believed to have come to Madras sometime during 52 AD. He was killed on St Thomas Mount just outside the city in 78 AD and was interned in San Thome beach where a church was later built. Several years later, another church was built further inland and his mortal remains were transferred from the old church to the new one. In 1606 the church was rebuilt as a cathedral and in 1896 it was made a basilica. The beautiful stained glass window at the basilica portrays the story of St Thomas and the central hall has 14 wooden plaques depicting scenes from the last days of Christ. In the cathedral is a 3 ft high statue of Virgin Mary, which is believed to have been brought from Portugal in 1543.

Kanyakumari

The aura of the place is so mesmerizing that the tourists definitely like to take back little memoirs of Kanyakumari. Therefore, Shopping Tourism in Kanyakumari India is a very good place to look for handcrafted trinkets, palm leaf drawings, sea-shell crafts. Besides these, you can also shop for books of Swami Vivekananda and other mementos dedicated to this spiritual leader.

A religious destination of immense importance, Kanyakumari in Tamil Nadu is also frequented by hoards of tourists for the scenic beach and numerous tourist attractions that the land flaunts Shopping Tourism in Kanyakumari India. The southernmost tip of peninsular India, Kanyakumari must be visited on any tour to Tamil Nadu. Though not exactly known to be a shopper's paradise, Kanyakumari offers quite a few enchanting options to tourists for Shopping Tourism in Kanyakumari India Kanyakumari is an excellent shopping destination for buying various seashell items. Nothing better than to purchase beautiful seashell trinkets and souvenirs for your loved ones from this popular beach destination Shopping Tourism in Kanyakumari India ! While shopping in Kanyakumari, you can buy beautiful decorative items made of wood and bamboo. Palm-leaf utility articles are also good buys from Kanyakumari.

On the beachfront at Kanyakumari and within the temple premises there are several handicraft shops which sell many seashell products. The Tamil Nadu Co-optex Sales Emporium, Indco Products. Tamil Nadu Crafts and Poompuhar are some of the well known shopping centres where you can buy various handicraft items, textiles and other materials. Shopping in Kanyakumari must also include multi-coloured sea sands and small curios made of numerous kinds of sea-shells. Traditional saris and other dress materials are also easily available in some of the shops at Kanyakumari Shopping Travel Tours What better gifts and souvenirs to carry home form this popular beach destination than beautiful trinkets made from seashells! While shopping in Kanyakumari, you will come across beautiful decorative items made of wood and bamboo.

Shopping Tourism in Tanjore India

The city of Tanjore in Tamil Nadu is a haven for craft lovers. The city draws much of its fame from the exquisite handicrafts and handlooms that its skilled artisans produce. Weaving, painting, jewellery, woodworks are some of its renowned handicrafts which make for wonderful shopping in Tanjore. Since long past has been a princely state and under the patronage of the royals, tradition of art and craft attained a glorious height in Tanjore. Do remember to take back some artifacts while shopping in Tanjore.

Silk weaving is a major traditional craft in Tanjore. A lot of people are engaged in the profession. They specialize in weaving silk saris with broad border and unique motifs laden all over with Zari work. The saris are huge hit for weddings and religious occasions. Pick up graceful Tanjore silk saris while Tanjore Shopping Travel Tours Another must-buy in Tanjore is traditional paintings. Richly adorned paintings of mostly Hindu gods are quite popular with those who want to do

Tanjore Shopping Travel Tours Check out Thalaiyatti Bommai (literally the head-nodding doll), which serve as great souvenirs of a Tanjore Shopping Travel Tours Thanjavur Plates (with sombu, coconut), brass and bronze idols, bowls and vessels are other items for shopping in Thanjavur. There are many shopping joints within the city. Several government run shops and private ones dot over the townscape, which you may explore for great variety and right price.

Visiting the craftsmen at work and buying directly from them is also a good option for Tanjore Shopping Travel Tours Shopping in Tanjore is an amazing experience. During your tour to Tanjore, you can go out shopping at the several markets in Tanjore. There are several shopping joints within Tanjore including government run emporia and private shops. You may also visit the craftsmen at work and buy directly from them. You can avail of a variety of authentic articles at good prices at all these places. Tanjore was formerly a princely state and under the patronage of the royals, tradition of art and craft reached a glorious height. Tanjore is renowned for its exquisite handicrafts and handlooms produced by its skilled artisans. Weaving, painting, jewellery, woodworks are some of its famous handicrafts which make for great Tanjore Shopping Travel Tours A prime traditional craft of Tanjore is silk weaving. While shopping in Tanjore, pick up some lovely Tanjore silk saris, weaved with broad border and unique motifs laden all over with Zari work. These saris are hugely popular for weddings and religious occasions.

Madurai Shopping Complexes

For a city sipped with history and tradition, it is not surprising to have an amazing corpus of traditional and ethnic. Products ranging from handicrafts to textiles and metallurgical artifacts. It is particularly known for the cottons and the batiks. If one is looking to explore all these products under one roof. Prithu Mandapam Market is the place to be Madurai Shopping Complexes. Madurai is also a nice place to shop for the traditional objects from greater Tamil Nadu as well. These are available in the West Tower Street, Handloom House, Khadi Crafts, etc. in addition to this, there are numerous flea markets and shops selling curios outside major tourist attractions.

While shopping in Madurai, you can buy locale manufactured cottons and batiks from Puthu Manadapam Market Madurai Shopping Guide. Just outside the eastern entrance of the Meenakshi Temple

Madurai Shopping Guide. The interesting things about the rows of tailoring shops here is that they can stitch a dress for you in an hour or two. You can also pick up the famed Madurai silk and handloom sarees from big textile showrooms like the famous Hajeemoosa Textiles Madurai Shopping Guide. If you want to buy souvenirs in wood or brass, you should visit the Cottage industries emporium and other government emporiums nearby Madurai Shopping Guide. Madurai is also famous for its ethnically crafted jewellery if you want to indulge. In the pleasure of buying gold and silver ornaments. Madurai has also been a textile centre for long Madurai Shopping Guide. Here skilled tailors can reproduce your dress with cottons and printed fabrics at Puthu Mandapam. You can also visit the government Poompuhar Handicrafts shop Madurai Shopping Guide. The Cottage Arts Emporium and the Madurai Gallery for hand-woven silks and cottons.

Chidambaram City Travel Packages

Shopping in Chidambaram is restricted to local handloom and textile products. There are daily markets around commonly visited places like the Nataraja temple where tourists can buy souvenirs. They range from stone carved images of Shiva in the *Ananda Tandavam* posture, replicas of the temple, laminated or framed images of the gods and deities etc. apart from these, during the festivals there are large fairs throughout the city where villagers from the nearby areas set up their stalls.

One could buy trinkets of local jewellery, or refresh their taste buds with the local sweets and snacks. Beside these there are state handicrafts and khadi houses.

Chidambaram Tourism-Chidambaram is one of the most ancient and most celebrated of shrines in India. It is of great religious as well as historic and cultural significance. Tour to Chidambaram is the seat of the cosmic dancer Nataraja (Ananda Tandava pose; the Cosmic Dance of bliss). It is one of the Pancha (five) Bhutasthalas signifying the five elements of wind (Kalahasti), water (Tiruvanaikka), fire (Tiruvannamalai), earth (Kanchipuram) and space (Chidambaram). Tours to Chidambaram-There are several tourist attractions in Chidambaram. The Nataraja temple is located in the centre of the town and covers an area of 40 acres. The roof of the sanctum sanctorum is covered with gold plates. The presiding deity of the temple is represented by air, one of the five elements of the universe and is known as Akasa

Lingam. The Thillaikaliamman temple is on the northern end of the town. It was built by Kopperunjingan, who ruled between 1229 A.D. and 1278 A.D. Pichavaram is just 16 km from Chidambaram and ranks among the most exquisite scenic spots with abundant and varied tourism resources. Chidambaram Tours and the Annamalai University is a residential university founded by Raja Sir Annamalai.

Chettiar. It is on the eastern outskirts of the town and is a great centre of Tamil learning and Carnatic music, with facilities in various disciplines including Medicine, Engineering, etc. Chidambaram Tourist Attractions-The nearest airport to Chidambaram is Tiruchi which is 168 km. away. It is connected by rail with Tiruchi, Madurai and Chennai. It is also well connected by roadways with all major towns and cities.

Shopping in Rameshwaram City India

Rameshwaram Shopping is highlighted by the availability of wonderful handicraft items of the region. This is a haven for a variety of exquisite handicraft and decorative items. They can be bought from the many shops near the temples. These are made by the local craftsmen and are god souvenirs to take home. There are items made from palm leaf, beads and seashells. You can purchase exquisite handicraft items. The Rameswaram silk sarees are very popular among the ladies. There is a lot of variety and textures available at reasonable prices. Shopping in Rameshwaram City India markets in Rameshwaram are stuffed with these exotic decorative masterpieces. Which are very popular among the tourists, visiting this place throughout the year.

Numerous shops near the temples of Rameshwaram sell exquisite showpieces made of seashells, beads, palm leafs, etc. The Rameshwaram shops are the ideal destinations for shopaholics and fashion freaks Rameshwaram Shopping Guide. The Khadi crafts available in the shops in the city attract them Rameshwaram Shopping Guide. The women swear by the famous Rameshwaram Silk Sarees and do not miss the opportunity to buy a few for their near and dear ones. Rameswaram is on an island in the Gulf of Mannar Rameshwaram Shopping Guide. Connected to the mainland at Mandapam by rail and by one of India's engineering wonders, the Indira Gandhi Bridge Rameshwaram Shopping Guide. The bridge took 14 years to build and was opened by Rajiv Gandhi late in 1988.

The town lies on the island's eastern side and used Rameshwaram Shopping Guide. To be the port from which the ferry to Talaimannar

(Sri Lanka) departed before passenger services Were suspended more than a decade ago as a result, there are now very few foreign visitors. The island is situated on the west of the Pamban bridge and is thronged by the marine biologists for research and observation. It is 20 km from Rameswaram via Mandapam Rameshwaram Shopping Guide. The island is famous for coral reefs and houses a wide variety of sea creatures in its reefs. This Lord Vishnu temple stands at the southern tip of Rameswaram in Dhanushkodi. It is the only temple structure that survived the 1964 cyclones Rameshwaram Shopping Guide.

Ooty Shopping Guide

It is an ideal place to shop. You can get Exclusive Nilgiri products including Nilgiri tea, fruits, natural oils like Eucalyptas. Toda embroideries and tropical plants are alsoeasy to get. The cooperative Super Market and Municipal Market are the best places if you are looking for local fruit and general groceries. If looking for Indian handicraft and other material items then you need look no further than Kairali of Kerala Handicrafts and Poompuhar of Tamil Nadu Handicrafts. On the slopes of the great Nilgiri range, the region grows some of the best qualities of coffee and tea in India. The sprawling plantations and the heady smell are feast to senses. You may choose to buy some coffee or tea while shopping in Ooty.

The ace craftsmen of Tamil Nadu are skilled in making fantastic Jewellery, painting, pottery, and stone crafts. Look for such artifacts as you go on shopping in Ooty. You may also come across some tribal crafts in the shops. The local bazaars are replete with private shops and Government run emporia, where you can shop till you drop Shopping Places in Ooty India. Many hotels have shopping arcades where of course the price would be a bit on higher side Shopping Places in Ooty India. The shopping malls of Ooty are flooded with natural products of forests Shopping Places in Ooty India. Ooty is a paradise for those who love shopping. Surrounded by tea gardens, the tourists can smell the enchanting scent of fresh tea leaves while taking a stroll in the long winding paths of Ooty. The fresh tea leaves are purchased by the tourists as a relic of the beautiful place of Ooty Shopping Places in Ooty India.

Another prominent itinerary in the list of items while shopping in Ooty is the pure and sweet honey which is available in all the stores and shopping centres of the place Shopping Places in Ooty India. The natural oil of Eucalyptus has a great demand among the shoppers because of its medicinal value. The markets of Ooty are full of fresh fruits that impart a colourful look to the place Shopping Places in Ooty India.

The exquisite piece of the embroidered items by the tribal community of Toda represents the rich traditional art and craft of South India. The delicately designed jewellery of Silver is another attraction for the tourists who purchase such items as souvenirs for their near and dear ones Shopping Places in Ooty India.

Shopping in Ooty offers the tourists to choose from a plethora of several eatable items and handicraft products that reflects the salubrious climate and the enriched regional culture of the place Shopping Places in Ooty India.

Mamallapuram Shopping Guide

Mahabalipuram is a favourite shopping haunt for South Indian artifacts, both wooden and granite based. The stone artifacts made by the locals are a collector's delight. They can be bought at the small side roads. They make excellent souvenirs and are reasonable and very attractive. They also reflect the creativity of the local craftsmen. Mamallapuram has revived the ancient crafts of the Pallava stonemasons and sculptures and the town wakes every day. To the sound of chisels chipping away at pieces of granite. Some excellent work is turned out.

The yards have controls to supply images of deities and restoration pieces. To many temples throughout India and Sri Lanka. Some even undertake contract work for the European market Shopping Places in Mamallapuram India. You can buy examples of this work from the Poompuhar Handicrafts Emporium or from the craft shops Shopping Places in Mamallapuram India. Which line the roads down to the shore temple and to the Five Rathas Shopping Places in Mamallapuram India. If you want a hammock, this is quite a good place to buy one Shopping Places in Mamallapuram India. For a book exchange service try Himalaya Handicraft on the main street. Exquisite soapstone images of Hindu gods, woodcarvings, jewellery and other similar products are also for sale. There are several Kashmiri shops too Shopping Places in Mamallapuram India. Mamallapuram is a place where one can shop for beautifully carved images of Hindu Gods in soft stone or wood. Decorative articles made from sea shells are widely available here Shopping Places in Mamallapuram India. There are some Kashmiri shops selling Hammocks here. There is even a Himalayan Handicraft emporium here which offers some good handicraft items from the Himalayan states.

Dharapuram Shopping Guide

This is definitely not a shopper's paradise. Only the local artifacts are available here. The local souvenirs are available at reasonable prices in the small shops and also by the road side. It also has a spillover from Erode and the neighbouring cities of textiles and hosiery. This, however, is not a place on would recommend for shopping. It is basically a sleepy town with not much activity. The cities nearby are rich in exports, like Erode for Hosiery and Coimbatore for silks.

Erode also has a number of textile mills. When Tippu fell to the British, the East Indian Company took over the administration. Its famous for its aanjaneya temple. Tamil Nadu. In ancient times Dharapuram was called as Viradapura which has significant links to Mahabharata. Dharapuram and Coimbatore got the status of Municipality on a same day.

Dharapuram Municipality is promoted 1st grade municipality on May 6, 1983. Dharapuram Town is situated along the bank of River Amaravathi with an extent of 7.02 Sq.km. The town has attained the status of a Municipality in the year 1916 and functioning as the First Grade Municipality from 09.05.1983. The town developments completely depend on the agricultural activities and Commerce and Trades. Once upon a time Dharapuram was a Capital for South NOYYAL Dt, and Bhavani was a North Noyyal Dt. That time Erode was a village Dharapuram City Tour Guide.. It is a sleepy village at the foot of the Nilgiris Mountains Dharapuram City Tour Guide.

It is about 90 Kms from Coimbatore, in the district of Erode. It is situated on the banks of the river Amaravathi. This is a tributary of Cauvery. One side of it is fairly garlanded by Kodaikkanal Mountain Ranges Tamil Nadu Travel Tourism India. Dharapuram City Tour Guide town is residing on the banks of the holy river Amaravathi, a tribute to Cauveri. It has a rich history with the famous Hindu dynasties being a part of it. Tamil Nadu Travel Tourism India.

Kerala Shopping Guide

Shopping in Kerala is as exciting as touring the mystical place. Kerala is famous for its local crafts and you will find a traditional touch in each and every craft item in Kerala. Apart from the usual knick-knacks, there are many eatables that you can buy in Kerala Shopping Guide. The famed banana chips are available in each and every shop in Kerala. While in Kerala Shopping Guide, shopping can be done in major cities like Kochi Kerala Shopping Guide.

Trivandrum, etc. In all major cities, you will find not only the flea markets but also glittering malls and showrooms. Kerala is famous for gold and every road in Kerala's major cities will have a huge jewellery shop. You will be amazed to see the amount of gold that is bought by people. Indian gold is pricey so check the on going rates before you buy anything Kerala Shopping Guide. Apart from jewellery, Kerala is well-known for its ivory carvings, pottery, brocade fabrics and earthenware products. It is an unforgettable experience to shop for those small traditional items in Shopping Places in Kerala India.

Also famous are the Indian spices that are available in Shopping Places. You can choose from turmeric, pepper, ginger powder and other exotic spices that are available only in Kerala. The most famous shopping centres in Kerala are in Trivandrum on the M.G. Road. You can buy the famous wooden "Kathakali" face as a remembrance of this beautiful place. You can also buy the traditional Indian attire known as "Sari".

Kerala is famous for its variety in saris and you can find some really good colours and designs here. Do not hesitate to bargain a bit on the prices Shopping Places. Owing to the abundance of forests and coconut groves in Kerala, wood, coir and coconut shells traditionally remain the base of such handicrafts. A whole range of souvenirs and trinkets are made from these Shopping Places. Artifacts made of teak, deep-wine rosewood and fragrant sandalwood may arrest your eyes while shopping in Kerala. Buffalo horn is also popular with Kerala artisans as a raw material for the handicrafts. But the sea-fringed state of Kerala is also the land of spices. Since long past Kerala has carved a niche of its own in the global spice market for its rich flavored spices. Spices are used in medicines, preservatives, perfumes and above all in cooking.

Cochin

Cochin is a haven for shoppers from all parts of the world. You can buy here some authentic metal-ware, camel-bone carvings and also wood-made structures. Unsurprisingly, there are also articles that are made of coconut and bamboo cane Cochin Shopping Travel Tours. If you are looking for handicrafts then there are many options like jewellery stores and garments and handmade fabrics. The major hubs for shopping are MG Road, which is located at the centre of the city Cochin Shopping Travel Tours.

There is also Marine Drive for shopping lovers (do not confuse it with the one in Mumbai). Weekdays are the best days to shop, as most of the shops are closed on Sundays Cochin Shopping Travel Tours. As travellers loiter around the old city, the cosmopolitan character clearly comes to the forefront that are well reflected in the Mansions and structures built in the place Cochin Shopping Travel Tours. Discovered by the Portuguese, the island city with the lagoons and canals with the fishing hamlets is today one of the busiest port of India Cochin Shopping Guide.

Cochin lies on the direct route to the countries of east Europe and Australia and is proud to possess all the three forms of transport in one particular region Cochin Shopping Guide. Fort Cochin: Called the Old Fort, the Fort Cochin is the first and the foremost fort built by the Europeans in India and is among the most important travel attractions of the city. Initiated by the Dutch, the Fort was also developed by the Britishers Cochin Shopping Guide.

The Fort as a whole consists of many amazing structures Cochin Shopping Guide. The Fort houses the memory of Vasco Da Gama, the first European to land on the coast of India in the year 1498. The old fort comprises a huge Portuguese style mansion, the St. Francis church and the basilica of Santa Cruz Cochin Shopping Guide.

Chinese Fishing Nets: The huge Chinese cantilevered fishing nets were brought by the Indian traders from the royal court of Kubla khan, the famous Mongol Emperor and founder of the Yuan Dynasty of China Cochin Shopping Guide. These nets were erected by the traders in around 1350 to 1450 AD and are set up on the teak wood and bamboo poles. The nets offer an interesting sights when they are lowered in to the sea to catch the big cats underwater Cochin Shopping Guide.

Mattancherry Palace: Constructed in the year 1557, the magnificent Palace was presented to Raja Veera Kerala Varma of Cochin as a gift by the Portuguese Traders. Complete with extraordinary murals and scenes from the epics of Ramayana and Mahabharata, the palace also displays the Dutch maps of Old Cochin. The royal coronation and the palanquins are splendidly presented. Renovated in 1663 by the Dutch, the palace show case the wonderful attires of the Maharajas who ruled the place from earlier times.

St. Francis Church: The St, Francis Church has the reputation of being the first church built by the Dutch in the year 1503 AD. It is also the burial place of Vasco De Gama, the portuguese trader and sailor, the first European to discover India. The great traveller was buried here in 1524 before his remains were taken to Lisbon, Portugal in about 1538.

Bolghatty Island: The narrow and elongated island widely known for the famous Bolghatty Palace was constructed by the Dutch in 1744. The island hold the only picturesque golf course of Cochin among its prime attractions.

Calicut Shopping Guide

Shopping in Calicut is a pleasure for people from all across the world. Its most popular joint for shopping is Sweet Meat Street – yes, it is a street which goes back to the ear when there used to be streets lined with stalls of sweetmeat. Here, you can get fancy clothes at reasonable rates and prices. Also, Mavoor Road is one such place where you can get fancy and good clothes. Big Bazaar Road is your cup of tea if you are looking at wholesale spice market. Then there is Comturst Store near town hall that sells handloom fabrics. These are manufactured locally in the factories.

Climate: Due to its nearness to sea, the place has a hot and humid climate. Summer starts from March and continues until May. Maximum temperature recorded in the month of May is 36°C and minimum temperature recorded in the month of December is 14°C. Southwest monsoon arrives in the first week of June and average annual rainfall is 254 cm Calicut Shopping Guide.

Past: There is not much known of the early history of Calicut except for some prehistoric rock-cut caves that have been found at many places of the district. During the Sangam age, the district was under the Chera administration until AD 1122. This was the time when this region was a major centre of trade between Kerala and the outside world Shopping Places in Calicut. The city of Calicut came into existence in the 13th century when Udaiyavar, the king of Ernad, conquered the area around Ponniankar and built a fort at a place called Velapuram, now known as Calicut. Interestingly, the name Calicut is derived from 'calico,' the fine variety of hand-woven cotton cloth said to have originated from this place Shopping Places. Outer world came to know about India in 1498 when Vasco da Gama came to Calicut and obtained permission to carry out trade from here. Quickly in succession came the English and Dutch. Disputes over the control of Calicut continued for a long time until 1792, when the East India Company went into an agreement with the local Zamori rulers to directly administer this area. Kerala was declared a state in 1956, and Calicut today is one of the most important centres of trade and business in this progressive state.

Sites To Visit: Kappad is the place where Vasco da Gama set foot for the first time when he came to India on May 27, 1498. There is a small stone monument at the beach to commemorate that event.

Pazhassirajah Museum is located on the East Hill. It is run by the State Archeological Department. Ancient mural paintings, antique bronzes, old coins, models of temples, and megalithic structures are on display here Shopping Places. Situated next to Pazhassirajah Museum is an art gallery displaying paintings of Raja Ravi Varma. Dolphin's Point is a good place to watch dolphins playing in the sea early in the morning. On this beach are also situated Calicut Town Centre, Lions Club, and a lighthouse. Two crumbling piers, more than hundred years old, stand out into sea at Kozhikode beach. The beach is easily accessible from the city and provides a good view of the setting sun. The place also has a Marine Life Aquarium open whole day.

The Science Planetarium at Jaffarkhan Colony is the best place to unravel the mysteries of universe and enlightens about the planets and stars. The Science Centre has an interesting array of games, puzzles, and scientific gadgetry, which can keep a person busy for the whole day. The planetarium and Science Centre are in the same complex. Mananchira, which was the palace tank of King Mana Vikrama, has been now turned into a traditional architectural splendor with carpeted green grass and surrounded by ethnic buildings. The place also has a musical fountain.

Sites Nearby: Beypore (11 km) is a small coastal town known for its shipbuilding industry for centuries. It is still a favourite destination to buy large boats. Vadakara (48 km) is a commercial centre of martial arts and the birthplace of Tacholi Othenan, a legendry hero of North Malabar.

Ninety-eight kilometres away from Calicut is Tellicherry and Sultan Battery famous for their breathtaking scenery. Thusharagiri is famous for its waterfalls and lush green forests. It is at a distance of 11 km from Kodenchery, a place abounding in rubber plantations, coconut, pepper, ginger, and spices of all sorts. There is a dam at Kakkayam, located around 45 km from Calicut. The place offers challenging trekking and rock-climbing through river path and numerous waterfalls.

Shopping Tourism in Alleppey India

Alleppey is a haven for shoppers. It has all the ingredients to make it a shopping paradise. Here, you can shop for some very authentic coir products and carpets. You can also see how coir are manufactured here. The city has many shops that sell coir matting and carpets. You can get it all at very reasonable prices here. However, being tourists you may have to bargain it with the local shopkeepers.

However, the quality of coir products is so good that most of you may not paying a tad higher price for it. Alleppey is also a magnificent destination if you are looking to purchase pepper, coconut oil or cardamom. Indian Holiday offers an excellent range of Alleppey tour packages to make your India trip a bit more special. The architectural splendor and the modern outlook of this capital city make Alleppey the dream destination for tourists.

Alleppey the backwater destination of Kerala is famous for its beautiful backwaters houseboat cruises and seafood. If you are looking for an idyllic retreat amidst the emerald green waters, palm fringed shores and lush acres of greenery then Kerala Backwaters is the ideal destination for you. Alleppey is widely known for its good quality coir products and carpets, and shopping in Alleppey for these products will be a fascinating experience. You can get glimpses of the coir manufacturing process at Alleppey-right from the coconut husk to the final rope/coir yarn stage. The numerous shops that sell coir matting and carpets are frequented by a regular number of tourists and the fine quality, variety and reasonable prices make these a much sought after product while shopping in Alleppey. Alleppey is also famous for the pepper, coconut oil, areca nut, cardamom, and sugar available here. In the markets in Alleppey you will also find hoards of fresh fruit and vegetables, which you will be more than delighted to buy.

Tourist attractions: The central area of Alleppey town is called Mullakkal, where you will come across a number of gold and silver shops. Renowned for gold and silver ornaments, these shops are places worth visit on your shopping spree.

Kumarakom Shopping Travel Tours

Shopping in Kumarakom is a damn good experience for people from all parts of the world. You can go shopping to Kottayam, which is 15 km from the city or can shop in the interiors of the city . There are many craftsmen in Kerala, so you will find a lot of handcrafted items in this culturally rich state. There are camel bone carvings that are reasonable and also look very striking. You can also purchase many reasonable and high-quality handcrafted items of wood, coconut shell, cane and bamboo.

There are also many other items like jewellery and garments that are worth having a look at Kumarakom Shopping. Although not one of the hottest shopping destinations in Kerala, Kumarakom is a pleasant place to indulge in some leisurely shopping when you are free and not wandering into the depths of the wildlife sanctuary or cruising down the charming backwaters. Shopping in Kumarakom can be a nice experience because the various items available here are generally of good quality and would tempt you to pick souvenirs from the shops scattered in the town.

Some of the best buys while shopping in Kumarakom include metal-ware, camel-bone carvings, wood carvings. Articles made of coconut shell, bamboo and cane, embroidered screw-pine (pandanas palm) mats, grass mats, and various other types of handicrafts items. The people of Kerala are wonderful artisans and all these finely crafted items are much sought after by tourists visiting Kumarakom Shopping. Shopping in Kumarakom can also include various antique items, jeweller. Readymade garments, and ethnic hand-woven textiles, which are also easily available in the local markets. You will also find various gift items typical of the state of Kerala. These can range from products as diverse as lampshades and fashion accessories like earrings, to brass lamps, 'kathakali' masks.

Other decent buys at Kumarakom include fresh and aromatic spices which are quite abundant here. But if you want to indulge in an extensive shopping spree, then Cochin-at about 70 km from Kumarakom, will be the perfect shopping haunt for you.

Munnar Shopping Guide

Not a surprise, the best thing you can buy here is tea. Tea is brought to shops here direct from estates. Besides being reasonable and high on quality. It is easily available and you can smell it and tell that there cannot more fresh aroma anywhere in the world. Like many other parts of Kerala, you can also find here a lot of handcrafted items.

At a reasonable rates and of high-quality. Besides, tea you can also shop for spices here as there is rich spice plantation. If you are a real tea lover, you can even visit factories and carry a few leaves as samples, and can also taste various flavours.

The markets are minus glitz and glam of a showroom—a local bazaar set up. Besides the local veggies, woollens, tea, coffee, spices, spices, seasonal fruits etc. are seen arranged not-so-aesthetically in the narrow lanes of the this bazaar. The majority of bazaars are owned by the private owners but the presence of Government Shops can also be felt in the market. Munnar's best buys are all its local products.

Munnar is all meant to buy tea and better quality tea, which cannot be procured anywhere else in the country. Tea and history is 25 years old. Several tea kiosks and shops are full-fledged engaged into tea selling. As many the smaller and larger tea shop are owned by local people. Lay your hand on the best quality tea such as colonial tea (lowest Rs 140 for half kg), Lemon Tea, Green Tea, etc. Unlike tea, strawberries are seasonal pick ups. Fresh and best in quality, strawberries are sold at chosen outlets.

Spices are available in abundance in Munnar. Every shop and other nook and corners are engaged in selling tea and spice such as cardamom, cinnamon, nutmeg, clove, etc. So be it spice shopping or tea shopping in Munnar it will always be an interesting experience for the tourists. Top Tea Station in Munnar has a collection of rare fruits like the passion fruits and tree tomato.

Shopping Tourism in Trivandrum

Trivandrum being the most important city of Kerala, economically and culturally. Certainly has a shopping experience to offer to people of all tastes. You can shop here for valued handcrafted items such as jewellery, garments and household items. Things may be little expensive here as they are being sold in commercial markets. However, you can choose from a wide range of fabrics and materials like wood, ivory, coconut. Chalai is the local market here. You may have bargain a little bit here to get reasonable prices.

But all in all you will get good and long-lasting stuff. A Trivandrum tour is left incomplete if you return without shopping in Trivandrum.

More often than not shopping is an integral part of a tour. Everyone wants to take back some artifacts, utilities or souvenirs after touring a region. The rich tradition of art and crafts make for a great shopping in Trivandrum. Metal work is an ancient art in this part of Kerala. The ace craftsmen of Trivandrum make exquisite items out of bell metal. Pick up some kitchenware, brass lamps and many other objects d'art while shopping in Trivandrum.

Coir products are also a wonderful speciality of Kerala. Floor coverings, doormats, floor Matting and rugs come in a range of colours and designs, which are made of coir or coconut fibres. These along with coconut shell crafts are huge favourites with those who want to do some shopping in Trivandrum. Wood carving and horn carving is also interesting art forms in Kerala. You may be on the look out look for beautiful artifacts carved out from animal horns as you go on shopping in Trivandrum. Don't forget to pick up miniature snake boats and kathakali masks while shopping in Trivandrum that make for fantastic souvenirs of a Trivandrum tour. You would find many shopping joints in Trivandrum. Some are run by the state government while others are private ones. Drop in at M.G. Road in the city to where you may come across large variety of local handicrafts for shopping.

Thrissur Shopping Guide

As Thrissur is well known as the cultural centre of Kerala, this city abounds in religious and cultural items all around. The rich cultural and traditional activity here makes it well organized in the production of artistic and craft products, which also forms major shopping articles available here for tourists. These handicrafts are mainly based in producing wonderful woven silk cloths and jewellery. Coir handicrafts, crafts of coconut shells, carvings of horns, carvings of woods, works of brass, carpet making and other household articles comprises the major portion of handicraft products. The Kathakali Mask is the best bought souvenir of visiting.

Thrissur in Kerala is renowned for its mesmerizing variety of silks. Bell metal curios, brass work, textiles and gold jewellery are typical buys, the shopaholic would find hard to resist when in Thrissur Shopping Guide If you are making a choice for a true memorabilia of the place from a wide array of display. Thrissur's very own culture to take home the true flavour of the region. The silk produced in Thrissur are possibly the best buys while in the city. A variety of materials in myriad hues are sure to attract the tourists and visitors. Artifacts made of brass are also popular for their intricacy and use in common everyday life. Exquisitely crafted ornaments and embellishments in gold with in distinctly South Indian designs and alignments are also preferred by many Shopping Places.

The shops of Thrissur are welcoming with well behaved sales person who are always ready. With a smile to help you decide what is best for you if you find yourself lost in the huge variety available. The best part is, you can shop at your own pace for delightful souvenirs to take back home. Surabhi, Kairali or other government emporiums are good places to shop for things that are related to the culture and tradition of Kerala.

Periyar Shopping Guide

There are not much of shopping centres in Periyar. This place is mainly dedicated to the wildlife sanctuary and its staunch visitors. People visiting this place rarely ask for shopping centres too Periyar Shopping. In fact, there is no particular product of Periyar sold or available in the city.

Sprawled over an area of about 780 sq. km. in the Idukki District of Kerala, Periyar is one of the major tiger reserves in India. Renowned worldwide as being home to a large number of wild elephants and tigers, and a host of other animals and birds.

Although not one of the hottest shopping destinations. Periyar offers some pleasant options for tourists to indulge in some leisurely Shopping in Periyar. In fact, an avid shopper will find it impossible to return from a trip to the Sanctuary without shopping. But, if anyone is bound to shop in Periyar, he can shop for spices, which is the best thing available in this city. Periyar is a place with variety of spices. It is also exported to other places of the nation Shopping Places in Periyar India. Cardamom, Cinnamon, Pepper, Ginger, Anise, Mace and Nutmeg are some important spices a visitor can shop for. The most sought after items for tourists visiting the sanctuary is a wide variety of exotic spices. The slopes of the Western Ghats at Periyar grow a number of spices like pepper, cardamom, cinnamon, ginger, nutmeg, mace and anise. Spice trading having been a mainstay of the local economy of the region, spice-scented air at Periyar welcomes tourists and tempts them to shop for some excellent quality fresh spices that are grown in abundance here. While shopping in Periyar, you can also buy T-shirts with exclusive Periyar Wildlife Sanctuary motifs of tigers and elephants. These can serve as excellent souvenirs for your loved ones back home. But if you want to go on a shopping spree in Periyar, you can head for Kochi, located about 190 Km from the sanctuary. At Kochi you can find numerous shops and a large variety of items to buy including souvenirs and local handicrafts. Kumily, located nearby, is a famous shopping centre and spice trade centre Shopping Places. A wide variety of spices and handicrafts are also available at the shops in Kumily.

Kollam Shopping

One can find many places like markets and malls in Kollam for shopping. Some of the most popular items for shopping in this city are jewellery, products of handloom and handicrafts and the textiles. The most common shopping centres in Kollam are Rani Fancy, Rani Gold Covering and Fancy Centre. Chungath Prince Jewellery, Sky Jewellery, Sunny Jacob Jewellery. Dazzles, Lifestyles, Supreme Textiles and Sudarshana. Kollam is also a place of Ayurvedic centre as it has a good collection of medicinal herbs grown in the forests of this place.

Thevalli Palace: This is a beautiful and historically renowned palace situated on the banks of Ashtamudi Kayal (backwater) Sasthamkotta 26 Km. northeast of Kollam city. Sasthamkotta is situated on the bank of Kallada river. There is a temple dedicated to Lord Sastha. Sasthamkotta lake The place in known for the Sasthamkotta fresh water lake. The natural gift is set amidst scenic surroundings covered by hills on the three sides.

Thenmala: 70 km from Kollam, Thenamal is a small hill town amidst thick forest. Thenmala is an interesting picnic spot to enjoy natural scenery. The main attraction is trekking. Boating facility also available. Best Season-September to January

Thenmala Deer Park: The another attraction of Thenmala is the Deer Park. Thenmala Rock are about 5000 year old, which are worth seeing.

Kottarakkara Kathakali Museum: Kottarakkara Thamburan Kathakali Museum, is the memorial of Kottarakkara Thamburan (King) the father of the Kathakali. Exhibited here are various models of Kathakali, Kathakali classes and ornaments. Mahatma Gandhi beach & park at Kochupilamoodu, Thirumullavaram beach and Ashramam picnic Village, are some of the important spots of local sight seeing. Mahatma Gandhi beach lies just 2 Kms. from the town. It is fascinating place for an evening. Thirumullawaram Beach is 5 kms. from the town.

Palakkad Shopping

The city of Palakkad is not much popular or characterized with market infrastructures. The city doesn't have any particular distinct product of its own. This city is not commercially built up to the level. It is an agro-based civilization. Generally goods like textiles, handicrafts, handloom products and agricultural products take the main share of Palakkad markets Palakkad Shopping Info. As for the history of Palakkad goes, very little is known about it. Evidence in form of relics suggest that Palakkad existed during the Paleolithic age. First millennium AD saw the Perumal rulers exercising their control over the land Palakkad Shopping Info. This control was later disintegrated into smaller divisions by the Perumal governors.

Accounts of William Logan, the Scottish author of the Malabar Manual also mentions Palakkad as one of the Malabar region that was captured by the Pallavas of Kanchi. Another record describes a war that was fought by the king of Palakkad in 988 AD to stop the invading army of King of Kongunadu at Chittur. The victory of Palakkad in that war is still celebrated in the form of a festival. Palakkad Shopping Guide 1757, yet another invasion by the Zamorins made the then Raja seek the help of Mysore ruler, Hyder Ali.

Hyder Ali obliged and eventually secured Palakkad for himself and later his son, Tipu Sultan. However, with the defeat of Tipu in the third Anglo Mysore war of 1792. Palakkad Shopping Guide along with other Malabar territories (belonging to Tipu) passed of to the British. The British made Palakkad a part of the Malabar District of Madras Presidency which post independence became a part of the Madras state. In 1956, when Kerala came into existence, Palakkad became a part of it.

Shopping: Palakkad has a quiet a good number of options for shoppers. There is a big bazaar (Valiya Angadi) where shops sell items like traditional bell, peacock villakus, thooku or hanging villakus, nilavillakus and utensils. Tranvancore sarees, Kerala souvenirs and jewelleries are other options for shoppers.

Shopping Places in Wayanad India

Despite the beautiful natural delights of Wayanad, this city also has beautiful shopping centres in and around the city. The major count of the products sold here are the spices of Kerala. The handicraft and handloom products of this city are a good bought that one can get as a memorandum for visiting the city. The crafts here are mainly done with coconut shells, ivory, canes, wood and metals. Other items like garments, textiles and furniture are also available in excellent quality and at suitable costs. One can also get fresh nutritious vegetables, fruits, fish and chicken etc. One should not forget to get the mask of Kathakali to commemorate your visit to this city. Evidence in form of relics and edicts indicate inhabitation of the area as early as in the New Stone Age. However, recorded history is available only from the time of the 18th century.

In earlier times the land was ruled over by the Veda rajas and later it came under the Pazhassi Raja of the Padinjare Kovilakom of the Kottayam family. During the reigns of Hyder Ali of Mysore, Wayanad was came under his rule, however with the defeat of his son, Tipu Sultan, at the hands of British, the entire Malabar region went to the British. This was followed by an intense revolution led by the Pazhassi Raja. The revolution ended only after the death of the raja himself.

Thiruvananthapuram Shopping Guide

This city of Thiruvananthapuram is an excellent place for shoppers. One can find almost all sorts of articles relating luxury, household, garments, jewellery, gifts, foods and many more. The SMSM Government Emporium is the right place for shopping souvenirs and handicraft items. Varieties of handicraft and handloom wonders are available in various range of quality and cost.

Rosewood sculptures or sandalwood sculpture, carved items, bronze creations, fabrics and the Kathakali mask are the best buys of the city. Chalai is a market where local people come for marketing. All type of items for regular utility is available in this market. Kerala depicts the rich heritage and culture of South India. From its remarkable temple architecture to the beautifully sculpted idols, it displays the excellence of the artisans of Kerala. Metal Work is an ancient art of the city of Kerala, which has been carried on for generations. Then you can pick up some of these kitchenware, decorative items and brass lamps from Kerala. The coir products of Kerala are equally famous. From floor coverings. Doormats, rugs or mats, the coir products are found in almost all the shops of Kerala. They are made of coir or coconut shell fibres. Along with this beautiful coconut shell crafts are also available. Shopping in Thiruvananthapuram or a tour to Thiruvananthapuram remains incomplete If you do not buy the miniature elephants or the snake boats which are the typical symbols of Kerala. The miniature Kathakali masks are also beautiful souvenirs.

Andhra Pradesh

Shopping Places in Hyderabad India

The City of Nizams has many shopping centres. It has historically been a rich trading and commerce centre. Hyderabad is a haven for those who love to buy handicrafts. It also sells many kinds of perfumes which have been famous since the times of Nizams. You can go shopping in Charminar Area, where you will find ethnic garments, jewellery and handcrafted items. Some of the shops here remain close on Fridays. There are also many street-side bazaars, where you will also find many locals shopping. Book lovers will find the Abids Bazaar a nice place. You many find here old books which have become a rarity.

Shopping in Hyderabad city is one remarkable experience one wishes to have too often. The markets in the city are provided with all that makes the heart pound and the purse to lose control. Shopping Places in Hyderabad continues to be one of the best to provide precious stones and antiquities in the sub continent and at large. The best buys in the city include jewellery, pearls, handicrafts, apparels, leather goods and traditional crafts. Abids, Basheer Bagh, Nampally, Begum Bazar, Laad Bazar and MG Road are main shopping areas in Hyderabad city. These places feature some of the best stores and showrooms in Shopping Places.

The pearls and jewellery for which the place has been notorious over years can be purchased from Laad Bazar. At Laad Bazar are present a lot of shops that sell the mentioned products and more including semi precious stones, glass beads and colourful bangles. Shilparamam, an arts and craft village presents exquisite pieces and objects. The traditional handlooms, textiles, carpets can be had from this place and that too for genuine prices. Some other related items merchandised in the city include brass ware, Nirmal paintings, Kondapalli toys and Bidri ware. Bidri is an ancient art and in modern times can be found in forms like vases, ashtrays, ornaments, nameplates etc. The souvenir and handicrafts centre opened by Andhra Pradesh Tourism at Ravindra Bharati and Mahtaab Restaurant are great places to shop. Some other popular places to look for the things include Handloom House-Nampally, Kalanjali-Nampally, Lepakshi-Tank Bund, Central Cottage Industries Emporium-S.D.Road Secunderabad.

Vijayawada City Travel Packages

The malls and the markets of Vijayawada are almost busy for the whole weeks but still busier are the Sundays. The street is overcrowded with shoppers in the city. The people moves all around the city to find their shopping items. All items of need are available in the city. Generally the most displayed items of the city include the electronic goods and garments for all. The most interest inculcating part in the city to shop is the heavy discounts and free gifts on purchases. The most rushing day of shopping is on the day before Makar Sankranti. Shopping in Vijaywada is truly a memorable experience. One can shop for anything ranging from handloom products, handicrafts, furniture to pearl jewellery, silver jewellery and textiles. Apart from these, there are also things like exquisite antiques, leather goods, pearls as well as semi precious stones. Vijaywada is also well known for beautiful toys that are made in the nearby villages of Kondapalli and Machlipatnam. Vijaywada is the Kalamkari paintings and kalamkari works. Some of the most popular markets for shopping in Vijaywada are around MG Road. Eluru Road, Besant Road and Governorpet. Other than these popular places Vijayawada Shopping Guide. There are a number of shopping malls and market places in Vijaywada where you can shop to your hearts content.

Ranging from handloom products to handicrafts, furniture to textiles, pearl jewellery to silver jewellery, you can set off with anything and everything in Vijayawada. Besides these knick-knacks, the city has wonderful antiques, leather goods, pearls as well as semi precious stones to offer. Kalamkari paintings and handiworks are things not to be missed on your visit to Vijaywada, the third largest city of Andhra Pradesh.

Regarding shopping places, MG Road, Eluru Road, Besant Road and Governorpet are some of the popular markets in Vijaywada. There are many shopping malls that dole out maximum number of things under one roof. In the nearby areas, Kondapalli is a nice place to get colourful toys, made from light-weight wood. You can also browse the local markets, where you can find most of the items at reasonable price.

Shopping Tourism in Warangal India

Warangal is an excellent place for shopping, and its handicraft are world famous. It is famous for Metal crafts, Banjara Fabrics, Warangal Rumals, and Nakashow Paintings. Visitors would surely like the Warangal

Carpets, which have huge demand in India. People of Warangal are associated with wooden industry, therefore its wooden handicrafts move very fast. Apart from wooden craft, Pembarthi Metal crafts attract tourists. Cloth symbolizes the culture of country and everyone would wish to get involve in it. Warangal "Banjara Fabric" is capable to entice visitors. Embroidery is done to make it look nice. Banjara Fabric is available in variety of colours. Another exquisite item to buy from Warangal is its Warangal Rulams. For those who love shopping, the Warangal city of Andhra Pradesh has some good deals to bargain for. Since the region is famous for handicrafts like brass ware, carpets, scroll paintings etc., your question regarding 'what to buy' would never arise. Infact, it would be unfair not to have a glimpse of such amazing artifacts. Once seen, it is sure that you would not be able to resist buying those amazing knick-knacks.

Another fact about these handicrafts is that they are made by observing traditional techniques and methods. Till day, artisans in local villages practice the time-honored art. The exclusive carpets from the region are popular amongst the national as well as the international markets. Regarding the shopping places in Warangal, you can browse the local markets. Though they have limited range of products, it is exceptionally good and you will get not go home empty-handed. For special and selected items, you must explore the shopping places that are known for particular products. Like Khadi Gramodyog Bhandar at Subedari and Hanamkonda is the best place to get premium Khadi items that offers authentic items at reasonable rates. Podduturi Complex, near Warangal, is a nice place to shop for Lepakshi handicrafts. To get the best brassware and gift items, Hanamkonda is the right place to opt for.

Vishakhapatnam Shopping Travel Tours

The main shopping centres of Vishakhapatnam are located on the main road stretch of Jagadamba Junction to Old Post Office, Kurupam Market, Dwarka Nagar, Daba Gardens and One-Town Area."

The best deals in the famous Narayanpet, Kalamkari, and Pochampali, printed fabrics and wall hangings can be found in Khadi Grammena Udyog. Lepakshi, Girijan Co-Operative Society and Eastern art Museum are other such places. Where you can get exclusive handicrafts of Vishakhapatnam. Wooden toys called Etikopaka are also famous of this region. You can find a great variety for young and old alike at

Kondapalli. Vermillion boxes and bangles are also found here. Perhaps industrial centre is the exact term for Visakhapatnam.

However, with its sun-kissed beaches and beautiful landscape, the city is also a big hit in the tourism market of Andhra Pradesh. Though Vizag is not a shopper's paradise, it has some quality things to set you on a shopping spree. Indeed you must be pondering over the question of 'what of buy', so here comes the answer.

From this port city, you can purchase jewellery, handicrafts, clothes and traditional South Indian metal utensils. Apart from curios and artifacts, sandalwood products-varying from wood carvings to sculptures-are really nice antiques to splurge. Other famous things of the region are spices, pickles, spices, soaps, perfumes, musical instruments, handmade paper and Indian tea. While shopping from the local market places, keep in mind that you are required to indulge in some bargaining. Before purchasing anything, it is better to confirm rates at other shops too.

To get handicrafts, Lepakshi Emporium Eastern, Art Museum and Girijan Cooperative Society are good places that offer most of the famous state works. Dabagardens is a great place to buy sports gears, ranging from cricket sets to skates.

If you want to buy jewellery, then Kurupam Market is the popular gold and silver souk. Owing to the proximity of many shops in markets, you can get great bargains. Markets at Waltair, RTC Complex, TSR complex, Jagadamda Junction, Kurupam and Dwaraka Nagar are quite popular amongst the people.

Karnataka

Karnataka Shopping Guide: Shopping Guide in Karnataka is an adventure and involves a lot of fun. Karnataka is regarded as a shopper's paradise from all parts of the world. Shopping is almost regarded as exciting experience. Lively, busy and active, Mysore's street markets are an essential part of Karnataka life. They are grand for bargain hunting and all sorts of goods are on sale, from clothes to antiques. The state boasts amazing handicraft by the rural artisans, old antiques and the fantastic silk and cotton weaves and much more.

Shopping Malls in Karnataka is world famous for sandal woodworks. Exquisite sandal wood carvings can be found in this state. Other than this you can shop for metals, stone and wood stuffs. The artisans of

Karnataka are traditionally skilled in making striking objects. The woven silk fabric of Mysore is also worth a buy as you shop in Karnataka. Besides these Mysore Paintings and Bidriware are also a must buy while shopping in Karnataka. Several Government Emporia and exclusive private shops mark all over the state of Shopping Places in Karnataka. Shopping in Karnataka and Shopping Malls in Karnataka takes a delightful turn as you travel to lovely Udupi that is admired for its mythological figures cast in metal, shop for crafts cast in bell metal in Mangalore, buy metal crafts in Bidar, Sravanbelgola and Nagamangala that is renowned for its bronze objects.

Shopping tours in Gulegudda in Karnataka open up a lavish land of Ilkal saris, Lambani jewellery and Kinnala paintings Shopping Places in Karnataka India. You can also shop for the famous Mysore paintings with their subtle patterns in a riot of vegetable dyes and gold leaf work.

Shopping for pendants, delicate baskets, and wooden caskets with inlay work, sandalwood pens and exotic bookmarks is a delightful adventure in Shopping Places.

Sandalwood: Sandalwood of Karnataka is renowned for the exquisite carvings on wood. The sandalwood products range from idols of deities and finely wrought chariots to decorative pieces such as paper cutters, boxes, name cases, trays, photo frames, and combs.

Mysore Silks: Mysore is famous for its luxuriant silk sarees. These sarees enchant one and all with a riot of colours and traditional patterns woven in real gold threads and brocade. They are a must have on everyone's shopping list.

Metalware: Metalware craft has taken distinctive forms in different regions of Karnataka.

Bangalore Shopping Guide

Bangalore is also well abound in places of Shopping. There is a beautiful hill called Nandi Hill at a distance of about sixty kilometres from Bangalore. Nandi Hill is popularly known for it's being health care resort. The lakes and the valleys viewed from this hill resort are awesome. It is tourist's delight to visit this resort during summers. Moving for about 28 km from the city is the big Banyan tree. It is also the major amazing factor to the visitors. This big Banyan at Romahalli is spreading over and area of three acres to surprise. There are lot many more places for Shopping in Bangalore.

Commercial Street: Commercial Street is one of Bangalore's busiest shopping areas. While garment, hosiery and textile stores are in a majority here, you can also find shops selling shoes. Art supplies, stationery, novelties, jewellery, travel kits, sports and general goods. The side streets are also worth exploring. You never know what you might find there Bangalore Shopping Guide. Things may be inexpensive, especially if they are unbranded Bangalore Shopping Guide. The clothes may not be of very good quality but you can bargain on some great deals here.

Brigade Road: Brigade Road is a favourite hangout for youngsters as they have a variety of shopping options available accompanied by entertainment Bangalore Shopping Guide. One can get just anything here: Electronic equipments, kitchen appliances toys, music, garments and shoes. There are malls like Fifth Avenue and Mota Royal Arcade, which are worth exploring. You'll get a variety of products that range from cheaply priced to very expensive.

M.G. Road: It's a very popular commercial area and has many sari stores. The Raymonds and Cotton World showrooms are also located here. Jamal is the place to go for buying Bone China and cutlery. Gangaram and Higgin Botham are very popular bookstores, also located at M.G.Road. Shopping Centres to look out for on M. G. Road are Shrungar Shopping Complex, Barton Court, Public Utility Building, Spencer's Super Market, the Coir Board showroom, Natesan's Antiquarts, Kids Kemp, Saree Kemp, Cauvery Arts and Crafts emporium and others Shopping Places in Bangalore India.

Residency Road: If you are looking for steal furniture or handicrafts, Residency Road is the place to go to Shopping Places in Bangalore India. Some of the state emporiums are located on this road: Gangotri, the Uttar Pradesh Government Handicrafts showroom, offering brassware, wooden furniture, jewellery, etc. Mriganayani, the M. P. Government Emporium, Utkalika, the Orissa Government Handicrafts Emporium and Gurjari, the Gujarat State Handicrafts Emporium Shopping Places in Mangalore India.

There are other markets that specialize in the products they sell; Richard Square is famous for cutlery and crockery, Avenue Road is known for its stationery, stainless steel ware and silver jewellery, Chickpet is famous for its silk sarees, silver and gold jewellery and textiles.

Mysore Shopping Guide

Mysore: Visitors can also opt to go around the city of Mysore for sight seeing. There are various beautiful and worth visiting place around the city of Mysore. The temple of Somnathpur is one among the most visited place around Mysore. The construction of this temple looks like a star, which is reflecting the typical design of Hoysala architecture. It is well preserved till date. The Bandipur National Park is a popular wildlife sanctuary near Mysore. One can have a look over the park having an elephant safari.

Mysore Silk: Like Srigandha (sandalwood), Mysore Mallige (Mysore jasmine) and Mysore Badane (Mysore brinjal), Mysore is also famous for its Silk. Silk sarees and Magutas are being traditionally worn since a long time, both on religious and auspicious occasions. Silk sarees come in a large variety, the cost of saree depending upon the content of gold in it.

The sarees are tastefully gold laced on its both edges and the pallu which is wrapped over the body. Not only private weavers in well-known centres like Molakalmur and other places but also the Government Silk Weaving Factory in Mysore produce excellent varieties of silk sarees, Magutas and ties.

The silk products of the Factory still commend wide acceptability for its genuine quality, gold lace and colour. Right from taking out of yarn from the cocoon upto weaving the yarn into colourful garments takes place in Mysore. The Factory has a show-room in its premises at the Manandavadi Road and also at the shopping area of K.R. Circle. Discount on sarees is offered during some seasons. Private showrooms in Mysore sell sarees produced by private weavers.

Handicrafts: Mysore is a reputed place for handicrafts. Artisans, both in their homes and at work centres produce a variety of items. The elegant and attractive items of handicrafts mostly are wood-based, made out of sandalwood, rosewood and teakwood. With the ban on ivory, production of handicrafts in ivory has unfortunately disappeared. Mysore continues to produce a large quantity of sandalwood and hence sandalwood articles are the best items for purchase.

A variety of articles, including a large number of figures of gods and goddesses, are available either in sandalwood or rosewood. They are manufactured by some of the best craftsmen either individually or at craft centres established by reputed private firms. The inlaid works of rosewood like teapoys, coffee tables and other items of furniture are attractive and pleasing.

Different sizes of elephants are also produced out of rosewood, sandalwood and teakwood, so also figures of gods and goddesses. Jewel boxes, table-top items and a large variety of small items, ideal for gifts and presentations. The Cauvery Handicrafts Emporium of the Karnataka Handicrafts Development Corporation is an ideal place for purchase these and other items like silk sarees, jewellery and other handicraft and artefacts.

Agarbathies: Besides handicrafts, sandalwood items and oil, silk fabrics, Mysore is also famous for Agarbathies or incense sticks. Varieties of agarbathies are manufactured by leading agarbathi manufacturers and small vendors. Most of the branded agarbathies are of excellent quality and Mysore is still the home of the best variety of these incense sticks. The incense sticks are still traditionally manufactured like the age-old times.

Stone Carving: Stone carving is another traditional art item of manufacture in Mysore. There are a number of sculptors, who carve excellent pieces of idols of gods and goddess, apart from other figures, mostly needed for temples and other auspicious places. Some of these master sculptors, who have their own centres in the city, have won State and National awards and reputed for their masterly works in stone. Some of their works have been installed in other places of the country. A few of their pieces have also been exported to other countries, mostly for installation in temples and religious centres.

Shopping Places in Hassan

Hassan is having a good number of sites which serves the purpose of excursion for the tourists and localites. The most preferred tourist picnic spots near the city. It is a beautiful dam site built over the river of Hemavathy. It is 22 km far from the main city of Hassan. Moving for 40 km from the city of Hassan is the belur. It is also a beautiful city built over the river of Yagachi and posses the pride of being the first city capital of the Hoysalas. Chhanekeshava Temple is another pride of Belur. Shopping Places in Hassan India Halebid is another important site of excursion from Hassan. The place of Halebid is 39 km far from the city of Hassan.

Hassan located 194 kilometres from Bangalore is a serene town that can be accessed easily from the cities of Bangalore, Mysore, and Mangalore by road as well as rail. Apart from the various tourist attractions offered by Hassan, the place has also has a lot of shops that put up for sale a wide range of articles that pertains to the interests of the tourists. Hence, Shopping in Hassan is one of the important aspects of touring Hassan.

While Hassan Shopping Travel Tours Karnataka, the most common shops that you would come across are the ones that sell various items that are unique to this part of the world. Some of these items have defied the barriers of time and change in the preference patterns of people all over the world. The sarees and clothing materials made from pure silk have adorned women of all ages for centuries. The silk is created in the natural way by rearing silkworms in mulberry trees.

This Hassan Shopping Travel Tours Karnataka over the years, has flourished in leaps and bounds. A substantial portion of the annual production of silk is exported which yields valuable foreign to the economy thus helping it to grow even further.

The sandalwood available from the forests of Karnataka are popular not only in India but throughout the world due to its quality and fragrance. A variety of articles made from this rare wood are available in the Markets. Articles of ivory have always been the signs of pomp and sophistication among the socially affluent households. The Jungles of Karnataka being heavily infested by tuskers, in a place rich in ivory reserves.

The collection of items that you will come across while shopping in Hassan is generally decorative. Thus Shopping in Hassan, India, would certainly enrich your tastes and preferences and enable you to understand and appreciate the quality of craftsmanship and labour that has gone into the production of such articles.

Bijapur Shopping Guide

The visitors can go for Shopping to various places around the city of Bijapur. This city is surrounded by numerous beautiful places for excursion. Aihole, Pattadakal, Kadula Sangama, Badami and Basavana Bagewadi are some of the prime sites mostly of tourist's major choice of destinations. Aihole is at a distance of about 110 km from the city of Bijapur. Aihole is a place of temples that too well known for its architectural and masterpiece carvings on the temples. Apart from other beautiful Hindu temples, there lies the distinct Buddhist Temple spicing to the importance of Aihole.

Location: Bijapur is located in the northern part of the state of Karnataka, in the southern region of India. It is 613 km from Bangalore city and 486 km southeast of Mumbai (Bombay) city Bijapur Shopping Guide. The climate of Bijapur is temperate with summers (April-June) being moderately hot and winters are cool and pleasant (November-February). It experiences southwestern monsoon rains in the months of June to August.

Visiting Time: The best time to Bijapur is during winters.

The Past: The origin of Bijapur goes back to the early medieval period. The Chalukyan rulers of south India, between the 10th and 11th centuries laid the foundation of Bijapur. At that time, it was called as Vijayapura (the City of Victory).

The local Yadavas rulers ruled it for about a century. Ala-ud-din Khilji, the Sultan of Delhi, captured it and made it a part of his empire at the end of the 13th century. Khilji could not hold on to Bijapur for long and it became the part of the Bahamani Empire in 1347 Shopping Places in Bijapur India.

The golden period of Bijapur started with the decline of the Bahamani rulers, when, in 1489, Yusuf Adil Shah, one of the nobles under the Bahamani rulers, laid the foundation of the Adil Shahi dynasty and made Bijapur the capital of his kingdom. The Adil Shahis ruled Bijapur until 1686, when the last great Mughal ruler Aurangzeb defeated them Shopping Places in Bijapur India.

Tourist Spots: Fortified walls surround the old city. The main places to visit within Bijapur are its monuments, which belong to the reign of the Adil Shahi dynasty. The imposing Gol Gumbaz or the Round Dome, which is to the eastern end of the walled city, is the main attraction of this city. Mohammad Adil Shah built it in 1659.

This structure has the largest dome, unsupported by pillars, to be found in India and the second largest in the world. It houses the tomb of Mohammad Adil Shah. From the turrets of the Gol Gumbaz, one can have a panoramic view of the city. The medieval complex near the Gol Gumbaz has important buildings. There is an archeological museum and well-maintained gardens near the Gol Gumbaz. Ibrahim Roza, which is on the western outskirts of the city, is a beautiful tomb built by Adil Shah II for his queen.

It is an important structure and is known for its highly decorative carving. The citadel, which is situated at the centre of the walled city, is a small, fortified area with a moat. It has palaces, pleasure gardens and public halls belonging to the Adil Shahi rulers. Though most of the monuments are in ruins, the remnants of Gagan Mahal are worth seeing.

The Sat Manzil (seven-storied palace), Jala Manzil (water pavilion) and the Bara Kaman (twelve arches) are important spots near the citadel. Jama Masjid, the mosque built by Ali Adil Shah I, is an important place to visit. The Taj Bawdi (water tank), Upli Burj (watch tower), the Mehtar Mahal (palace built by sweepers) and Asar Mahal are other important places to visit in Bijapur. The Malik-e-Maidan (monarch of the plains) cannon, which is one of the largest surviving bell-metal cannons in the world, is placed on the city walls and is an important attraction of the city.

Hospet Shopping Markets

The tourist of Hospet has many places to visit in the places nearby the city of Hospet. Some very important mentionable amongst those places are the Chitradurga Fort. Hampi, Queen's Bath, Vithala Temple, Raghunath Temple Hospet Shopping Markets India. Virupaksha Temple, King's Balance, Achyutraya Temple, Lotus Mahal. Royal Residence, Museum and Art Gallery, and Tungabhadra Dam site. The Tungabhadra Dam is at a distance of around six kilometres from the main city of Hospet.

This dam has a prime importance to the people of the city. The garden of this dam is a prime destination for the tourists. Hampi is the main place of excursion for the tourists from Hospet. What brings recognition to Hospet as a tourist destination is its proximity to Hampi, which is a World Heritage Site.

Its just few kilometres from Hospet making it a perfect option for excursions Hospet Shopping Markets. Chitradurga and Harihar too are situated at a short distance.

Shopping in Hospet can be a pleasurable experience as this place is rich in heritage and past glory Hospet Shopping Markets India Hospet Shopping Guide. Hospet bears testimony to its past and all the things available here bear a mark of the bygone times Hospet Shopping Guide. From Hospet customers carry home huge amounts of hand-crafted items, beads, pendants, carved tables, screens, dinner gongs, boxes, caskets, mythological figures.

A host of stationery items, trays, decorative panels made of sandalwood. Inlaid furniture and sandalwood carvings are favourite pick ups for affluent tourists. Shopping in Hospet can be a marvelous experience as it has much to offer to its visitors. It is said that Hospet is a shopper's paradise for all who love to buy indigenous products or historical artifacts local to the place.

Shopping in Hospet is very different experience as this place offers you a varied range of hand-crafted local items all fresh and local.

In Hospet you can shop in the following places:

- Andhra Handloom House, near Gandhi Chowk,
- Karnataka Handlooms, Station Road,
- Tamil Nadu Cooptex, near Gandhi Chowk.
- Departmental Stores, Tungabhadra Departmental Stores, Station Road.

Coorg Shopping Travel Tours

The Coorg visitors will be lucky enough to visit some other amazingly beautiful tourist places nearby Coorg. There are numbers of such beautiful places in an around the city of Coorg. The Omkareshwara Temple is one among those beautiful sightseeing.

The Irrupu Falls along with the Abbey Falls looks marvelous and every visitor of Coorg opts to visit this wonderful water world. The charm and misty environment created by the droplets of water here resembles to heaven Coorg Shopping Travel Tours. Raja's seat is another must visit site of the city Coorg. This place is especially dedicated to the lovers of nature. Coorg is a beautiful hill station located near Ooty. Nestled amidst sprawling acres of greenery etched on the Western Ghats, Coorg is the dream destination.

Meandering roads, valleys dotted with coffee plantations and the aroma of coffee refreshing the senses allures the tourists to this heaven in South India offers online information. Coorg is not a shopaholic's paradise. Located near Ooty this is a small hill station in South India has acres of coffee plantations. Tourists who are interested in shopping in Coorg mostly buy coffee and spices. So all you connoisseurs of different kinds of coffee.

Coorg is also famous for spices like pepper and cardamom and fruits like oranges. So if you are planning for some shopping in Coorg then buy some of the best quality coffee or the spices. Coffee estates throughout Coorg manufacture coffee and this locally produced coffee is exported to different places as well as distributed throughout the country. If you wish to buy some Tibetan artifacts as souvenirs to take the memories back home then visit the Kushal Nagar market in Coorg.

This place is famous for the souvenirs and different collectibles generally attracting the tourists. If not coffee, spices or the Tibetan decorative items then Coorg is also famous for another thing and that is honey. While shopping in Coorg you can also some honey. One of the India's largest producers of honey, Coorg is located quite near to the Honey Valley which supplies honey to all over India and other places. So taste a bit of this sweet honey and take back the memories of your idyllic retreat in Coorg in South India.

13

Significance of Relation between Retailing and Tourism

Tourism in India

Tourism is one of the largest service industries in terms of gross revenue and foreign exchange earnings. Its role and importance in fostering economic development of a country and creating greater employment opportunities has been well recognized worldwide. It has been an important vehicle of widening socioeconomic and cultural contacts throughout human history. A wide array of interests – entertainment, sports, religion, culture, adventure, education, health and business – drives tourism. With the world becoming more integrated with the growth in overall economy, communication and transport the demand for tourism can only go up. Tourism promotes broad based employment and income generation.

- Investments in tourism infrastructure fuels generation of employment and income. This leads to a cycle of further growth in demand of tourism and subsequent flow of investments in the sector.
- Adding to the demand of a variety of products and services, tourism offers potential to exploit synergies across a number of sectors – retail being one of the most visible beneficiaries.
- In India, the tourism industry has the potential to grow at a high rate and ensure consequential development of the infrastructure. It has the capacity to stimulate other economic sectors through its backward and forward linkages and cross-sectional synergies with sectors like agriculture, horticulture, poultry, handicrafts, transport, construction, and retail specially.

The share of India in international tourist arrivals has progressively increased from 0.46% in 2004 to estimated 0.55% in 2007 (Min. of Tourism, Annual Report 07-08). Foreign Tourist Arrivals (FTAs) rose from 3.46 million to about 5 million during the same time.

Below are given two tables, Table 1 and Table 2 which show the year-on-year growth of foreign tourist arrival (FTA) in India 2005 till 2007 and the estimated growth for 2008 respectively.

Table 1: Foreign Tourist Arrivals In India During 2007 And Corresponding Figures For 2005 & 2006

	Foreign Tourist Arrival (Nos.)			Percentage Change	
Months	**2005**	**2006**	**2007**	**2006/05**	**2007/06**
January	385977	459489	532088	19.0	15.8
February	369844	439090	498806	18.7	13.6
March	352094	391009	444186	11.1	13.6
April	248416	309208	333945	24.5	8.0
May	225394	255008	267758	13.1	5.0
June	246970	278370	310104	12.7	11.4
July	307870	337332	377474	9.6	11.9
August	273856	304387	360089	11.1	18.3
September	257184	297891	325893	15.8	9.4
October	347757	391399	440715	12.5	12.6
November	423837	442413	510987	4.4	15.5
December	479411	541571	575148	13.0	6.2
Total	3918610	4447167	4977193	13.5	11.9

Table 2: Foreign Tourist Arrivals In India During 2008 and Corresponding Figures For 2006 & 2007

Foreign tourist arrival (nos.) Percentage Change;

Months	**2006**	**2007@**	**2008@**	**2007/06**	**2008/07**
January	459489	532088	584765	15.8%	9.9%
February	439090	498806	560658	13.6%	12.4%
March	391009	444186	509926	13.6%	14.8%
Total	1289588	1475080	1655349	14.4%	12.2%

@ Provisional Estimates;

Retail in India

India tops At Kearney's list of most attractive markets for global retailers for the last two years (India Retail Report, 2007). India is for sure at the peak of attractiveness for retailers right now as its USD 270 billion (Rs.1200, 000 crore) retail market continues to grow at the rate of 13 percent and all indicators seem to suggest that there can only be further acceleration from here on. What is even more heartening is the fact that India's miniscule organized retail market has gained the momentum required to propel it to the next phase of real rapid expansion: at prevailing prices, this segment grew 42 percent in 2006. Organized Retailing has increased its share from thee percent in 2004 to 4.6 percent and is valued at Rs.55,000 crore (USD 12.4 billion). All that Indian retail now needs is an un-interrupted supply of investment.

Investments in Retail Sector

A report by investment banker Goldman Sachs, credits India with the potential to deliver the fastest growth over the next 50 years with an average rate of more than five per cent a year for the entire period. All these are clear portends in terms of investments and returns. By the end of 2008, FDI (foreign direct investment) is expected to touch the magical figure of USD10 billion with investments in infrastructure development and capital market continuing to flow in at a rapid pace. India is investing over US $130 billion in infrastructure by the end of this decade. Indian retail industry itself has attracted investment of over Rs.200 billion (over USD 4 billion) in creating infrastructure, systems & shop-fit. The additional retail space is expected to add Rs.300 billion (USD 6.67 billion) of business to organized retail.

In this land of 15 million retailers, most of them owning small mom and pop outlets, we are likely to have no less than 100 million square feet of shopping centre space by 2007-08, generating retail sales to the tune of over Rs.50,000crore.

Industry studies indicate that today's total of 50 hypermarkets will grow to 1,200 across India by 2011, at which time there will be 3,000 supermarkets, twice as many as there are today. And that will require USD 25 billion to be invested in the retail sector over the next five years, as compared with the USD 2 billion that trickled in over the last one decade – 35 percent of that investment is expected to come from foreign investors and retailers.

Relation between Retailing and Tourism

Although retailing and tourism have shared a long and successful journey, often it is known only by those who are intimately familiar with both or either industry. As per an essay by Maria Fok, "Beyond our imagination – the retailing and tourism relationship" (Woolsworth, NSW), up to 81% of visitors to Australia consider shopping as one of their primary leisure activities. Tourism generated $77 billion in consumption in one year in Australia out of which $17.7 billion (23%) was retailing expenditure by the tourists.

We know of countries like Hong Kong, Singapore and Dubai, which have successfully leveraged retailing to develop tourism. Globalization has made the same products available in most countries at the same time. Shopping is becoming less differentiated on a locality basis. Tourists buy from retailers all forms of goods and merchandize. Apart from necessities like food & beverage, prominent categories are gifts and souvenirs. Tourism services providers are also speciality retailers of a particular category – hotels, restaurants, tour operators, ticketing agents, guides etc. At a commercial level there is a mutual interdependence that is fundamental to both industries for revenue generation and growth.

- Tourism and retailing contribute significantly to any economy both directly and via the multiplier effect as expenditure in both industries filter throughout the economy and pull other sectors in process.
- Tourism drives growth and development in Retailing. Retail districts have always been places of special significance in urban settings. The development of "Themed Market Places" as a viable format of retail has only been possible with the focus on tourists as shoppers. Dilli-Haat in New Delhi is a prime example of the same. It showcases ethnic Indian clothes and artifacts for selling to tourists.
- At the same time Retailing drives growth and development in Tourism. "Incredible India" has been established as a brand by government initiative, which can be used as a marketing tool available to retailers to promote the Indian authenticity of their products. This development can enable retailers to incorporate tourism into their on-going business strategy and deliver a more uniquely Indian retail experience to tourists.

Tourism and Retailing share many fascinating similarities.

- The labour force of both industries share the common characteristics of being on average young, working on part time and casual employment basis, relatively low levels of formal education and high turn over rates.
- Both of these industries need to comply with some common government policies and regulations. Government responsibilities which affect both include zoning laws, road and transport infrastructure, health measures, food standards, consumer affairs, labour management laws etc. Government's policies on visitor entry from any country directly impact the sales level in both the industries.
- Tourism and retail are similar in that they are commonly marketing and managing the brand of their products. In the case of retail the products are generally tangible goods whereas tourism products may include package tours with focus on special interests such as shopping. As a good business strategy, food retailers may consider innovative packaging which focuses on portability and shelf-life; making it attractive for tourists to take products home.
- Tourism and Retail are highly 'people' oriented industries where the growth of customer relationships is of paramount importance. The two industries use strategic customer loyalty programs and relationship marketing in order to grow their customer base and aim for repeat business.
- Tourism promotes understanding and learning which can enhance the way retailers do business. In travelling across the globe, individuals gain insight and exposure to new ideas, learn the advancements in retail overseas and broaden their vision of the changing needs. Travel also exposes retailers to identify new vendors, global outsourcing possibilities and development of networks.
- Airports are a converging point for tourism and retail relationship. Retail attractions are positioned to maximise tourist exposure and increase their likelihood of spending. Though retail is not the prime driver of facility visitation by the people at airports, there is an increasing emphasis on including a retail experience for tourists. Retail is a growing source of revenues

for airports as airport retailers target a captive audience, which is cash rich and time poor.

- Within big urban centres like Delhi, a lot of tourist movement happens through convenient city transportation systems like Delhi Metro. The Metro stations provide a very good opportunity for retail business. There is already recognition of this phenomenon by major retailers like Big Bazaar and McDonalds who are teaming up with builders like Parsvanth and Delhi Metro Rail Corporation to create retail stores for them at prominent Metro stations.

Using Events to Promote Retailing and Tourism

The 2010 Commonwealth Games in New Delhi is presenting a golden opportunity to leverage the interdependence of both of these sectors. As an Example, we can study the effect of Sydney 2000 Olympics "The retail sector in Australia received a significant boost during the Games. Sales in tourist locations increased by 40-80%. It is estimated that the Games resulted in a net increase of $164 million in retail turnover (during September 2000 alone). Major spending was in clothing, souvenirs, hospitality and services sector (takeaway food). These sectors saw turnovers increase by $152 million in New South Wales in the month of September 2000. The district of Darling Harbour in Sydney enjoyed a 209% increase in sales as it became the main party-hub with restaurants, bars and nightclubs registering record business during the games. The speciality formats called as The Olympic Concept stores alone sold $54 million worth of merchandize in the three-week Games period. The value of retail merchandise spread well beyond the Olympic Concept stores with total retail sales of licensed merchandise estimated at $1 billion."

The tourism and retail industry in India should join hands to cash on the opportunity which Commonwealth Games 2010 is presenting to cash in on the synergies of the two sectors.

Opportunities of Investment in Indian Tourism Industry

Tourism makes a significant contribution in India's foreign exchange earnings, which grew from US$ 6.17 billion (Rs.27944 crore) in 2004 to an estimated US$ 11.96 billion (Rs.49413 crore) in 2007 (Min. of Tourism, Annual Report 07-08).

The nodal organization for the development of tourism in India is the Ministry of Tourism. The Ministry plays a crucial role in formulating national policies and incentives as well as in coordinating the efforts of the State/Union Territory Governments and the private sector for promotion of tourism. It also catalyzes private investment; strengthens promotional and marketing efforts; and helps in providing trained manpower resources. The ministry, in order to develop tourism in India in a systematic manner and to facilitate investment (both foreign and domestic) into the sector, has made several policy announcements and incentives. The most important being the National Tourism Policy, which has been formulated with the aim to:-

- Position tourism as a major engine of economic growth;
- Harness the direct and multiplier effects of tourism for employment generation, economic development and providing impetus to rural tourism;
- Focus on domestic tourism as a major driver of tourism growth;
- Position India as a global brand to take advantage of the burgeoning global travel trade and the vast untapped potential of India as a destination;
- Acknowledge the critical role of the private sector with Government working as a pro-active facilitator and catalyst;
- Create and develop integrated tourism circuits based on India's unique civilization, heritage and culture in partnership with States, private sector and other agencies;
- Ensure that the tourists to India gets physically invigorated, mentally rejuvenated, culturally enriched, spiritually elevated and 'feel India from within'.

As per all such initiatives, now 100% FDI is permitted in hotels and tourism through the automatic route. Also, the estimated foreign exchange earnings during 2007 were Rs. 49413 crore as compared to Rs. 27944 crore during 2004, showing an annual growth of almost 25%. These measures along with the embedded advantages of investing in India provide numerous opportunities to the investors in the tourism sector.

Ownership and Co-location opportunities in Tourism and Retail

This synergy for tourism and retailing can bring:-

- Cost savings in combining facilities and overheads,

- Better buying terms for greater combined volumes of food & beverages,
- Marketing and branding integration,
- Savings on insurance (operations cost),
- Operational efficiencies, restructuring and rationalization of support offices,
- Developments like co-location of facilities which will provide retailers with greater footfalls and convenience for tourists and locals. The clustering of these facilities may evolve in the future into major one-shop entertainment, leisure and retail super-centres.
- The industry similarities provide huge potential for sharing of intellectual capital and resources or joint investment in IT, marketing and customer-loyalty programmes.
- Airports and Metro stations will be a focal point for both industries simultaneously.
- More development of Themed Markets at places of religious or historical significance is another potential opportunity for the two sectors.

There is a growing interest of private equity consortiums in retailers, tourism related industries and airlines. Depending on the entities in the PE consortium, there may be possibility of common ownership in future leading to control and financial support for some operations in the retail and tourism infrastructure development. As an example, we can see in Australia, the retail giant Woolworth Ltd.'s acquisition of the Taverner Group which includes tourism industry operations such as hotels, hospitality and gaming facilities.Common ownership possibilities will mean the way in which business is conducted will come under more scrutiny from investment consortiums which will offer new sources of funding for growth and investment and commercial insight from their involvement in vast ranging industries worldwide.

Scoping of Risk

The scope of risk associated with investment opportunities in Indian tourism sector are. These risks are mainly classified into two broad categories i.e. commercial risks and non-commercial risks. Commercial risk can be further divided into three different categories i.e. financial market risk, operational risk and business risk.

The Need for Risk Management Instruments

Managing success in Indian tourism is dependent upon the involvement of the financing community. Here, investors and lenders are averse to risks and this may lead to unexpected reductions in a firm's or project's cash flows, value, or earnings. This is the basic reason for application of risk management instruments in this sector. The risk management process can be described as the process by which an enterprise tries to ensure that the risks to which it is exposed are those risks to which the enterprise wants/needs to be and thinks it is exposed. One can use any of the four possible responses that the parties involved in an investment opportunity. They may adopt to deal with these risks.

Risks may be:

- Avoided
- Mitigated
- Retained or
- Transferred.

The investment project in retailing and tourism sector, the risk management is continuum the first two responses (avoidance and mitigation) may be categorized as risk control and the latter two (retention and transfer) as risk financing. These are important aspects of risk management in Indian tourism sector. Now a days, this became a critical issue with the management that what risks and how much, the enterprise should bear as a part of its normal business and what risks the enterprise should transfer to one or more market participants.

Bibliography

Andrew, N; Flanagan, S & Ruddy, J: *Tourism Destination Planning*, Dublin, Dublin Institute of Technology, 2002.

Apostolopous, Y and Leivadi, S: *Sociology of Tourism, The: Theoretical And Empirical Investigations*, London, Retailed, 1996.

Ashworth, G J and Dietvorst, A G J: *Tourism and Spatial Transformations: Implications For Policy and Plan*, Wallingford, CAB International, 1995.

Ashworth, Greg and Larkham, P J: *Building a New Heritage: Tourism, Culture & Identity in the New Europe*, London, Routledge,1994.

Baum, Tom: *We're all Going on a Summer Holiday: Images of Tourism Past and Person*, Buckingham, University of Buckingham, 1995.

Beeho, A & Prentice, R: *Conceptualising The Experiences of Heritage Tourists*, 1997.

Beeton, Sue:: *Film-Induced Tourism*, Clevedon, Channel View, 2005.

Belie et al.: *Tourism and the Inner City: An Evaluation of / Impact of Grant Assist*, London, HMSO, 1990.

Benefice, Brian G, and Cooper, Chris: *Geography of Travel and Tourism*, The, London, Heinemann, 1987.

Bolshevism, Germy: *Coping with Tourists: European Reactions to Mass Tourism*, Oxford, Berghahn Books, 1995.

Boniface, Priscilla and Fowler, Peter: *Heritage and Tourism: In the Global Village*, London, Retailed, 1993.

Bosselman, Fred P: *In The Wake of the Tourist: Managing Special Places in Eight Countries*, Washington, DC, Conservation Foundation, The, 1978.

Briguglio, L and Vella, Leslie: *Competitiveness of the Maltese Islands in Mediterranean in Tourism*, Chichester, John Wiley, 1995.

Brown, Dona: *Inventing New England: Regional Tourism in the Nineteenth Century*, Washington DC, Smithsonian Institution, 1995.

Brunt, Paul: *Market Research in Travel and Tourism*, Oxford, Butterworth Heinemann, 1997.

Burkart, A and Medlik, S: *Management of Tourism*, The, London, Heinemann, 1975.

Chambers, Erve: *Native Tours: The Anthropology of Travel and Tourism*, Prospect Heights, Waveland Press, 2000.

Chandler, Harry and Carter, John: *Chandler's Travels: A Tour of the Life of Harry Chandler*, London, Quiller Press, 1985.

Clark, Colin: *Tourist Services and Guidance: Heritage and Information*, Strasbourg, Council of Europe Press, 1989.

Coccosis, Harry and Nijkamp, Peter: *Sustainable Tourism Development*, Aldershot, Avebury, 1995.

Cohen, Erik: *Towards a Sociology of International Tourism*, 1972.

Dann, Graham M S: *Language of Tourism*, The, Wallingford, CAB International, 1996.

Davidson, R and Maitland, R: *Tourism Destinations, London*, Hodder and Stoughton, 1997.

Davidson, Rob: *Travel and Tourism in Europe*, Harlow, Addison Wesley Longman, 1998.

Ecotec: *Calderdale: Tourism Impact Study*, Calderdale, ECOTEC/Calderdale Council, 1990.

Edensor, Tim: *Tourists at the Taj*, London, Retailed, 1998.

Edgell, David L: *International Tourism Policy, New York*, Van Nostrand and Reinhold, 1990.

Elliott, James: *Tourism: Politics and Public Sector Management*, London, Retailed, 1997.

Fairgrieve, James: *Geography in School*, London, University of London Press, 1926.

Foster, Douglas: *Travel and Tourism Management*, London, Macmillan Educational, 1985.

Frechtling, Douglas C: *Practical Tourism Forecasting*, Oxford, Butterworth Heinemann, 1996.

Gamble, P. R: *The Educational challenge for Hospitality and Tourism Studies*, Tourism Management, 13, 1992.

Ghimire, Krishna: *The Native Tourist*: Mass Tourism within Developing Regions, London, Earthscan, 2001.

Goeldner, C. R: *The Evaluation of Tourism as an Industry and a Discipline, Paper Presented to*, International Conference for Tourism Educators, Guildford, University of Surrey, 1988.

Gunn, Clare and Var, Turgut: *Tourism Planning*, London, Retailed, 2002.

Hall, C Michael *Tourism Planning: Policies, Processes and relationships*, Harlow, Prentice Hall, 2000.

Hall, Colin and Jenkins, John: *Tourism and Public Policy*, London, Retailed, 1995.

Hall, Colin Michael: *Tourism and Politics*: Policy, Power, & Place, Chichester, Wiley, 1994.

Harrison, Lyndon: *Tourism Means Jobs*, Chester, Lyndon Harrison, 1996.

Harron, S and Weiler, B: *Ethnic Tourism*, Belhaven/Wiley, 1992.

Inkpen, G: *Information Technology for Travel and Tourism*, Harlow, Addison Wesley Longman, 1998.

Inskeep, Edward *National and Regal Tourism Planing*: Methodologies & Case Studies, London, Routledge/WTO, 1994.

Irwin, William *The New Niagara: Tourism, Technology, And the Landscape of Niagara Fal*, University Park, PA, University of Pennsylvania, 1996.

Jack, G and Phipps, A: *Tourism and Intercultural Exchange: Why Tourism Matters*, Clevedon, Channel View, 2005.

Jakle, John: *Tourist, The: Travel in Twentieth Century North America*, University of North Nebraska, 1985.

Jennings, Gayle: *Tourism Research*, Chichester, Wiley, 2001.

Judd, D R: *Promoting Tourism* in US Cities, 1995.

Karski, A: *Urban Tourism* - A Key to Urban Regeneration?, 1990.

Kotler, Philip et al: *Marketing Places: Attracting Investment, Industry & Tourism etc*, New York, free press, 1993.

Labarge, Margaret Wade: *Medieval Travellers: The Rich and Restless*, London, Hamish Hamilton, 1982.

Laws, Eric: *Tourist Destination Management: Issues, Analysis & Policies*, London, Routledge, 1995.

Leed, Eric J: *Mind of the Traveller, The: From Gilgamesh to Global Tourism*, New York, 1991.

MacCannell, Dean: *Tourist, The: A New Theory of the Leisure Class*, London, Macmillan, 1976.

Machin, Alan: *Retracing the Steps: Tourism as Education, Janus*, Fin, ATLAS / FUNTS, 2001.

Opperman, Martin and Chon, Kye-Sung: *Tourism in Developing Countries, London*, International Thomson Business Press, 1997.

Patullo, Polly: *Last Resorts: The Cost of Tourism in the Caribbean*, London, Cassell, 1996.

Pearce, Douglas: *Tourism Today: A Geographical Analysis*, Harlow, Longman, 1995.

Pearce, P L: *Social Psychology Of Tourist Behaviour*, The, Oxford, Pergamon, 1982.

Peters, M: *International Tourism*, London, Hutchinson, 1969.

Ringer, Greg: *Destinations: Cultural Landscapes of Tourism*, London, Routledge, 1998.

Ritchie, Brent: *Managing Educational Tourism*, Clevedon, Channel View, 2003.

Robinson, H: *Geography of Tourism*, A, London, Macdonald and Evans, 1976.

Robinson, M, Evans, E & Chalazion, P: *Tourism and Cultural Change, Sunderland*, Business Education Publishers Ltd, 1996.

Rogers, H Anthea and Slinn, Judy A: *Tourism: Management of Facilities*, London, Pitman: M & E, 1993.

Schwaninger, M: *Trends in Leisure and Tourism for 2000 - 2010*, Prentice Hall, 1989.

Scottish Tourist Board: *Visitor Attractions: A Development Guide*, Edinburgh, Scottish Tourist Board, 1991.

Seaton, A V et al: *Tourism: The state of the Art*, Chichester, John Wiley, 1994.

Shaw, G and Williams, A: *Tourism and Tourism Spaces*, London, Sage, 2004.

Stevens, Terry: *Island Tourism*: Malta, , WTO, 1993.

Trench, R: *Travellers in Britain*, London, Aurum, 1990.

Tribe, John *Corporate Strategy for Tourism, London*, International Thomson Business Press, 1997.

Urry, John: *Tourist Gaze*, The, London, Sage, 1990.

Van den Berg et al: *Urban Tourism: Performance and Strategies in Eight European Cities*, Aldershot, Avebury, 1995.

Van Harssel, Jan: *Tourism: An Exploration*, New York, Prentice Hall, 1994.

Veal, A: *Leisure and Tourism*: Policy and Planning, Wallingford, CABI, 2001.

Wahab, S A: *Tourism Management*, Tourism International Press, 1975.

Walle, Alfred H: *Cultural Tourism*: A Strategic Focus, Boulder, Co, Westview Press, 1998.

Wilkinson, Paul: *Tourism Policy and Planning: As Studies from the Caribbean*, Elmsford New York, Cognizant Communications Corporation, 1997.

Yale, Pat: *From Tourist Attractions to Heritage Tourism*, Huntingdon, Elm, 1991.

Zarkia, Cornelia: *Philoxenia: Receiving Tourists*-but *not Guests-on a Greek Island*, Oxford, Berghahn Books, 1996.

Index

□□□